IT'S ALL ABOUT
STUDENT LEARNING

Cuesta College Library main entry; accessible entry is to left rear.

IT'S ALL ABOUT STUDENT LEARNING

Managing Community and Other College Libraries in the 21st Century

Edited by David R. Dowell and Gerard B. McCabe

LIBRARIES UNLIMITED LIBRARY MANAGEMENT COLLECTION

LIBRARIES UNLIMITED

A Member of the Greenwood Publishing Group

Westport, Connecticut • London

Library of Congress Cataloging-in-Publication Data

It's all about student learning : managing community and other college libraries in the 21st century / edited by David R. Dowell and Gerard B. McCabe.
    p. cm. — (Libraries Unlimited library management collection)
 Includes bibliographical references and index.
 ISBN 1-59158-149-4
 1. Community college libraries—United States—Administration. 2. Academic libraries—United States—Administration. 3. Libraries and students—United States. 4. Libraries and education—United States. I. Dowell, David R. II. McCabe, Gerard B. III. Title. IV. Series.
Z675.J8I87 2006
025.1'977—dc22   2005020896

British Library Cataloguing in Publication Data is available.

Library of Congress Catalog Card Number: 2005020896
ISBN: 1-59158-149-4
ISSN: 0894-2986

First published in 2006

Libraries Unlimited, 88 Post Road West, Westport, CT 06881
A Member of the Greenwood Publishing Group, Inc.
www.lu.com

Printed in the United States of America

The paper used in this book complies with the Permanent Paper Standard issued by the National Information Standards Organization (Z39.48–1984).

10 9 8 7 6 5 4 3 2 1

Copyright Acknowledgments

The editors and publisher gratefully acknowledge permission for use of the following material:

Appendix 8, AACC Position Statement on Library and Learning Resources Center Programs reprinted with the approval of the American Association of Community Colleges.

Photographs of Cuesta College reprinted with permission.

Photographs in Appendix 9 courtesy of MiraCosta College.

CONTENTS

CONTENTS

CONTENTS

INTRODUCTION

David R. Dowell

This project began with a focus on community college libraries. Most of the chapter authors were recruited with that premise in mind. After the chapter authors had completed their work, however, it increasingly became clear to the editors that most of the topics covered are also relevant for libraries that serve small four-year colleges. These schools would be classified as Baccalaureate Colleges under the Carnegie definitions. The indispensable characteristic of the library managers for whom this book is intended is that they direct libraries in colleges, whether two-year or four-year, that maintain an almost exclusive focus on student learning rather than on faculty research. It is that unity of mission that guided the compilation of the chapters that follow. Before we examine the commonalities, however, we should recognize that there are some differences.

COMMUNITY COLLEGES

Community college, as the term is used in this book, refers to a broad range of two-year, postsecondary schools. Historically they were called junior colleges; in a few places they still are. In some states they focus primarily on vocational education. In others their mission is to prepare students for transfer to four-year colleges. In some cases they are also assigned the task of taking leadership roles in community and regional economic development—particularly workforce training. Increasingly they are becoming vehicles for lifelong learning as they approach their potential to provide education by the community, for the community, and in the community.

This evolution of mission is not complete or uniform. In some areas, community colleges were created specifically to meet one or more of the previously mentioned functions. In others, they developed as an extension of the K–12 school system into a K–14 system and only later were split off into separate institutions and given their own governance system.

In size community colleges vary from student bodies of a few hundred to tens of thousands. At the latter end of the spectrum there are community college campuses with more lower-division undergraduates than can be found on the largest research university campuses. The educational backgrounds and aspirations of these students are broader than for any other type of higher education. Open enrollment policies of many community colleges mean that they must provide precollegiate skills to those adults who did not get them earlier in their life experiences. However, the California Community College system enrolls more post-baccalaureate students than any other system of higher of higher education in the world. As a result, this system sometimes claims to be the world's largest graduate school.

The mission of the twenty-first century community college in the United States has been evolving for the past hundred years. Today's community colleges trace their ancestry to the six students who in 1901 enrolled in what was to become Joliet Junior College in Illinois. This venture was an outgrowth of the local high school—a heritage that still has a noticeable impact on today's colleges in many parts of the country. Even today the procedures and traditions of some community colleges seem to be caught in an arrested state of adolescent development frozen somewhere along its evolutionary metamorphosis from its K–12 roots to institutions that fully embrace the mores of the mainstream of academe. The nature of their creation continues to have an impact today.

In the early twenty-first century community colleges continue to evolve:

> Community colleges are centers of educational opportunity. They are an American invention that put publicly funded higher education at close-to-home facilities, beginning nearly 100 years ago with Joliet Junior College. Since then, they have been inclusive institutions that welcome all who desire to learn, regardless of wealth, heritage, or previous academic experience. The process of making higher education available to the maximum number of people continues to evolve at 1,173 public and independent community colleges. When the branch campuses of community colleges are included, the number totals about 1,600. (American Association of Community Colleges, 2004)

It is not the purpose of this work to redefine the widely accepted levels set forth within the Carnegie Classification of Higher Education. Community colleges fall into the category of Associate's Colleges within that nomenclature:

> These institutions offer associate's degree and certificate programs but, with few exceptions, award no baccalaureate degrees. [This group includes community, junior, and technical colleges.] This group includes institutions where, during the

period studied, bachelor's degrees represented less than 10 percent of all under-graduate awards. (The Carnegie Foundation for the Advancement of Teaching, 2000)

However, the institutions described in this work have a mission that transcends this definition. They are colleges of their communities, by their communities, and for their communities in which they are integral and unifying forces. They serve as avenues for lifelong learning and community development. As such they do not educate just first-time collegians. As mentioned previously, the California Community Colleges enroll more post-baccalaureate students than any other system of higher education in the world. In some states there is periodic pressure for two-year colleges to evolve into bachelor's degree–granting institutions, four-year colleges to evolve into comprehensive universities, and comprehensive universities to evolve into research universities. Sometimes this pressure is internal from within the colleges, but other times it comes from legislators seeking to provide more educational opportunities that are more conveniently located for constituents. At this writing there is a bill moving through the Arizona legislature to create "four-year community colleges." Often this solution is perceived to be cheaper, since two-year colleges are funded at significantly lower rates per full-time student than are four-year colleges and universities. In other states institutional roles are more tightly defined with little possibility of change.

Publicly funded community colleges have latent political clout within their states that is rarely harnessed. All state legislators are likely to have a community college within their districts. The same cannot be said for four-year institutions. The harnessing of this potent political force is rarely accomplished except in moments of extreme threat. The very diffusion of control to individual communities that allows each institution to be uniquely positioned to meet local needs also makes it difficult for them to speak with a clear, collective, and unambiguous voice at the state level. Within this conflict of role definition lies much of the challenge for securing future political and therefore fiscal support.

According to figures released by The Carnegie Foundation, two-year colleges are by far the most numerous type of institution within higher education. They make up more that twice the number of the next largest category. The 1,025 publicly funded associate colleges make up only 61.5 percent of the total number of the schools thus classified, but they enroll the vast majority of the students (The Carnegie Foundation for the Advancement of Teaching, 2000). They are the primary focus of this work. although many of the issues discussed apply equally to the private schools in this category. In fact, much of the subsequent discussions apply to any college for which the primary focus is teaching and not research.

BACCALAUREATE COLLEGES

Baccalaureate colleges are primarily undergraduate colleges. However, things are not always as clear-cut as they appear. Of the 606 Baccalaureate Colleges listed by The Carnegie Foundation, almost 10 percent of them fell into the sub-category of "Baccalaureate/Associate's Colleges." "These institutions are under-graduate colleges where the majority of conferrals are below the baccalaureate level (associate's degrees and certificates). During the period studied, bachelor's degrees accounted for at least ten percent of undergraduate awards" (The Carn-egie Foundation for the Advancement of Teaching, 2000). It would appear that these institutions might already, in some cases, be very close to being the four-year community college envisioned by some members of the Arizona legislature.

However, the distribution by form of governance for these four-year colleges is very different than for the two-year institutions. The vast majority of the bach-elor's degree institutions were privately controlled. Overall, only 15 percent of them were publicly funded. This compares with 61.4 percent of the associate's degree granting schools. As might be expected, the Baccalaureate/Associate's Colleges were more likely to be publicly controlled; but only 15 of 57 such hybrid institutions were state supported (The Carnegie Foundation for the Advance-ment of Teaching, 2000).

Although public versus private control does not define the function of col-leges, it is an important characteristic. So is whether the college is urban or rural. Four-year colleges are more likely to be residential campuses than their two-year counterparts. All of these features profoundly affect all aspects of the schools. However, both baccalaureate and community colleges share one critical feature: Their primary reason for existence is to help students learn rather than to create new knowledge. That is what the teaching faculty does; it is what the libraries should be doing as well.

FROM TEACHING TO LEARNING

In recent years there has been a shift of focus from input measures to output measures. These have affected different parts of the country and different parts of undergraduate education at different rates. By now all regional accrediting agencies have incorporated elements of this paradigm shift into their standards. Many of us first heard of this movement a decade or two ago through efforts to reconceptualize the role of classroom faculty "from the sage on the stage to the guide on the side." In some ways this is just a new way of saying the old expres-sion "If the student has not learned, the teacher has not taught." In other ways the current emphasis on measurable student learning outcomes takes this dialog a step or two further. Accrediting agencies are asking colleges to document the dialog that is taking place on campuses about student learning outcomes. As this dialog becomes institutionalized, the spotlight shifts from a focus on faculty and teaching to students and learning—measurable learning. Symbolic of this change, some colleges have attempted to institutionalize this by changing titles. For example, instead of having a Vice President for Academic Affairs or a Vice President for Instruction, they now have a Vice President for Student Learning;

instead of a Dean of Humanities they now have a Dean of Student Learning, Humanities; and so on. Only time will tell whether this change of vocabulary is but a passing fad or whether it is going to transform the educational process in some significant way.

In some ways libraries may have been ahead of the curve in renaming themselves learning resource centers. However, it is difficult to document that this change in nomenclature has had a significant impact on our ability to help our students learn. In many colleges learning resource centers are reverting back to using the term *libraries*, often reflecting that, in the vernacular used by students and faculty, our departments continue to be thought of as libraries.

Although the following statement was written as a definition of community college libraries, it equally applies to four-year colleges as well:

> Community colleges are comprehensive institutions that provide a full array of educational programs. Library programs, as part of that full array, are indispensable to the teaching/learning mission of the community college. In today's world, libraries are not just a place, because many library resources and services are online and accessible from anywhere. Community colleges continue to need libraries as a physical space, as long as students need assistance to conquer the digital or information divide and there is a need to house and provide access to materials not available electronically. (American Association of Community Colleges, 2002)

More importantly, many library faculties have taken leading roles in helping their colleges incorporate information literacy into the competencies students are expected to learn. It is not the purpose of this book to discuss in any comprehensive way the dynamic of information literacy. It is important, however, that information literacy and student learning remain at the forefront of the minds of library managers as they attend to the seemingly mundane but important tasks that are discussed in the chapters that follow.

LIBRARIES FOR LEARNING

Libraries in colleges differ from those found in universities in that their collections and services are designed to support the curriculum of the college. In collection development there is no need to build a research level collection so that someone can write a dissertation 20 years from now. The emphasis is on supporting the current curriculum. When there is a windfall of money to support an enhancement of the collection, community college library directors should not feel torn between whether to use it to buy more journals to support the research of faculty and graduate students or to support the classroom needs of undergraduate students. Too often in a university there is an unconscious assumption that if the in-depth needs of graduate students and faculty researchers are met, then of course the needs of the undergraduates will be far exceeded. Good librarians know that this is not the case. However, they sometimes have to struggle to communicate this to university faculty who are selected, assigned, retained, and rewarded almost solely on the basis of research output. Such faculty members are predisposed to urge the spending of any available dollar on additional research journals and conference proceedings. It is easy for them to forget that their undergraduate students do not need to know what has happened in their discipline in the past five minutes. They need to know what the discipline is. They need broad coverage of the subject instead of in-depth coverage of a minute subdivision of that discipline.

Community and baccalaureate colleges are institutions in which by far the primary reason for being is to help students learn. Unlike research and comprehensive universities, colleges disseminate knowledge and make no pretense of being in the business of creating knowledge. They hire, assign, retain, and reward faculty on the basis of ability to affect student learning—not on the basis of research output. This learning is delivered locally, consumed locally, and evaluated locally. Since library services are generally delivered, consumed, and evaluated locally as well, they fit in more comfortably in colleges than in other levels of higher education.

True cutting-edge research often cannot be evaluated locally. If it is specialized enough, there may be only a dozen or so similar researchers around the world who truly understand whether a piece of research is truly earthshaking or if the researcher is just blowing smoke. In order to make promotion and tenure decisions in such a case, it is often necessary to involve some of these external specialists in the evaluation process because no one on the home campus is expert enough to make valid judgments at the frontiers of a discipline.

Several decades ago Alvin Gouldner distinguished between two categories of staff members. The first he called "cosmopolitans," whom he defined as being "low on loyalty to the employing organization, high on commitment to specialized role skills, and likely to use an outer reference group orientation." He contrasted that with "locals," whom he described as staff members "whose loyalty to the employing organization is high, have a low commitment to specialized role skills, and are likely to use an inner reference group orientation" (Gouldner 1957, 290).

Last year Kenneth Green updated Gouldner's definitions and applied them to the Internet and distance education:

> It's easy to simplify and extend Gouldner's characteristics of cosmopolitans and locals in academe. For example, in campus communities, cosmopolitans identify with their disciplines over their institutions. While they may work at Acme College, they are, first and foremost, biologists, Chaucer scholars, economists, mathematicians, psychologists, sociologists, and zoologists. In contrast, while locals may teach these subjects, they identify themselves as Acme faculty ahead of their disciplinary affiliation. Cosmopolitans are more likely to work in universi-

ties and other elite institutions; in contrast, locals may be employed in teaching institutions, including community colleges. Cosmopolitans are more interested in research than locals, who would focus more on teaching, student contact, and committee work. (Green 2004, 37)

ROLE OF LIBRARIANS

In colleges for which teaching is the primary focus, librarians are on much more equal footing with classroom faculty than in research universities. Certainly the educational credentials of librarians are on par with those of any group of classroom faculty in most colleges. In addition the role of librarians is in helping students learn information literacy skills is more compatible with the tasks of locals than it is of cosmopolitans. As a result librarians are more comfortable in exercising their full rights and responsibilities as faculty members in this environment. They have no reason to take a backseat to any group on campus unless they impose this position on themselves.

MOVING FROM LIBRARIAN TO MANAGER

The library hierarchies in such colleges are very flat. Sometimes there is only one librarian who serves as director whether or not that is the official title. In all but the very largest college libraries, there are no formal manager-in-training positions such as assistant directors or assistant deans through which frontline librarians can make a systematic transition from professional to managerial activities. In collective bargaining environments, this distinction is often codified and even more difficult to bridge in an incremental and orderly manner.

As a result librarians often find they have become managers but with little preparation, no orderly transition, and no clear mentors close at hand to guide them through their new responsibilities. One only has to sign on to appropriate Listservs to validate this observation. The cries for help emanate daily. The chapters that follow do not serve as an encyclopedic management text for new library managers; rather they provide information on a series of situations that will confront all college library managers sooner or later.

A quick look at the demographics of our profession shows that we are not immune to the changes that are going on in the society of which we are a part. Librarians, particularly college library directors, will be retiring in unprecedented numbers in the next 5–10 years as the baby boomers exit the full-time workforce in increasing numbers. This phenomenon in the general population is compounded because of some historical factors within librarianship. After the shortage of librarians during the 1960s that followed the widespread acceptance of the MLS as the appropriate entrance credential, the 1970s produced a bumper crop as schools moved to address this need. The librarians who were a part of that surge into the field are now approaching retirement en masse.

MANAGING COMMUNITY AND OTHER COLLEGE LIBRARIES IN THE TWENTY-FIRST CENTURY

The following chapters are more experientially based than the preceding discussion. They were selected to give college library managers—particularly new managers—resources to assist them as they try to lead their libraries to ever-higher success in fostering student learning. Although hardy souls may wish to read this text from cover-to-cover, most managers probably will choose to consult particular chapters and/or appendices at the time of specific need.

REFERENCES

American Association of Community Colleges. 2002. "AACC Position Statement on Library and Learning Resource Center Programs." Approved by the AACC Board of Directors November 8, 2002. http://www.aacc.nche.edu/Template.cfm?Section=Position_Statements&template= /ContentManagement/ContentDisplay.cfm&ContentID=9634&InterestCategoryID=224&Name =Position%20Statement&ComingFrom=InterestDisplay. Accessed July 16, 2005.
———. 2004. "About Community Colleges." http://www.aacc.nche.edu/Template.cfm?section=AboutCommunityColleges. Accessed July 16, 2005.
The Carnegie Foundation for the Advancement of Teaching. 2000. "The Carnegie Classification of Institutions of Higher Education." http://www.carnegiefoundation.org/Classification/. Accessed July 16, 2005.
Gouldner, Alvin W. 1957–58. "Cosmopolitans and Locals: Toward a Latent Analysis of Social Role Parts 1 and 2." *Administrative Science Quarterly* 2 (3), 4: 281–306; 444–480.
Green, Kenneth C. 2004. "Digital Dilemmas: Cosmopolitans, Content and Productivity." http://www.educause.edu/ir/library/pdf/ffpfp0104.pdf. Accessed July 16, 2005.

I

INDISPENSABLE: A QUALITY STAFF: ORGANIZED, INSPIRED, AND RIGHT FOR THE JOB

1 ORGANIZATIONAL STRUCTURE OF LIBRARY/ LEARNING RESOURCE CENTERS

Michael D. Rusk

INTRODUCTION

This chapter examines the building blocks that make up a community college library. To understand the organizational structure of libraries and learning resources centers (LRCs) it is necessary to understand how they evolved as part of the community college since the first was founded around the turn of the twentieth century. What were some of the underlying attitudes that guided community colleges through the years? Where are community colleges likely to grow in the future? These questions and others are the focus of this chapter on the structure of libraries and LRCs. Examples of organization charts included here are general diagrams only and do not reflect particular institutions.

Judy Born, Sue Clayton, and Aggie Balash published an outstanding study of community college organizations in 2000. Titled *Community College Library Job Descriptions and Organizational Charts*, this work, based on a survey of 268 libraries, contains a wealth of data on job titles, responsibilities, reporting structures, and departmental relationships in community college libraries. It is recommended to anyone wishing to go beyond the information in this chapter and delve into the variety of structures in libraries today.

ORGANIZATIONAL IDENTITY IN COMMUNITY COLLEGES

Community college libraries are unique entities that provide both general and specialized services for their parent institutions. A study of the organiza-

3

tion of libraries and LRCs in two-year colleges yields such a variety of structural models that it is difficult to point to basic themes common to all. There is even a bewildering variety of names applied to the library that imply roles in the institution that are distinct from the traditional role played by the library of an upper division college or university: Library, LRC, Educational Resources, Information Services, and Library Media Services are all encountered when studying the unique entity commonly known as the library in a community college.

For the purposes of this overview, we refer to the library/LRC to describe the blend of traditional, print-oriented library services and its associated instructional media services. This pairing of library and media, or audio-visual services, is one of the few common themes of community college library/LRC programs and may be a major factor in distinguishing the library in the two-year college from its university counterpart.

The structural norms found in library/LRC programs today are deeply rooted in the cultural past that gave birth to the first two-year college in Joliet, Illinois, in 1901. Early community colleges were viewed as grassroots institutions, closer to the needs of the working class in the rapidly expanding economy of early twentieth century America.

> Because community colleges contribute to the continual process of human development and have grown out of the needs of the masses they have been called 'democracy's college,' 'opportunity college' and like the land grant colleges, 'the people's college'. (Roueche and Baker 1987, 5)

Early libraries in community colleges were conceived as supporting two primary institutional goals: (1) college transfer, or preparing students with the first two years of study leading to completion of a bachelor's degree at a university; and (2) vocational training or the provision of short-term, targeted courses and degree programs aimed at students desiring to climb the ladder of success. In the area of college transfer, the community college offered access to higher education for students who were not able to attend a university. Vocational training, in contrast, served to enrich local labor pools while preserving the dream of economic success for students either unable to or disinterested in pursuing a bachelor's degree.

Another formative factor in the growth and structure of libraries/LRCs was the diversity of student skill levels that resulted from increased access to higher education provided by the people's college.

> Once they were admitted, many students found themselves in considerable academic trouble. Since they were deficit in one or more basic skills, they had trouble meeting the rigorous demands of college courses. (Roueche and Baker 1987, 7)

The need for high academic standards, which community colleges needed to compete well with four-year and comprehensive institutions, and the goal of providing access to college for large segments of the population, many of whom were deficient in academic skills, presented challenges felt especially in the library/LRC programs, whose job it was to provide the resources for academic success.

LIBRARIES AND ORGANIZATIONAL IDENTITY

Libraries/LRCs in community colleges have followed the same paths toward a defining organizational identity that community colleges have over the years. The stresses caused by the conflicting goals of vocational training and college transfer have caused librarians to seek creative means of meeting student needs, and library/LRC structures have often taken unusual shapes as a result.

Library/LRC programs have tended to support the mission of college transfer more than vocational training. Book and periodical collection building resemble the collecting and cataloging methods of university libraries, and professional and clerical staffs are usually organized in similar departmental structures. Vocational training tends to be less general and focused upon up-to-date methods in use in the workplace; this may have led to the early incorporation of audiovisuals for both faculty presentations and student study in the library/LRC. This movement led to the creation of departments for managing and accessing audiovisual resources in community colleges before they were introduced in university libraries.

Finally, the library/LRC was considered one of the physical assets of the community college and, like other support areas, separate from the academic apparatus of the institution. The American Council on Education in 1921 issued the first published standards for evaluating community colleges. Standard 8 read;

> The material equipment and upkeep of a junior college, including its buildings, lands, laboratories, apparatus and libraries, and their efficient operation in relation to its educational program should also be considered when judging an institution. (Witt et al. 1994, 89)

In our exploration of the structures of library/LRC programs, it must be understood that the community college as a parent institution derives from a complex, even contradictory, organizational identity, and this factor has been the primary reason that library/LRC programs have taken the unusual and varied shapes seen in community colleges today.

GENERAL LIBRARY/LRC STRUCTURE

Background

The structure or the functional division of labor in an organization is reflective of the fundamental reasons why an organization exists. Libraries/LRCs in community colleges have the twofold purpose of serving the information needs of students while providing resources and equipment that support faculty in the classroom. These objectives overlap normally, so that teachers can augment their own knowledge, which they in turn impart in their courses, and can also use research tools helpful to the students working on assignments.

Library/LRC programs developed from community colleges' need to support students desiring to transfer to a bachelor's program in an upper-division college upon completion of their first two years of study. Print collections and later audiovisual collections were acquired, cataloged, and made accessible in scaled-down versions of traditional academic libraries that tended to divide duties into public services, technical services, and audiovisual (AV) services. Though there continue to be numerous variations, this three-part structure can be discerned in the organization charts of most community college library/LRC programs today.

Sample Organization

The organization chart presented in Figure 1.1 is an abstraction of most of the general functions provided by library/LRC programs for a single campus college.

The three-part breakdown into public, technical, and AV services is the lowest level generalization underlying library/LRC structural plans. Keep in mind that there is considerable variation in the placement of certain functions; interlibrary loan, for instance, is often considered technical instead of public services. Also, AV, sometimes called media, resources may be cataloged and shelved into the stacks alongside print resources, changing the 'AV collections' box to the public services area. The chart in Figure 1.1, however, will serve our purposes as a basic map of the general structural building blocks of the library/LRC in most community colleges today.

Library/LRC programs have grown in the 1980s and 1990s with the development of richly diverse multimedia environments, microcomputer technology, and networking. Responding to change brought on by the Internet, new services and staff with technology-rich skill sets have pulled the library/LRC organization chart in many directions and brought about sweeping changes in the basic three-part structure.

Public Services

Public service functions lead the way in providing services to the students or faculty who come into the library/LRC. In most community colleges, a faculty-level professional librarian will be present to oversee clerical and support staff who carry out functions such as circulation, reserves, interlibrary loan, maintenance of book and AV stacks, access to periodical back issues, and services related to fax and photocopy machines. Though there are many ways to divide public service functions in a library/LRC it is most common to find the general area designations of *Circulation* and *Reference* assigned to the plethora of activities carried out on the floor to deliver library/LRC services to the user.

The focal point of the public services functional division is the reference element. Whether called reference area, department, office, or desk, this is the

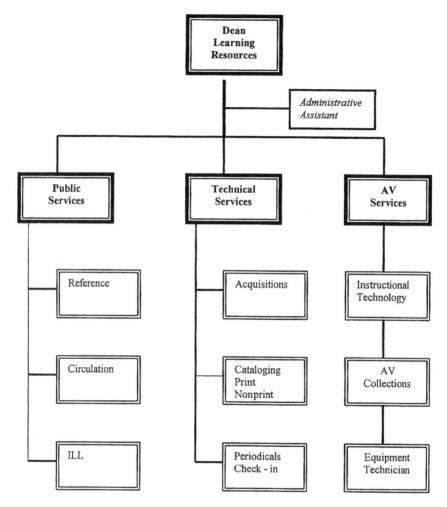

Figure 1.1 Library/LRC Organization (Single Campus)

primary domain of professional staff who are on hand to be the essential link between students and resources in the collections. In addition to assisting with use of resources, reference librarians carry out collection development, bibliographic instruction, evaluation of online databases, and specialized services to faculty needing research beyond what they can do themselves.

Interlibrary Loan (ILL)

The ILL function in library/LRCs is normally managed by a professional librarian with extensive bibliographic and networking skills. OCLC WorldCat and other bibliographic utilities have made possible a far broader base of service than was possible in the 1960s and 1970s, when ILL was primarily carried out among sets of libraries in defined geographical areas. ILL services interface with the functions of the reference desk by providing document delivery for articles located on bibliographic databases. For this reason the ILL office is often located near the reference areas in the library/LRC. One or more clerical staff members normally assist in the ILL office, and there is often a courier service to deliver materials between libraries in the vicinity.

Many library/LRCs combine ILL with other functions and make it the responsibility of a single staff member, sometimes designated Library Assistant and often reporting to a public service librarian acting in the role of supervisor. The terms "ILL/Reserves" and "ILL/Acquisitions" appear in some organization charts. These designations often indicate that the ILL function is assigned to a single staff member who has multiple duties and carries out ILL to a narrowly defined group, usually students. Here a fundamental question arises as to the breadth of ILL services in a library/LRC: Who are the recipients of ILL services? How far can ILL services be extended? There is a difference in magnitude between an ILL office that retrieves articles and books for students who are working on assignments and a larger-scale ILL effort that can support students, faculty, and staff with information needs like in-depth research. Faculty seeking advanced degrees make extensive use of ILL. If ILL is offered as part of the library/LRC services, it should be equipped on a larger scale to handle the demand.

Technical Services

The set of functions normally associated with technical services includes the acquisition, cataloging, and processing of materials for the shelf. Nonprint or AV processing can involve a check of the item itself to make sure the order was correctly filled as well as actually viewing an instructional video, DVD, or slide set to ensure that items delivered are of the expected quality.

Online ordering via the Internet has made manual systems obsolete for ordering books and media and has dramatically shortened the time between order and delivery, a common problem for acquisitions departments in the past. Some libraries /LRCs have eliminated the acquisitions area entirely. Instead, librarians order material online through vendors such as Baker & Taylor (Title Source II) or Blackwell (Collection Manager) and have the materials shipped directly to them. Processing and cataloging are provided by most vendors so that online ordering systems make it possible for a librarian needing books on a subject to place an order online and actually have the fully processed item in hand and ready to give to the patron in a matter of days.

Integrated library systems, high-speed local processing, and services delivered over the Internet have affected the structure of technical services in community college libraries/LRCs more than any other factor. Organization charts often show a librarian with a title such as Technical Services Librarian, with assistance by one or more skilled technical staff carrying out the function of acquisitions and cataloging, which has been the traditional technical services role.

Some libraries/LRCs include the function of records management and archiving in the technical services department. Staffs are generally composed of an archivist or librarian assigned to that role supported by one or more clerical staff and reporting to the librarian in charge of Technical Services.

Audiovisual Services

No area of the library/LRC has experienced such rapid change as the AV or media area. From humble beginnings as the room where projectors and tape recorders were stored to a broad-based electronic media support department, these sets of services have grown to include closed-circuit television systems, satellite downlinks, video production, and support for high-tech presentation systems in classrooms campuswide. In many instances media services have broken away from the library/LRC entirely and become a separate department headed by a professional with experience and training in the area of instructional media. Titles such as Instructional Technology Director, AV Specialist/Videographer, Media Support Coordinator, and Media Services Manager appear on the organization charts for some libraries/LRCs, and many have split away entirely and report to a distance learning department or instructional technology area.

There remains a need to provide for cataloged media collections, and often a Media Services Librarian will provide support for faculty requesting materials to use for instruction and for students who are using media software as part of assignments or to create their own presentations for class. Cataloging media software is a specialty that is generally assigned to a skilled technician in the technical services area working alongside professional librarians responsible for the library/LRC catalog and bibliographic data management.

Administration

An individual, most often with the title Library Director, generally heads libraries/LRCs in community colleges. Other titles, including Director of Library Services, Director of LRC, and Director of Library/Media Services can be found, as well as Dean of Learning Resources Center.

Regardless of title, this midlevel administrator often reports to a Vice President of Academic Affairs and is responsible for the overall functioning of the library/LRC department collegewide. Institutions with multiple campuses, each having a library/LRC, typically report to the library/LRC director or dean through a head librarian or Library Services Coordinator for that location.

Job descriptions for library/LRC directors or deans generally include all responsibility for management of their organization and strategic planning for the future. The director/dean often handles budgeting and expenditure of funds for library resources, supplies, and equipment though personnel funds may be administered by the college accounting or comptrollers office. Other duties of library/ LRC directors and deans often include participation in partnering arrangements with other departments to provide a common base for services. Often a distance learning department will partner with the library/LRC and another area such as faculty development to provide support for courseware development, resource sharing, or support for online classes and other services brought on by the deployment of instructional computer software on campus.

Library/LRC directors and deans often have numerous administrative duties added to their job descriptions, and these duties can extend beyond the services maintained by their department. Universities as well as community colleges have shown a tendency to designate a single office as the resource office for copyright information. This office is often that of the Library Director. Other duties such as records management liaison between the institution and the governing body, such as the state, also may fall to the head of the library/LRC.

Multicampus Structures

Community colleges with multiple campuses are meant to bring higher education closer to the people who need it; however, they are faced with providing the services of a fully functioning college on a campus that is part of a larger system and that may share some support services with other campuses. Computer services, security, purchasing, and network support are some functions that may be centralized on one campus yet have services that support all campuses in the system, as shown in Figure 1.2.

Library/LRC programs in a multicampus environment also centralize some functions for efficient support institutionwide. Public services such as reference, circulation, and some media activities tend to be the basic service set of campus libraries/ LRCs. Technical services such as acquisitions, cataloging, serials control, and systems administration are often centralized on one campus to eliminate duplication of effort and to ensure consistency. Media services may have a centralized distribution system for sharing resources among campuses, and some functions requiring deeper skills, such as video production and instructional television, may be concentrated on one campus but provide services to all. Smaller media units on campus provide software and equipment support for instruction and viewing stations for students working on assignments.

Though there are benefits to centralization of administration and technical support, some institutions aim for fully functioning library/LRC programs on each campus. Benefits are gained from being able to handle all support needs at the campus level without having to call upon services centralized elsewhere in the college, but the inevitable overlap of functions that results from duplication of services and staff on each campus can prove expensive in the long run.

Library/LRCs in multicampus environments tend to have the mission of being a single program with several campus components. Staffs working in librar-

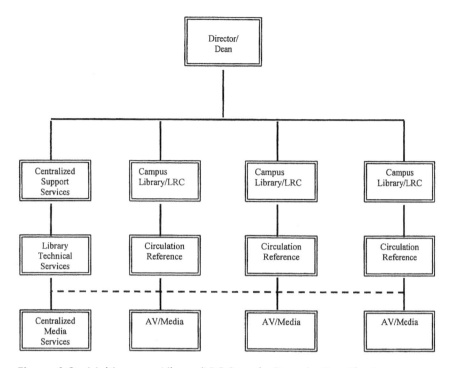

Figure 1.2   Multicampus Library/LRC Sample Organization Chart

ies/LRCs that are spread over a large area tend to work as a team with their peers on other campuses. Staff rotations are common and beneficial to keep skills fresh and bring about teamwork among widely distributed staff. Organization charts for libraries/LRCs in multicampus institutions show highly similar staffing on each campus with functions and titles reflecting closely related or duplicated duties. Efficiencies are gained in a multicampus library/LRC program by fostering a sharing environment for resources and equipment so that books, articles, and especially costly instructional videos can be used on more than one campus and save costs of buying several copies. Automated library systems often take into account that materials may be actively shared between service units and provide control systems to make the distribution of resources efficient. For example, see Figure 1.3 for the organization chart for Tulsa Community College LRC.

VARIATIONS IN LIBRARY/LRC STRUCTURE

Information, data, and library services are delivered in a wide variety of ways on community college campuses. Some libraries/LRCs are stand-alone operations with an entire building dedicated to the purpose. Other libraries/ LRCs are part of a larger physical structure and often have close relationships with related areas

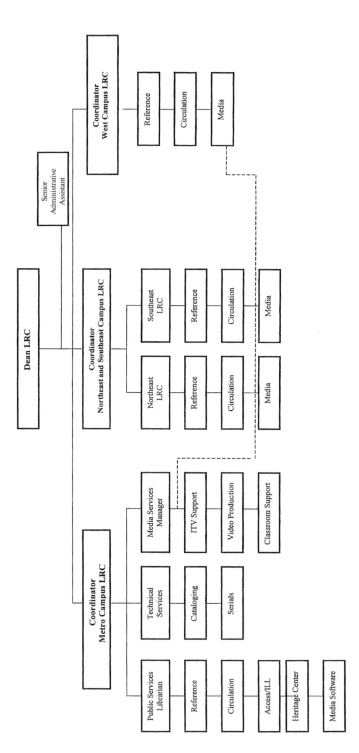

Figure 1.3 Organization Chart—Tulsa Community College Learning Resources Center

such as distance learning, instructional television (ITV), and computer and language labs. Also many institutions have areas specializing in instructional support for faculty who use multimedia in class and often create their own presentations. Though traditional structures can be discerned in most library/LRC organization charts, new functional units can be seen growing out of the existing structure to accommodate new roles for staff working with high-technology systems and instructional design software.

Many forces affect an organization's structure. Budget constraints, consortium arrangements, mergers with other departments on campus, and the development of new instructional programs are just a few of the activities that can bring about change to an organization chart. But no force has brought about more rapid change than the growth of computer technology and its related networking infrastructure. The impact of technology has been felt in two primary areas in community colleges: and library/LRC programs have been quick to respond by finding new ways of organizing their staff and resources to meet the challenges.

The impact of computer and networking technology began to appear in the 1970s and 1980s with a tremendous demand for training to meet the labor needs of business and industry for computer programmers, systems analysts, and management information system professionals. Library/LRC programs supported this effort by strengthening collections in the areas of computer science and adding periodicals and other materials to help keep faculty and administration up to date on new developments taking place as the national computing infrastructure grew.

The second impact of new technology in community colleges was felt in the 1980s and 1990s as computer and networking systems were implemented to bring about efficiencies in the college infrastructure itself. As the presence of microcomputers in college offices grew, libraries/ LRCs purchased workstations for professional staff and for student use in the reference area. Online Public Access Catalogs (OPACs) migrated from terminals to microcomputer workstations and bibliographic databases were purchased on CD-ROM that could be either loaded individually by the user or juke-boxed for ready access to several disks by a single workstation. Library/LRC directors in the 1990s found that purchasing new workstations to replace older units and keeping up with the demands for software and online databases became a major budget item that often came at a time when library/LRCs were experiencing cutbacks in funding.

Librarian Specialties

As computer technology advanced on campus, the library/LRC was quick to adapt by adding electronic resources to the reference areas and by integrating microcomputer workstations into the offices and technical service areas. Most community college libraries/LRCs had invested in an automated library system by the mid 1990s, and this became yet another factor forcing change in the organization chart. Early automated library systems such as NOTIS, Gaylord, and VTLS placed requirements on librarians that were difficult to meet. New systems emerging in the mid and late 1990s, such as Endeavor's Voyager, Innovative Interfaces Inc., SIRSI, and DRA, required the appointment of a systems administrator from among the ranks of the library/LRC to oversee configuration, to provide liaison with technical support staff both on campus and from the system vendor to troubleshoot problems, see to file maintenance, and help with staff training.

Systems Librarian

As automated library systems made possible a wider integration of the libraries/LRCs, electronic databases users found the resulting increase in access to these resources to be invaluable for assignments. Some community college libraries/LRCs developed a professional level position to address the increased demands for specialized computer related skills to support the new electronic resources and the computing base deployed in the public service areas. Job titles for this position include Information Services Librarian, Electronic Resources/ Reference Librarian, Information Services Librarian, and numerous others. The responsibilities for this position may include the following:

- Maintain library/LRC computers;
- Assist students in using online databases;
- Serve as liaison with automated library system vendor, OCLC, and other technology-related entities;
- Organize contracts and licenses for electronic library materials; and
- Liaison with computer staff to maintain a library/LRC server.

The Internet has had a fundamental impact on instruction in community colleges and in the delivery of library/LRC materials. This has changed some of the original responsibilities of the systems librarian. Institution-level programs such as WebCT and Blackboard have made it possible for online databases to be accessed through a college instructional portal. Oversight for this activity involves the librarian assigned to technology or systems to work directly with related areas such as Distance Learning, Instructional Media, or Telecommunications.

Most libraries/LRCs have found that the Web page has become the face of the library to many students. A well-constructed Web page is vital to the successful delivery of services in electronic format. Experience shows that once a Web page has been designed and implemented it requires continuous updating to stay useful. This task is often assigned to the systems librarian, who works with other Web page staff elsewhere in the college to integrate the library/LRC site into a larger institutional Web site.

Finally, some mention must be made of microcomputer-based instructional labs located on campus. Though a lab may be part of an instructional division, many libraries/LRCs have served as the host for the college computer lab. Some libraries/LRCs have incorporated their own computer room for student use of electronic resources and bibliographic instruction. Often the library computer lab is used by instructional areas for classes and by college departments for training in a variety of computer-related skills. Though normally maintained by one or more technicians, the computer lab in the library/LRC will often be placed under the jurisdiction of the librarian assigned to systems (see Figure 1.4).

It must be emphasized that community college organization charts show a wide variety in placement of the librarian assigned to oversee the electronic resources and computing base of the library. In many if not most instances the systems function is assigned to a public or technical services department head who works with all departments to maintain the automated library system and the online databases. It is not anticipated that library technology will ever decline in complexity, making the role of the systems librarian only more of a burden until it must necessarily split into more than one position or be taken over by another department of the college assigned to broad technical support functions that include the computing base of the library/LRC.

Media Specialties

The variation in structures represented by community college library/LRC organization charts is once again seen in the areas of media or AV services. In the past a single media area could serve the needs of instructional areas for hardware and software, but advances in multimedia technology have increased the complexity of demands and brought about sweeping change in the organization chart. New systems such as closed-circuit television, satellite downlinking, interactive authoring of software, and video production changed the nature of work for the traditional media technician. A parallel path of change is seen in new media formats including videodisk and CD-ROM in the 1990s and DVD in the early 2000s. On the library side, technical service librarians continue to catalog materials in new formats much as they have in the past, but more advanced formats

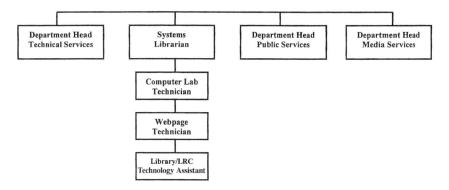

Figure 1.4 Technology Librarian Placement in Organization Chart

such as streaming video, multimedia packages, and faculty course packs stored on campus servers could challenge these practices.

Traditional media services on many campuses have assumed an expanded role due to two primary factors. First, traditional media departments offered a centralized service with technicians delivering equipment from a "ready room" or equipment area. Advanced projection technology in the 1990s, however, changed the central distribution model for media services to a distributed model with equipment permanently mounted in classrooms or instructional areas in which they are used. A ceiling-mounted video projector connected to a microcomputer enables instructors to provide first-rate, high-tech presentations for their students. Other equipment, such as document cameras, VCRs, and electronic screens may also be present in a multimedia classroom. This distributed model requires media staff to be out in the field maintaining equipment in classrooms rather than working from a central area. In addition to presentation systems in classrooms for instruction, media services staff are also called upon to maintain and operate sound systems for specialty areas such as boardrooms and auditoriums. This change from centralized to distributed media services has brought about changes in the structure of media departments in response to entirely new sets of service needs.

The second factor affecting structures of media areas is the growth of instructional design and the need to support faculty and students who wish to use computer technology to create courseware or to fulfill an assignment. Organizations charts in many libraries/LRCs will include a position for Instructional Technology Design Coordinator, Instructional Technologist, Instructional Technology Systems (ITS) Manager, or Education Technology Coordinator, which represents positions defined according to new demands for creation, maintenance, and delivery of instructional materials in computer-based formats. In many instances an Instructional Technology department will be shown as an entirely separate function, having split from the library/LRC to report to a dean of distance learning or telecommunications (see Figure 1.5 for an example).

Media services will continue to challenge the traditional structure of the library/LRC as new technologies improve the teaching process and the demand for technical support continues to rise. Some colleges are finding creative ways to provide support for computer and media systems campuswide by using cross-trained technicians in ad hoc teams to solve technical support issues and carry out large-scale equipment installations. An approach that seems promising is the deployment of media, computer, and lab technicians to support a centralized Help Desk. In this model technicians are managed in teams that provide rapid response to technical problems raised by calls to the Help Desk and routed to the appropriate technician on duty. Many Help Desk software programs issue a ticket when a call is made. This ticket serves as the caller's check to see if their request is being answered and as a work order for the technician that describes the problem to be solved. Finally, the ticket serves as documentation of a technical problem that, when viewed alongside hundreds of other tickets, may show

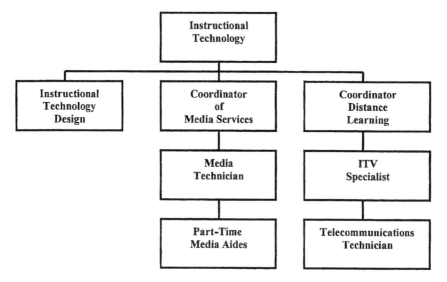

Figure 1.5 Media Services/Instructional Support Sample Chart

trends in equipment problems being reported. Seen in context, this could lead to prevention.

LIBRARY/LRC STRUCTURE: THE FUTURE

Any organization is subject to change from stresses in the institution and in the changing nature of its product. In the case of libraries, the product is information services plus the context n which they are delivered. Community college libraries/LRCs deliver information in the form of books, periodicals, microfiche, media, and electronic data accessible via computer. The context in which this information is delivered consists of the study areas of the library, AV viewing rooms, computer workstations and, sometimes, the computer room in the library. All of these items compose the essential product provided by the library/LRC to its parent institution, and this product is undergoing dynamic change.

The Virtual Library

At some point most library/LRC directors realize that their upper administration is not reading the same professional literature that the librarians are. Both groups are aware of the digital transformation taking place with regard to information normally housed in libraries, but librarians are sensitive to the fact that the print environment is not going to disappear overnight. Librarians tend to see the change as gradual and requiring a deepening of the staffing and material structure of the library/LRC to support the growing digital domain.

Upper administrators, in contrast, may view the virtual library concept from an entirely different angle. The term "library without walls" creates uncomplicated images in the minds of top management eager to cut costs in facilities and staffing. A library without walls is perhaps also a library without expensive books and staff—a notion sure to get the attention of fiscal officers on the lookout for cuts in costs.

The perception that digital libraries don't need facilities is reinforced by the rapid growth of online degree programs. Some colleges claim to be entirely online institutions offering degree programs in specific areas. Courses are supplemented by resource packs assembled from various sources and are often themselves supplemented by online access to an electronic library from a third party source.

Most librarians are aware of what is really needed to deliver quality services to students studying in a community college. A virtual or electronic library is a desired aspect to provide information to students taking online courses or coming to the library/LRC to find research material for assignments, but it is effective only if supported by a traditional library infrastructure. Online databases and electronic research tools do not run themselves. Librarians organized into efficient departmental structures are still needed to acquire, maintain, and teach the use of digital information. A virtual library will be useful only if it is part of a larger nonvirtual structure.

Another aspect of the virtual library paradigm is virtual reference. This is the ability to use computer and network technology to bring the learner at a remote location into contact with a reference librarian on duty in the library/LRC. It is the missing piece in the virtual library idea. Though still in the early stages, virtual reference services are yet another example of advanced technology nested within a traditional library service structure for optimum effectiveness.

Library/LRC organization charts will change to accommodate digital information services as the shift away from the print environment accelerates. Traditional departments such as Acquisitions and Circulation may disappear from organization charts in some community college libraries/LRCs because they are primarily oriented toward purchasing and circulation of print materials. New structures will appear based on services related to electronic information resources, and these may stretch beyond the physical library to other learning areas, labs, and offices on campus.

The Agile Organization

Library/LRC programs are one of the few parts of the community college where true innovation takes place. In many instances it was the library/LRC that purchased the first fax machine or where CD-ROMs were first used for data. Authoring software for producing computer-based learning modules often appeared first in the library/LRC media department, as did new media formats such as videodisks and later DVDs. The library/LRC may have been the first place on campus to install and use a satellite dish for teleconferencing or to operate an electronic bulletin board. Librarians in some community colleges in the early 1990s were finding access to a totally new entity called the World Wide Web and found ways to gain access to it even in its early, prebrowser form to locate information for their users. In so doing, librarians were the first on campus to access the Internet and to begin to teach their faculty peers how to use it.

There is a reason why libraries/LRCs are often the source of early innovations in community colleges. Library/LRC structures are generally organized around functional designs that resemble the processes that move information in the form of books, periodicals, and media through the steps required for ordering, processing, and final delivery to the customer. Lying beneath the organization chart of the library/LRC is the fundamental management paradigm of the supply chain, and librarians, usually without realizing it, have learned to operate efficiently in that environment.

> Companies are developing new strategies with the goal of reinventing themselves into agile, nimble organizations—companies capable of not just reacting to challenges in their markets but of creating the type of change that can sustain profitable growth. (Fox 1999, 1)

Business and industry are organizing their internal structures around the concept of the agile organization. An agile organization is one with the ability to quickly match supply with demand while maintaining a high level of quality control. These changes take some predictable forms:

- Cutting backroom paper-based processes
- Integrating all transactions and documentation on the Internet
- Moving the product as close as possible to the customer
- Communication between all departments in the chain
- Finding core competencies and outsourcing everything else

Libraries/LRCs may find the agile organization concept useful in devising structures for the delivery of digital information to their users both on and off campus. Libraries/LRCs may find themselves joined with learning labs, instructional television, language labs, and other resource areas in co-managed structures that allow librarians to teach the use of electronic resources beyond the traditional library setting. Cross-trained teams of technicians from media areas and computer labs may work together to provide technical support to a broad user base campuswide. As mixed media resources are distributed over wide area networks to workstations throughout the college, traditional technical support units will be overextended if new structures are not developed to accommodate an expanded technology base.

19

This is only a small glimpse of what the future will hold for library/LRC organizational structures. Agile organizations will use the Internet in the fullest possible way to expedite the work of all service areas, and this will bring about changes to organization charts that cannot be anticipated today. As the new digital information world continues to define itself, libraries/LRCs will reshape themselves into integrated learning centers distributing information in multiple digital formats to workstations campuswide and to learners working from home. The "anytime, anywhere" learning paradigm will be reflected by new organizational structures that are emerging today from the unique and time-tested organizational identity of the community college library/LRC.

REFERENCES

Born, Judy, Sue Clayton, and Aggie Balash. 2000. *Community College Library Job Descriptions and Organizational Charts:* CJCLS Guide #4. Chicago: American Library Association.

Fox, Mary Lou. 1999. *Charting the Course to Successful Supply Chain Management,* Ascet Vol. 1. Rockville, MD: Manugistics Group, Inc.

Roueche, John E., and George A. Baker III. 1987. *Access and Excellence: The Open-Door College.* Washington D.C.: The Community College Press.

Witt, Alan A., James L. Wattenbarger, James F. Gollattscheck, and Joseph E. Suppiger. 1994. *America's Community Colleges: The First Century.* Washington, D.C.: The Community College Press.

2 MANAGING MOTIVATION

W. Jeanne Gardner

It is important that the community college library be a player, helping the institution achieve its academic mission. Staff and resources are required to make the library a viable entity in student success. When I accepted the directorship at a small community college library, it was because I could see areas for development; I, a baby boomer, choose positions where there are things that need to be done. The collection consisted of about 5,000 volumes, most of which were outdated. Early in my tenure at the college, I vividly recall a student asking at the library orientation, "Why do we have to be here? You don't have any books." My response was that things were changing and I invited him to come back in three months and let me know if the library was still a waste of his time. The student didn't repeat his complaint.

The library has moved from a cafeteria corner to its own space in a new building, and its modest collection has grown to about 25,000 volumes. The collection is vigorously deselected to maintain a current collection serving 26 technical and health programs. In addition, the collection boasts more than 9,000 digital books, a full text journal database, and three reference databases. The library collection has come a long way.

The staff of three has become five and has been complemented by five work/study positions. Perhaps the biggest challenge of the position was learning to work with team members—to balance their needs and wants against the goals of the library and service to the students and faculty.

Someone once said, "There is a lot of difference between people in an organization working together and all of them just working at the same time." In the small academic library setting, for better or worse, everyone gets to know everyone else.

In this high-exposure atmosphere, it is more important to maintain a collegial atmosphere and sometimes more difficult to accomplish than it is in a larger organization, where people may see those outside their department once or twice a year.

The community college library is often small, with a small staff. The expectation is that the library team will provide services that contribute positively to student learning and student outcomes. Yes, circulation figures indicate that the collection is serving the needs of the students; use figures for online databases can also be used to support that claim. However, some of the library's best support can be the feedback on library evaluations. If users indicate that they don't use the library because a librarian (everyone in the library is viewed as a librarian) is unpleasant, then the director must ask him- or herself, "What am I not doing?" It is, unfortunately, not easy to hide the discourteous staff member on the smaller team. Good management and motivation of all staff members is necessary. The library is going to earn a good reputation and be an asset to the college and the students only when the users like interacting with the library staff as well as finding that the resources meet their needs.

Let's look at the two components that comprise the good or bad workplace: management and motivation. Management, for the purpose of this chapter, can be defined as: "The process of getting activities completed efficiently and effectively with and through other people" (Choo 2003a). Management is a term applied to the work unit and its leader.

Managing others is an art and a science. Some people have an excellent feel for how to manage others (the art), whereas other people must learn from experience and study of management theories to get their work group to perform (science).

Motivation is defined as " any direct or indirect, positive or negative inducement, influence, suggestion or other stimuli that can mobilize and direct the attitude and behavior of an individual or group toward the accomplishment of some specific goal or objective" (Banki, 1986, 590). Motivation is used to refer to improving human behavior in the workplace.

One of the best ways to be a good director is to know what motivates you. When you know the answers to the following questions as they relate to you, you have identified your motivational style.

Do you work best

- when you receive praise?
- when you receive/perceive threats?

Although your motivational style may work for you, it may not be the most effective for all of your staff. It is important to identify the motivational preferences of the other people in the work group. When this information has been collected and assimilated, the director has a better understanding of the team and is in a better position to manage and motivate the work group.

Peter Grazier has identified six factors that influence team motivation: purpose, challenge, camaraderie, responsibility, growth, and leadership (1998). Directors who take these six factors into account can, by strengthening their understanding of their teams' needs and applying these factors, build a better team.

Have you and your team identified your library's purpose? Think about the following:

- Who the library serves;
- How the patrons' needs are met;
- What patrons' needs aren't being met and how they can be addressed; and
- Whether each team member's specialties mesh with the needs of the team.

By establishing the library's purpose and keeping that purpose in the forefront as a benchmark for deciding services, the library teams' energies can be directed to promoting the library. This creates effective library services that strengthen the library's position in the academic institution.

The challenge factor addresses the need to stay current in regard to technology and library trends. The role of technology continues to expand as the library team tries to meet its patron's needs in the digital age. Online public access catalogs (OPAC) are de rigueur in today's library. This means that all staff must be proficient in the use of the OPAC. A majority of libraries offer online, full-text databases. These databases require that workers keep up with the database search strategies and database changes. Most libraries maintain a Web page. As libraries begin to make streaming media services—music, video programs, and digital curricula collections—available to their customers online, more staff training will be required.

Do you have in place a program whereby team members can participate in personal education and/or technical training?

In today's library world it is vital that team members be provided with the opportunity to update their technical skills in order to be in a position to provide the best service to the library's patrons. This training can provide the skills to enable the person to do current assignments in a different, more efficient way, or prepare to provide new services.

Camaraderie builds rapport and strengthens the work group. Fostering fellowship among team members enables the work group to learn about each other. This in turn leads to better understanding and appreciation of each individual's wants and needs as they relate to the workplace. Determining the team's preferences in this area and taking them into account when group decisions are made will provide for a more smoothly functioning unit.

Has your library team ever held monthly or weekly celebrations or attended outside events as a group?

23

Celebrating birthdays and other occasions such as Columbus Day, Cinco de Mayo, Halloween, or October Fest gives everyone a chance to get to know each other beyond their duties in the library. These celebrations don't have to be elaborate; they can be as simple as a pot luck lunch with the items built around the occasion being celebrated. It acknowledges that there is more to each person than what is presented in the day-to-day activities of running the library. These are informal times that permit team members to visit and learn more about each other. Attending plays, movies, art shows, ball games, or other group events build on the multidimensional facets that make up each team member.

Two workplace motivation factors are responsibility and growth (Grazier 1998). Is there an attempt made to ensure that each person in the library has a position that is challenging and provides a sense of responsibility?

Yes, attempting to ensure that each team member does certain job duties that bring with them a sense of responsibility is time-consuming in the short run. In the long run, however, the director does not spend as much time dealing with individual actions brought on by dissatisfaction with the job.

Does the library provide staff with the opportunity for personal education and a career ladder?

The personal education opportunity doesn't have to be funded by the library, nor does it have to be on work time. However, it should be offered and recognized. This is a good occasion to celebrate team members' personal triumphs—a course of training completed or a degree earned. If the library continuously hires from the outside instead of growing its own team members, staff will soon get the idea that any advancement will come only from their leaving the organization to work for another library. Considering the high cost of training a new worker, it is more cost-effective to keep team members and move them up the ladder or let them make a lateral move when they indicate their readiness for such a step.

When the library has a small staff it is good to develop a cross-training program. This ensures that the essential services of the library will continue if a team member takes an extended period away from the job. A cross-training program provides an opportunity for team members to acquire new skills and competencies.

Does the library provide team members with leadership opportunities? This can be measured by answering the following questions:

- Are staff members given responsibility for training or managing others?
- Is the environment win-win?

It has been said that the team is only as strong as its weakest link. When individual team members become more capable the team becomes stronger. When an atmosphere of trust is created and everyone is encouraged to try new things, the library team can provide more innovative library services. Yes, there will be times when something doesn't work out. However, when a mistake is viewed as a learning experience and not an opportunity for discipline, then the team members will feel free to try new ways of doing things and in so doing be able to grow.

Looking at what worked and what didn't in a proactive manner strengthens the team. This liberates the individual team member to be creative and innovative, enhances the library's position in its community, and provides the users with dynamic library services.

Coaching is a management style that works well with all employees. This means that managers must learn to be supportive, provide assistance or knowledge when it is needed, and make feedback regular and specific (Humphries 2004).

It readily becomes apparent that the role of the library director in motivating the team is an intricate balancing act. Once the director has identified the components of the team's motivational style, he or she can begin to look at other ways to enhance the workplace environment.

How one starts the workday can set the tone for the next eight hours. Identify which of the following reflects your preference:

- going directly to your office without speaking to anyone or
- greeting team members you meet on the way to your office

Although the library director may prefer to go to his or her office without speaking to anyone, this action could send a message that the director is in a bad mood or dissatisfied with the staff's performance. This in turn puts everyone on the defensive. When a work group is on the defensive, more energy is employed in worrying about the cause of the imagined or real bad mood, and less energy is available to expend on meeting the day's tasks.

Directors who greet each person they meet on the way to the office in the morning send the message that it is another good workday. This sets the tone for the day and enables the work team to expend more energy on accomplishing the task at hand.

Like nourishing a good family relationship, the director learns to work with the team members while permitting them to maintain their own styles. Varied work and personality styles and different interests and experiences add richness and depth to the team. What might be a traumatic style for one person can be an optimal style for another and be used to the advantage of the team when the need arises. An example of this is the person who prefers to work on a project at a leisurely pace versus the person who prefers to tackle a project at the last minute. If a request comes in with a short time line it might be assigned to the person who works best on a tight deadline.

Each team member should be valued. This can be supported in a variety of ways. The director can create an environment in which each person is treated with respect and each opinion is received with respect.

When each team member feels respected and a valued member of the group, he or she is more likely to contribute to the group effort. An atmosphere in which team members are made to feel comfortable expressing their opinions enables the team to discuss ideas openly and develop better solutions.

Table 2.1
Comparison of Female and Male Managers' Work Values.

The managerial woman wants:	The managerial man wants:
To be treated with respect.	Wages and benefits.
To have a supervisor she can respect.	Challenging work.
Wages and benefits.	Opportunity for advancement.
Challenging work.	Authority to make decisions.
Sense of accomplishment.	Sense of accomplishment.

Source: Choo 2003b.

The six factors that influence motivation in the workplace are much different than the long-standing assumption that people are motivated to work by the desire for or need for remuneration. These factors establish that motivators are present in the work group that are not tied directly to pay and bonuses.

Studies back up these factors as motivators. In 1994 Sharon Mason surveyed 7,629 Canadian individuals to see if there was a difference in the work values between managers and clerical workers (Choo 2003b). Table 2.1 presents (in order of importance) the results for managerial women and men. These results suggest that men and women work for different reasons; therefore there is no managerial "one size fits all" values style.

Table 2.2 shows that similar results were found when clerical men and women were surveyed.

Not only should directors learn what motivates each worker, but they should take into account different preferences between managerial men and women and clerical men and women. But wait, this survey was of Canadians. Aren't Americans different? According to research by Stanford University associate professor Chip Heath ("What Motivates People? You Might Be Surprised" 2003), maybe

Table 2.2
Comparison of Female and Male Clerical Workers' Work Values.

The clerical woman wants:	The clerical man wants:
To be treated with respect.	Opportunity for advancement.
Wages and benefits.	To learn new skills.
To learn new skills.	Wages and benefits.
A supervisor she can respect.	To be treated with respect.
Opportunity for advancement.	Challenging work.

Source: Choo 2003b.

Americans are not that different from their Canadian counterparts. The employees in the American study indicated they were motivated by four factors:

- benefits,
- feeling good about themselves,
- being praised for good work, and
- the opportunity to learn new skills

These surveys indicate that what motivates the person in the work setting is changing. No longer can the manager rely only on monetary rewards to satisfy the employee. For some people a large salary is important; however, this type of person probably didn't pursue a career in the library profession. Work no longer is solely about money. The reasons for working are more complicated than that, and motivating these people requires that the manager speak to more than salary and bonuses. Research indicates that one of the reasons people work is for the sense of belonging, acceptance, and friendship that can occur in the workplace (Grazier 1998).

Who makes up the current workforce? The typical senior manager in today's library is from the baby boomer generation. The circulation and technical processing staff could also be boomers, although Generation Xers (Gen Xers) are entering these departments as older staff retires. If the reference librarian is young and new, he or she is probably a Gen Xer. The young work/study students are Generation Yers (Gen Yers). Are these three generations going to find it easy to work together as a team? Let's see.

Do you:

- take teamwork seriously?
- prefer that everyone work separately yet create an end product?

If you chose the teamwork option, you are probably a Gen Xer; if you chose the working separately option, you are probably a boomer.

Baby boomers are those people born between 1946 and 1964. Boomers have a strong work ethic (Marston n.d.). They are easy to identify; they are the office workaholics. They don't watch the clock, they put in extra hours, and they emphasize getting the job done.

Baby boomer directors are finding themselves supervising Gen Xers, those people born between 1965 and the late 1970s. Gen Xers are more comfortable with diversity and see global issues more easily. Skeptics and cynics, they are entrepreneurial and seek fun and meaning in their work.

Another way the Gen Xers are distinguished from baby boomers is how they view others in their work group. Gen Xers see coworkers as their peers, minimizing the workplace hierarchy. C. Allen Nichols (2002, 38), a Gen Xer, demonstrates this when he wrote, "To me leadership is an attitude; it is not about a position. A leader can achieve defined goals by knowing what he or she wants to do, why it is important, and how to articulate those ideas to others to get the assistance and collaboration necessary to implement that change." The boomers view coworkers in a more structured hierarchy.

Other traits of the Gen Xers are as follows:

- They move into management for altruistic reasons. "Status" and "management" are not necessarily synonymous to them.
- They are comfortable with female managers. Both women and men, when surveyed, expressed a preference for a female manager.
- They have had more formal management training, making them skilled managers.
- They are technology-savvy because they grew up with computers; they are the first true information generation.
- They have a different communication style. Xers are inclined to be straightforward communicators.
- They are self-reliant. They move from job to job easily. Their loyalty is to their profession, not their employer.
- They tend to be rule-shy. Wanting to get things done quickly, they seek results. When rules or procedures get in the way they may be sidestepped (McGarvey 1999).

It is easy for the boomer manager and the Gen X worker to come into conflict. Each of the distinguishing characteristics of the Gen Xer is the opposite of the boomer. Boomers moved into management for power, prestige, advancement, and higher salaries. Boomers learned their management skills on the job and through workshops. Some of them added computer skills after they had been on the job 10 years or longer.

In the early days of computers the frontline employees in circulation and reference relied on the technology department to repair the computer whenever there was a problem. It is just since the mid-1990s that computers were put in boomers' offices and they were expected to use and maintain them.

Boomers tend to have a softer style of communicating with others. This may be a possible reflection of the hierarchical structure they worked in, which had specific rules of conduct relating to the individual's position in the work group. They learned chain of command, a top-down power structure with the president at the top, followed by vice presidents, deans, faculty, directors, and coordinators. Each person in this hierarchy knew his or her place.

So how can these two disparate generations work together? The first step is to understand each other. To do this the manager should focus on each individual in the team. Here is a good place to apply one of Steven Covey's seven principles, "Seek first to understand, then be understood" (Covey 1989, 239). Sit down with your Gen Xers. Listen to them and begin to learn what matters to them. Hear your Gen Xer out; then let him or her know where you are coming from. Be flexible and nondefensive in dealing with Gen Xers.

Use a mix of management styles that incorporates frequent training that relates not only to the person's job, but also to the Gen Xers' career.

Is instruction built around multimedia charts, photos, graphics, color, and sound? Is it interactive and computer-based?

This means no talking heads, memos, or handbooks (Humphries 2004). It may mean going to workshops or taking a class on using the laptop and the digital projector to present your ideas.

The last group entering the work force is the Gen Yers. This group has been alluded to but not discussed in depth. Gen Y spans 17 years, from 1979 to 1996. Pamela Paul (Nayyar 2001, 6) divided the Gen Yers into three age groups: young adults, teens, and 'tweens.

Circulation staff has dealt face-to-face with these young people when the students registered for their library cards. All library team members need to learn about them in order to provide the best patron services. Gen Yers are the new library work/study employees. Besides the tattoos, body piercings, and midriff-exposing clothing, are these young people different from other generations? You bet. They share many similarities with the immediate generation ahead of them, the Gen Xers. Their differences are in three categories—demand to learn, control of time, and loyalty to the boss (Marston n.d.).

Gen Yers believe that diverse knowledge leads to job security, creates opportunities, and is power. They want to have as much control over how they spend their time as possible. They will demand flextime, the ability to work from home, and balance between work and play (Marston n.d.). Given the Gen Xers' and the Gen Yers' computer abilities and their desire to control their time, it is no wonder that Web-based education has become so popular. Having to appear in a classroom and do the obligatory seat time to earn three, four, or five credits goes against their grain. Dialing into a Web class at their convenience is vastly more appealing.

The boomers, as library employees, had a concept of loyalty to the college library. They could be unhappy with the job or with the boss, but hung in because of the library. In turn, the college provided them with a retirement. In the current work climate, funded retirement plans are becoming a thing of the past. It is more common for the younger employees to have IRAs that they take with them from job to job.

What can the library team expect of the Gen Xer and the Gen Yer? They will demand that they be able to prioritize how they spend their time and that they have ongoing access to learning opportunities. If technology can get the job done, little tolerance will be exhibited for older, manual processes. These will be important considerations for the director to understand and work with.

There are things the manager can do that will make the transition to acceptance of the work group that is comprised of the boomer, the Gen Xer, and the Gen Yer. The first is communication.

Make sure people know what you expect of them. Set clear expectations. When requirements change, discuss the reason for the change. Get feedback to determine that the team members understand what you need (Heathfield 2003).

The team will function more effectively if everyone knows how he or she is doing. The semiannual performance appraisal isn't enough anymore. Team members want to know when they did a project well and when their results were disappointing. A daily or weekly scheduled feedback time may be utilized when a big project is underway and change is occurring quickly (Heathfield 2003). When the library is operating smoothly with no major changes, monthly feedback may be more appropriate.

Put in place a process that provides rewards and recognition for positive contributions (Heathfield 2003). A thank-you note is appropriate.

Have a fair system in place to deal with team members who do not perform effectively (Heathfield 2003). To do nothing puts the whole team at risk. Unless there are extenuating circumstances in the individual's personal life, the problem won't go away by doing nothing. It is devastating to team morale when the director does not deal with the person who is not a contributing team member.

Set up the minimum number of rules and policies that are needed to protect the library and the college and create order in the workplace. As soon as a rule is written the exception walks in the door. By establishing as few rules as possible the team members feel comfortable dealing with exceptions as they arise. It also keeps in the forefront the purpose of the library—to provide services that enhance the educational experience.

Hold a planning day, close the library, and as a team sit down and establish a professional code of conduct. This provides a guideline for staff to fall back on when dealing with inappropriate behavior. After developing the code of conduct, develop a list of expectations for the library users. It takes pressure off the circulation desk staff that is facing an irate student or faculty member who feels he or she is being denied the material needed for class. If your college does not have a policy for reporting inappropriate student behavior, talk with the Dean of Students about developing one. An incident report states the date, time, persons involved, and what occurred. It is then forwarded to the Dean of Students for action.

When policies need to be revised, again involve the whole team in the process. It will be easier for you as a director because the team members don't perceive that the new policy is handed down but rather something that was developed with their input and understanding.

All in all, the library director of the 2000s must be able to master many things in order to build a good team. He or she needs to know each team member's motivational style, be able to influence each member, keep the library's purpose before the team, continuously identify continuing education opportunities that the team members can participate in, value differences, communicate clearly, acknowledge achievements, and develop appropriate policies. If the director isn't able to do this, his or her Gen Xers and Gen Yers will move to another library where the director's style is more to their liking.

REFERENCES

Banki, Ivan Steven. 1986. *Dictionary of Administration and Management.* Los Angeles: Systems Research Institute.

Choo, Chun Wei. 2003a. University of Toronto Faculty of Information Studies Web page. *FIS 1230 Management of Information Organizations, #1 Historical Development of Management Thought, #4 What is Management.* [Online] Available: http://choo.fis.utoronto.ca/FIS/Courses/LIS1230/WhatIsMgm.html. Accessed 8 October 2003.

———. 2003b. University of Toronto Faculty of Information Studies Web page. *FIS 1230 Management of Information Organizations.* [Online] Available: http://choo.fis.utoronto.ca/FIS/Courses/LIS1230/WomenValues.html. Accessed 8 October 2003.

Covey, Stephen R. 1989. *The 7 Habits of Highly Effective People.* New York: Fireside.

Grazier, Peter. 1998. "Team Motivation." [Online] Available: http://www.teambuildinginc.com/article_teammotivation.htm. Accessed 6 October 2003.

Heathfield, Susan M. 2003. "Set Them Free: Two Musts for Motivation!" *Human Resources* (Fall 2003). [Online] Available: http://humanresources.about.com/library/weekly/aa032801b.htm. Accessed 14 October 2003.

Humphries, Ann C. 2004. "Motivating Generation X." [Online]. Available: http://www.christianwomentoday.com/workplace/genx.html. Accessed 1 October 2003.

Marston, Cam. n.d. "Managing Gen X and Gen Y." [Online]. Available: http://www.programresources.com/professional_speakers_tips/marston_managing_gen__x and_Gen_Y.html. Accessed 14 October 2003.

McGarvey, Robert. 1999. "The Coming of the Gen X Bosses." *Entrepreneur Magazine.* [Online]. Available: http://www.entrepreneur.com/mag/article/0,1539,231444,00.html. Accessed 14 October 2003.

Nayyar, Seema. 2001. "Inside the Mind of Gen Y." *American Demographics.* 23 (September): [Online] Available: http://search.epnet.com/direct.asp?an=7207792&db=aph. Accessed October 2003.

Nichols, C. Allen. 2002. "Leaders: Born or Bred." *Library Journal* 127 (August): 38. "What Motivates People? You Might Be Surprised." 2003. *PRIMEDIA Business Magazines & Media Inc.* [Online]. Available: http://rermag.com/ar/meetings_motivates_people_surprised/index.htm. Accessed 1 October 2003.

3 HUMAN RESOURCES FUNCTIONS IN THE TWO-YEAR COLLEGE LIBRARY

Eric E. Palo and Kathy L. Petersen

INTRODUCTION

Human resources (HR) management is one of the major responsibilities of any library director. In many ways, human resource materials written for library or college administrators can be applied to library directors at two-year institutions. There are some unique features of these schools, however, that create additional issues for two-year college library directors.

The HR responsibilities facing the typical two-year college library director are not much different from those facing the administrator of a college administrative department. Attracting qualified candidates, choosing wisely from among them, and training and developing one or more staff members may be the areas where the library director has the most control. Issues like wages/salary, benefits, methods of internal promotion, and perhaps even hours of work will probably be controlled by federal, state, and local laws, and by college policy or even bargaining unit agreements.

The fact that two-year colleges are not-for-profit organizations, supported by uncertain taxpayer dollars, can lead to compensation issues. At this writing, virtually every state in the United States is experiencing budget deficits. While resources are shrinking, demands for service are increasing, along with the volume of information libraries must try to manage. This increases the pressure to make good use of staff while remaining responsive and flexible in light of dwindling resources.

The size of two-year college libraries varies greatly. Some may be staffed by just one individual, and others may have a director and a staff of many professional librarians and even more support staff and student employees. But because two-year colleges can be quite small, the specialized advice and support that one might expect from the HR office at a larger college or university may not be as specialized or, indeed, may not exist at all. In this case the library director must take on all of the HR functions for the library.

It is typical that the HR functions in a library receive less attention from library managers than the professional librarian responsibilities such as collection development or reference, but in reality they are vital to the successful functioning of the college library. Staff costs are probably the largest portion of the library budget, and the best-equipped library is an ineffective operation if the staff aren't carrying out their duties effectively.

A general knowledge of HR operations will help a library manager to work effectively with the college's central administrative staff. Regardless of the size of the campus central staff, involvement in HR aspects of the library is an integral part of the director's role.

Because most community college libraries don't have middle management positions, there are few opportunities to gain experience before being thrust into the role of director for the entire library. Few students entering library school are aiming at a library manager position, and courses in library management, while offered at some schools, are rarely required. The typical librarian rarely sees him- or herself as a manager. Instead, the personal image is that of a professional with specialized knowledge, or a scholar or member of the faculty. Indeed, administration is often seen as step outside the chosen profession, and some librarians reject it as conflicting with their personal interests and/or values. This does not mean, however, that an individual has not gained valuable preparation for their administrative role in their schooling and work experience (Matthews 2002, 579).

The outline of this chapter follows the personnel process from developing a job description through hiring, supervision, evaluation, and reduction in force. In the real world, these steps are never quite so neatly sequenced, and a new manager will step into the middle of many of these processes when he or she assumes management responsibility. If there is one, the advice of the campus HR department should be sought whenever there is a question as to appropriate procedure. You can establish a better relationship with them if you see them as advisors rather than gatekeepers or rule enforcers. They will be overjoyed to have you talk with them about a situation or issue before it becomes a full-blown problem requiring damage control. You also must be certain to learn the policies and procedures of your particular institution, because these details will vary from institution to institution. A procedure that was taken for granted at a previous library may get you in hot water in your new library.

JOB DESCRIPTIONS, CLASSIFICATION, AND COMPENSATION

Regardless of the size of the library, staffing decisions will benefit from an analysis of the institutional and library priorities and the budget that is available to implement those priorities.

In many cases, the staff job description and title will be constrained by campus policies and bargaining contracts and, in some cases, by state regulation. However, a clear description of a position is the basis for much that follows in HR management. A well-thought-out position description should clearly explain the duties for job applicants and lead to hiring people with appropriate knowledge, skills and abilities. Once hired, the job description guides daily activities.

Job descriptions should be reviewed and updated on a regular basis. Ideally, this would occur once a year. Unfortunately, it is not unusual in some colleges for descriptions to stay the same for decades, failing to reflect new duties and technology. This does not become an issue until a problem arises, such as staff being expected to perform duties that are not listed in their formal description, or "job creep," in which a staff member takes on more and more responsibilities but is not appropriately recognized and compensated for his or her additional work. In the ideal world, all staff members would be paid according to their level of responsibility. However, in the real world, sometimes a library manager may be forced to deal with the dilemma of allowing people to work at a higher level without being able to compensate them, or even preventing them from performing to their level of expertise because they would be working outside their narrow classification.

A good job description starts with both the work that is actually being performed and the additional work that needs to be performed. If there is an incumbent in the position, or others who are performing similar duties, a wise manager will consult with them and involve them in the process of creating or revising job descriptions, while still retaining the final authority for what is forwarded to the campus administration for approval and implementation.

Library managers who want more information on how to analyze workload without disrupting staff, and to develop data upon which to base job allocations may want to read Mayo and Goodrich's book on staffing (2002). They walk the library manager through defining the project, conducting the analysis, and using the information collected to implement changes in order to effectively meet priorities. They even include sample forms.

It is important to clearly and concisely define what qualifications to ask for and what work is appropriate for each position in the library. We have seen too many cases where an overly long, or overly complex, or even outdated description was used to recruit for a position, only to attract candidates who did not have the necessary knowledge, skills, or abilities. In order to attract qualified candidates and provide something against which to evaluate their applications, it is important to decide before you start recruiting what credentials are really needed to do an effective job.

RECRUITMENT

When advertising open positions, it is important to ensure that the ad, whether written by you or by the HR office, clearly, even if briefly, describes the job duties and the requirements of qualified candidates. An ineffective or erroneous advertisement can necessitate reposting to comply with relevant rules and regulations, and delay the process several weeks at a minimum.

Automatically conducting a national search for a professional position may not be cost-effective. According to a recent survey reported by the Association of College and Research Libraries (2002), only 17 percent of library school graduates left the region of their library school for a job. More than 65 percent of new graduates worked in the same state where they went to library school. This has implications for how your advertising budget is distributed. If you have library graduate programs in your region, you may not need to spend a large amount in advertising in national publications. Lead time for national journals can also add weeks, or months, to a candidate search. Targeted advertising can be useful in recruiting a diverse candidate pool. Publications in your area that serve minority populations, specialized associations and e-mail lists, and direct communication with schools with higher minority enrollment are a few venues that you might consider. If you are advertising out of your area, know in advance what your campus policy is on paying, or not paying, interview expenses.

INTERVIEWING, REFERENCE CHECKING, AND HIRING

Interviews with potential employees are the most valuable source of information about how that candidate will perform the job duties and fit in with the rest of the staff. Schedule enough time to learn as much as you can about each candidate's knowledge, skills, and abilities. Interviews of less than an hour for support positions and less than two hours for professional positions may not yield all the information necessary to make the best decision. Using your carefully crafted job description, you can easily develop interview questions that elicit the information on which to select the appropriate candidate. Take the time to write questions that address your specific vacancy rather than using generic questions found in books or suggested by HR.

One of the most powerful interviewing methods is called behavioral or behavior-based interviewing. It rests on the principle that the best predictor of future behavior is past behavior. Interview questions focus on how a candidate handled a situation in the past. For example: "Tell me about a time when you had to deal with a difficult patron," "Tell me about a project that you had to organize and complete with minimal supervision," or "What is your experience teaching classes in information literacy?" Questions based on past behavior tend to elicit real experiences of the candidate, as opposed to a scripted response. You are more likely to get insight into the candidates' actual skills and experience.

Reference checking should be a part of any hiring decision, no matter how well you know the candidate, and no matter how positive an impression he or she made in the interview. Even though references may be difficult or impossible to obtain, you should make an effort to check references and document your attempt, even if unsuccessful. This documentation may protect you from being accused of making a negligent hire, should an individual turn out to be a problem employee. An extreme example of the pitfalls of inadequate reference checking came to light in 2003 when it was revealed that the Pennsylvania State University had unknowingly hired a person who had served 13 years in prison for three murders in Texas.

Good reference questions always relate to the specific job vacancy. Some standard questions will be a part of every reference call, but others should be focused on the knowledge, skills, and abilities required to perform your job. One valuable standard question is "Would you rehire this person?" Often a final question—"Is there anything else I should know?"—will reveal key information to help you make a decision.

Even though a candidate provides written letters of recommendation, following up with a phone call to the referee is always recommended. No generic recommendation letter can address the specific concerns, issues, and job responsibilities of your position. Also, letters of recommendation can, and have been, forged.

Sometimes there is a temptation to check with friends and/or colleagues who know the candidate, even though they are not listed by the candidate as a reference. Professional personnel practice would dictate that you ask the candidate first if they have an objection.

When you have decided on your final candidate, you must be certain to follow your college's policies in making a job offer. Authority to make an offer may reside with the library director, or may reside with a HR official, or perhaps someone at the vice president level. Procedure may vary, depending on the type of position you are filling. Regardless of the position, never make an offer without the authorization to do so, and with a firm salary or pay range established. Should you have to withdraw an offer, you may be liable for damages if the candidate had given notice at his or her current job. If you are authorized to make a job offer, follow a verbal offer with a letter outlining the title, salary, start date, schedule, benefits, and any other pertinent information that applies.

TRAINING AND DEVELOPMENT

"The greatest challenge facing library managers in the new millennium is … planning, implementing, and evaluating an ongoing, viable training program for library staff" (Massis 2003, 5). An effective training program begins with a thorough orientation for every new library staff member, including student workers. One cannot assume that new employees can independently figure out what to do. They need orientation to the mission and priorities of the library and the college, as well as the specific processes involved in his or her individual job and the appropriate way to perform the tasks of the job. In addition to the specific duties of their position, you want to introduce them to your organization and make them feel a part of both the library and the college.

If you have the luxury of a larger staff, you might consider establishing a formal mentoring process, pairing a new employee with a veteran employee. This does not, however, relieve the library director of his or her responsibility for orienting staff members, making them feel comfortable, and ensuring they are given the tools they need to do a good job.

Student employees are often treated too casually. In actuality, they perform many key functions in the library. Two excellent resources providing more in-depth advice are *Managing Student Employees in College Libraries* (Kathman and Kathman 1994) and *Training Student Library Assistants* (Morell, Yee, and Bullard 1991). Just as lines between professional and support duties are blurring, in many cases so are lines between regular staff and student workers. Training and development of student workers should not be overlooked.

No library director can avoid the occasional need to informally counsel employees regarding behaviors that are affecting their work performance. It is important that discussions focus on work performance and not on personal issues creating the problem. It is tempting to try to help your employees, but it is important to remember that you are not a professional counselor. Your HR department should be consulted for anything more than minor issues. Most colleges have access to employee advisory services, either on campus or on contract, that can help employees with any problem affecting their performance. If your college does not have access to such services, use your reference librarian skills and research community organizations or agencies where you might refer employees for professional assistance.

The library manager may spend most of his or her time dealing with problem employees. Don't forget, however, to acknowledge good performance as well. The smart director will give feedback to staff on a regular basis. Performance evaluation thus becomes ongoing part of the process and not a once-a-year activity.

TENURE AND FACULTY LIBRARIANS

In many two-year colleges, professional librarians hold faculty status. This means they may have 9-month appointments within an 11- or 12-month operation. It also means they will be evaluated according to tenure procedures. The tenure process is governed by college policies, state law, and, in some cases, bargaining unit agreements. Library managers need to understand the differences that tenure rules and bargaining agreements impose on supervision, work assignments, and hours of work. The tenure process determines how one gains and maintains tenure, and may impose an additional burden on a tenure-track employee that others do not bear.

Termination of a tenured employee will likewise have additional processes involved. As indicated previously in this chapter, check with your HR department. You need their advice and the informed knowledge of your supervisor before taking any action that could be construed as affecting the tenure process. In the state of Washington, for instance, tenure of community college and technical college librarians is governed by state law, and failure to adhere to the procedures can and have resulted in acrimonious grievances and protracted lawsuits.

SUPERVISION

According to Giesecke (1997, v), "[Supervision] can … be one of the most difficult things you have ever been asked to do." Successful supervisors have good communication skills, as well as technical knowledge of the functions to be performed and a sense of humor. The two-year college library administrator, like any other supervisor, must develop in all these areas.

New supervisors should be self-aware. Know your strengths and weaknesses, what you're willing to delegate and what you want to keep close. You can't do everything yourself. If you have subordinates, you need to let them do their jobs. You will be judged as much on their performance as you will be on your own. The job of the supervisor is to give employees the skills and tools necessary to do the job required. If they are well trained and well equipped, you don't need to micromanage. As a new supervisor, you need to be sure that you know what your employees' jobs are and that you and they have a common understanding of the expectations.

If you are new to the organization, respect what has happened in the past and make changes gradually after gaining thorough understanding of what led to current practices. Involve the staff in changes whenever possible, in order to gain their commitment to the process. This also provides information to everyone about the broader operation of the library. A successful supervisor is one who builds an organization that can continue functioning with little or no disruption in his or her absence.

If you are promoted to a supervisory role from within, remember that your role changes when you become a supervisor. Suddenly your friends are now your subordinates. You need to walk the difficult path of distancing yourself from your former coworkers while still remaining cordial. You may find that other deans or directors on campus have been through a similar experience and they can give you valuable insights into how to undertake your new role.

Making the transition to supervision requires a different mindset. College administrators tend to promote librarians for their specialized technical knowledge and assume they will understand the difference between their old professional role and the new managerial role. Understanding this new role is a key issue for any librarian promoted to the director level.

As a new supervisor, start the way you plan to go. You can always become less directive or less controlling over time, but it is extremely difficult to become more directive or more controlling after a period of leniency. If you have new ideas, be certain to communicate them clearly to your staff and involve them in any changes when you can. Don't forget to discuss major changes with *your* supervisor before introducing them.

EVALUATION AND DISCIPLINE

A library director may supervise professional staff, classified employees, student workers, and perhaps volunteers (any of whom might be working full- or part-time). Expectations for all employees must be communicated clearly by the library director and reflected in job descriptions and performance evaluation documents. (Yes, you should have a job description, even if an abbreviated one, for your student assistant positions and volunteers, too.)

The best performance evaluation does not come as a surprise to the employee. A supervisor will have routinely discussed performance issues with employees on an ongoing basis. The formal annual performance review then becomes a summary documenting the current state of affairs. Performance evaluations also need to be consistent across the unit and across time. Employees need to know that the behavior that was unacceptable last year is unacceptable this year, or behavior unacceptable in a classified staff member is also considered unacceptable in a faculty member. Changes in expectations must be clearly communicated in advance of any evaluation period.

Employee performance problems should be handled as soon as they occur. Problems don't go away if you ignore them. You aren't doing a favor to either the employee or the institution by delaying action on performance problems. Although it can be unpleasant to bring up performance issues, it is essential that you do so, to keep them from developing into serious problems in the future that would require serious action. Ignoring problems with one individual's performance inevitably affects other employees, whether you see an immediate effect or not.

Campus policies on discipline will affect how you handle employee problems. In all likelihood there is an outline of appropriate steps. These policies both provide the individual with a process that allows him or her a chance to correct the behavior and documents the steps taken which could eventually support terminating an employee. Never assume you know how to approach the disciplinary process without checking with the individual or department handling personnel issues. You should also be certain to advise your supervisor of any performance and disciplinary issues.

REDUCTIONS IN FORCE (RIF)

An unfortunate feature of library management in uncertain economic times is the need to cut library budgets and, perhaps, reduce the number of employees. If you are lucky, you will have vacant positions that can be sacrificed, but there will be occasions when you must lay off an employee. Should this be necessary, it is critical that employees understand the need for reductions and know how decisions were made. Open communication from the very beginning is critical. In all likelihood, it will not be the library director who decides which position is cut but, rather, a campuswide process that takes into consideration seniority, bargaining unit contracts, tenure rules, and institutional priorities.

The RIF process might result in someone from another unit losing his or her position but having "bumping rights" to a position in the library. Although this would more likely happen with classified positions, it is possible that professional staff might also be affected. This situation is a very stressful one for everyone involved. The person bumping in to the library knows he or she has forced someone else out of a job. The remaining library staff must say good-bye to a colleague and accept a newcomer in his or her place.

The director can help pave the way for the new employee by informing the staff of the decision and reminding them how they would feel if they were in that position. Urge your campus administration to provide support for RIF employees and training for supervisors taking in a bumping employee. Just getting together with other managers in the same situation and discussing the impact and how to mitigate it can be helpful.

OTHER CURRENT ISSUES

Collective Bargaining and Implementing Contracts

Personnel in two-year colleges are often hired under bargaining unit agreements or union contracts. Although you will have little influence over them, you need to be aware of the provisions in any collective bargaining agreements effecting people in your unit. You may have employees working in several different bargaining units. At Renton Technical College, for instance, with six and a half full-time-equivalent employees in the library, there are three different collective bargaining agreements covering the staff.

Documentation and Record Keeping

Documentation is an essential part of the library director's HR responsibilities. When in doubt, write it down, but remember that your records can be subpoenaed or used in legal or quasi-legal proceedings. Accurate documentation of actions affecting personnel is vital, even if it seems time-consuming. Before you commit anything to paper, imagine how it will look printed in the local paper. Documentation should be both efficient and sufficient. It should not take an inordinate amount of time and should consist of remarks about behavior and not opinions. For example, rather than stating that an employee is lazy, you should indicate that he or she consistently failed to meet deadlines. State records retention and campus policy will govern how long you should keep employee records.

Responding to Requests for References

Campus policy may govern whether you can provide reference information for former employees. If you are allowed to provide references, be certain to discuss only work-related behaviors. Provide factual information. Don't state an opinion, as someone once did to one of the co-authors of this chapter, when she said, "I think he was a drug dealer." If you provide a written letter of recommendation, again, provide factual information, not opinions. The most valuable letters of recommendation provide specific examples and discuss specific skills; "he typed purchase orders in record time" is more helpful than "he was a good typist."

SUMMARY

Managing people can be a frustrating and time-consuming experience, but no library can succeed without a well-qualified, motivated, and competently led staff. The functions described in this chapter are not glamorous and at times can be quite tedious, but they are essential to a well-run two-year college library. The library director who selects good staff and gives them the tools necessary to do their job will be successful. Those who neglect these functions open themselves up to grievances, and their institutions to lawsuits, and will be lucky keep their jobs. Finally, college administrators need to remember that they don't have to do it all alone. Make use of the HR department of your institution—they are there to help you. Decisions in the HR arena are especially vulnerable to informal and formal challenges, ranging from staff mutterings to lawsuits. If you do not have an HR department that you can consult, talk to your supervisor when in doubt. HR functions may not be fun, but they are vital and a successful two-year college administrator will learn them and keep up with them every week.

REFERENCES

Association of College and Research Libraries, Ad Hoc Task Force on Recruitment and Retention Issues. 2002. *Recruitment, Retention, and Restructuring: Human Resources in Academic Libraries.* Chicago: Association of College and Research Libraries.

Giesecke, Joan, ed. 1997. *Practical Help for New Supervisors.* Chicago: American Library Association.

Kathman, Michael D., and Jane McGurn Kathman. 1994. *Managing Student Employees in College Libraries.* Chicago: College Library Information Packet Committee, College Libraries Section, Association of College and Research Libraries.

Massis, Bruce E. 2003. *The Practical Library Manager.* New York: The Haworth Information Press.

Matthews, Catherine C. 2002. "Becoming a Chief Librarian: An Analysis of Transition Stages in Academic Library Leadership." *Library Trends* 50 (Spring): 578–602.

Mayo, Diane, and Jeanne Goodrich. 2002. *Staffing for Results: A Guide to Working Smarter.* Chicago: American Library Association.

Morell, D. Boone, Sandra G. Yee, and Rita Bullard. 1991. *Training Student Library Assistants*. Chicago: American Library Association.

SELECTED BIBLIOGRAPHY

Dewey, Barbara. 1987. *Library Jobs: How to Fill Them, How to Find Them*. Phoenix, AZ: Oryx Press.

Max, Douglass, and Robert Bacal. 2003. *Perfect Phrases for Performance Reviews*. New York: McGraw-Hill.

Rubin, Richard. 1991. *Human Resource Management in Libraries: Theory and Practice*. New York: Neal-Schuman Publishers.

Stueart, Robert D. and Barbara B. Moran. 2002. *Library and Information Center Management*. Greenwood Village, CO: Libraries Unlimited.

Urgo, Marisa. 2000. *Developing Information Leaders: Harnessing the Talents of Generation X*. London: Bowker Saur.

Vesper, Virginia and Gloria Kelley, Compl. 1997. *Criteria for Promotion and Tenure for Academic Librarians*. College Library Information Packet Committee, College Libraries Section. Chicago: Association of College and Research Libraries.

II

UNDERSTANDING STUDENTS: MAKING THEM AWARE THAT THE LIBRARY CAN HELP THEM

4 VIRTUAL REFERENCE AND WEB-BASED EXPERT SITES: APPEALING TO STUDENTS IN AN INFORMATION-RICH, DEMAND DRIVEN SOCIETY

Brandi Porter

Research suggests that in today's information-rich, demand-driven society, students care more about timeliness of information than quality of the information (Luther 2003, 36). For students in higher education who care about dependable information, dredging through the multitude of information to find quality is a challenge. Furthermore, it is unclear whether students know what quality information is or how to recognize it. For purposes of this project, "quality information" means factually supported information sometimes peer reviewed and providing more than an espousing of one's uninformed opinions to sway or sell beliefs or products.

Students are driven to information that is easy to access and produces quick results. They seek information to which they can access from anywhere, at any time. Whereas 10 years ago students would go to the library to gain access to information, now access is as easy as their computer and the World Wide Web. "Most students start their research on the Internet. Many of them believe they find all they need there though they are unaware of how to distinguish between scholarly and popular sites" (Curtis 2000, 122). In addition, more and more students turn to commercial, profit-driven sites to find reliable information. However, in many instances information on these sites is sponsored or the result ranking is bought. Therefore, the effect is that many times search results are what merchants want to sell. The repercussions of this affect not only the individual but the community as well. Students who do not know or care about value and critical thinking will continue to lack those skills as they move throughout their lives, work, and leisure. It is important to note that "with the transition from a manufacturing, physical, labor-oriented economy to a knowledge work-oriented one, we simply must prepare the majority of children for thought work, for inquiry" (Soloway and Wallace 1997, 16). Although this point emphasizes the importance of a knowledge economy for children, it is no less true for college students. These critical thinking skills are vital in an information economy, where knowledge is power.

Community college librarians, especially, often struggle to provide research assistance to undergraduate students in an era of staff shortages, students who lack basic information-seeking skills, and users who no longer are primarily in the library. Many community colleges are including distance learning programs as a staple of their educational offerings. Librarians, therefore, are facing a changing landscape in which to teach and assist students. With reference help a core function of service, many of these academic librarians are turning to virtual reference assistance in an attempt to provide quality reference service in the midst of this changing student environment.

PROJECT RATIONALE

Information abounds; we are living in an age that many describe as one of information overload. The ability to find quality sources among the wealth of information is more challenging than ever. Despite the overwhelming amount of information available to students, they often settle for the source that is easiest to find. Our society has become one of instant gratification, and in many ways students epitomize this revolution. Students are settling for less and less value all the time. "For many searchers, the quality of the results matter less than the process—they just expect the process to be quick and easy" (Luther 2003, 36). Hence, students are relying more on the quick retrieval of information than on the quality and reliability of resources retrieved.

Expert search systems and virtual reference services are emerging across physical and virtual distances to assist students in finding quality information. The possibilities range from commercial solutions to librarian-driven approaches (virtual reference). Commercial services include keyword retrieval–based searches from Internet search engines (such as Google), fee- and non- fee-based "expert" pages (examples are Askme.com and WebMD.com), and directory response systems based on compilations of previous search queries (a popular one is AskJeeves.com) (Pack 2000, 16). Virtual reference models fall into two basic categories: individual library response groups, which are centralized to one library, and consortia-built response groups, which utilize librarians who provide reference services from a variety of institutions. Students are turning to these expert and reference services despite the lack of these services addressing the issues raised here (Coffman and McGlamery 2000, 66). In this chapter I focus primarily on virtual reference systems and outline the merits and shortfalls of some of these systems; look at the roles that individuals, businesses, and librarians play in developing and marketing these services; and analyze the role that knowledge management plays. Virtual reference systems are online tools for synchronous transfer of information between librarian and student. Typical features of such systems include chat capabilities, pushing (showing) Web pages or electronic database pages between individuals, a created directory of popular searches and/or questions, and archived transcripts of sessions for both librarians and students.

There are some potential barriers to examining and using virtual reference systems. The ability to test and use virtual reference systems relies heavily on successful technical development and support of the product. Snags in technology will impede the knowledge sharing process. Also, it has yet to be determined what effect third-party database vendors will have on the achievement of sharing quality resources through virtual reference products (Quint 2002, 50). This is particularly true if libraries enter into consortia reference agreements, but not into consortia database purchasing agreements. Depending upon the means of sharing information with students, vendors may not allow individual libraries to share proprietary journal articles with students from other institutions. Currently, access to scholarly journal articles is a service that librarian-driven systems can offer; most commercial-based Web products cannot. The relevance of these resources compared to expert-based systems, which usually are not privy to such access, are explored in this chapter.

Libraries previously were primary centers for information gathering in higher education, and librarians played a critical part in the gathering of resources for students; but today with the advent of the Internet, there is no vested interest by merchants to ensure that quality information exists on the Web. A major component of the librarian's role in higher education could be in jeopardy if commercial services can take the place of reference service. Therefore, this chapter provides valuable information on issues that librarians need to consider and plan for as they move their reference services online.

LITERATURE REVIEW

Literature on this topic was reviewed using databases focusing on libraries, computers, and information science, and articles relating to the creation, marketing, and management of virtual reference systems. In addition, articles highlighting the most popular expert-based search pages and their use were included. Articles noting student use of popular search engines such as Google and Ask Jeeves were gathered for comparison to virtual reference systems. The literature illustrated various search options students use, how the tools focus on providing information and whether that information is reliable, and if and why they draw students to use the services.

The literature can be grouped into several categories: virtual reference products and comparisons to expert-based systems (including strengths and weaknesses), assertions from those in the library and information science fields on how they view these two types of services (complementary or competition), and finally measurement and evaluation of virtual reference and expert-based systems. Although many agree that students choose the Internet first for research (Curtis 2000, 122; Dougherty 2002, 44; Luther 2003, 36), the literature review is important to glean insights as to the reasons why students choose this avenue, and whether there is something information professionals can and should do about this trend. The assertion of this chapter is that students care more about timely information than quality information, many times settling for unreliable and poor information.

Needs and Challenges of Virtual Reference Systems

The literature review indicates that many college and university libraries have implemented virtual reference systems, and this service has existed only a few years. Many writers describe the challenges of starting systems and the process undertaken in the author's own library, but few mention any solid reason for adding virtual reference services in their library (Burek Pierce 2002, 45). A few similarities are articulated in library literature. For example, reference and use statistics for physical libraries continue to decline (Ballesti and Russell 2003, 15), and students are moving online in droves, so librarians should too if they are going to serve them (Breeding 2001, 42). However, simply moving reference services online may not bring students to the service and may be an indicator of why virtual reference systems already in place are not more popular.

The underutilization of virtual reference systems is noted throughout the literature (Ballesti and Russell 2003, 18). Libraries using virtual reference many times do not market the service very well. This could be attributed to the fact that librarians believe in the power of the service to speak for itself, and/or that it is added work to take on the task of public relations with new services. There is research to suggest that librarians fear an onslaught of use from marketing of the virtual reference service. "More often than not, libraries do not make a big splash advertising and marketing its [virtual reference] availability, largely because of fear that if they do, they will be overwhelmed with users who could swamp the small number of librarians assigned to handle the questions" (Small Helfer 2003, 64). Without proper marketing of virtual reference systems in libraries, it is difficult to assess whether students are choosing Internet-based resources for their research, or if they do not know about the librarian-driven options.

Literature on this topic also identifies strengths and weaknesses of both virtual reference and expert-based systems. Librarians tout the quality of their service, providing authoritative information from reliable sources, including scholarly journals. Expert-based systems note that they are available all day every day and have their own repertoire of experts in particular subject areas of interest. Each system has its weaknesses as well; for libraries it appears to be availability, and for expert systems, it is that they are profit-based businesses whose interest in the bottom line may not always be in the interest of the student trying to find quality information (Coffman and McGlamery 2000, 67).

The Coexistence of Systems

The literature is split on whether expert-based systems are competition for libraries (Bivens-Tatum, 2001, 1; Coffman and McGlamery 2000, 69), or whether they are a complement to libraries (Tomaiuolo, 2000, 61; McLaughlin, 2003, 1). The question is an important one and is at the heart of the value of virtual reference and expert-based systems. Librarians often view the reference services they provide as unmatchable to any other attempt to do the same; however, of the sum of the articles comparing librarian and commercial approaches to reference services all but two articles attained (Tomaiuolo 2000, 61; McLaughlin 2003, 1) looked at expert-based systems as competition to librarian-driven systems.

This chapter's ultimate aim is to provide a clear view of the role of virtual reference systems for academic students to best meet the needs of this clientele. Much of the library literature assumes that librarians are the only experts when it comes to information searching, retrieval, and evaluation. The point that has not been thoroughly explored, however, is whether these are two different systems both with value to students in higher education.

Research, Evaluation, and Measurement

A variety of articles exist on the explosion of expert Web-based systems (Coffman and McGlamery 2000, 66; Pack 2000, 16); however, there are few surveys of comparisons between existing systems, and they are not comprehensive. Of the only comprehensive survey found on expert-based systems (Janes, Hill, and Rolfe 2001, 1106), the authors surveyed 20 expert systems by posing more than 200 questions and using library students to evaluate them. The result of expert system reliability should be considered through the lens of the library students evaluating them, as librarian standards for the search and retrieval of information seem to be much higher than students looking for answers. In this respect there may be a biased opinion in the literature of the value, or lack thereof, regarding expert-based systems.

Two research studies were found comparing expert-based systems to two electronic reference systems. The first examined two librarian-based systems and one expert-based system and found that "although the general response rate from all the services was good, library-based services were found to be more trustworthy since they provided answers together with the sources" (McCrea 2004, 11). The electronic reference services in McCrea's study operated by e-mail, not synchronously. Ten questions were sent to each service for answers. McCrea ultimately concluded that "it appears that libraries have lost their monopoly of being providers of reference information, and it may be that, with their 'human face,' the commercial companies will be the resource of choice in future" (2004, 11).

In addition, an evaluation of three virtual reference systems to two expert-based systems was examined (Cloughley 2004, 17–23). Cloughley's study asked five basic reference questions (requiring simple fact answers) and five advanced reference questions (requiring expanded research for answers) of each service. The results showed that one expert-based system performed unsatisfactorily (long wait time; did not answer all questions), and one performed relatively well for the researcher (quick response; answered all questions, and on most stated the answer in the reply) (2004, 21–22). Of the reference services compared, two were e-mail based and one chat based. As one would expect, the chat-based service provided faster response but did not provide as much detail as one of the e-mail-based services (the other e-mail service had the slowest response time of all) (Cloughley 2004, 22). Quality of these services was good but lacked detail in some needed areas. Cloughley (2004, 22) concludes that "users can use search engines like Google to find information directly from the Web, but DRS [digital reference services] aim to bring a more human-centered approach by involving the expertise of information professionals." Ultimately, it is unclear from the research whether the digital reference services actually achieve this goal. However, the great piece of what is missing from the literature is student assessment of virtual reference systems: Do these services meet the needs of academic students in terms of response time and quality?

An additional study of two universities was recently completed to assess users' awareness and use of virtual reference services (Johnson 2004, 237). Johnson surveyed affiliates of the two universities and asked users if they had used virtual reference in comparison to other reference services, marketing approaches, and some visions for reference services in the future. The results showed that few users had actually tried virtual reference, but they thought it would be the most used type of reference service (as compared to face to face, telephone, or e-mail reference) in 10 years (2004, 237).

One research article also exists on analyzing information from virtual reference interactions to determine to what extent information literacy and information problem solving are achieved in these transactions. The examination focused on three models: Association of College and Research Libraries (ACRL) Information Literacy Competency Standards, Sears' Classification of Reference Question Types, and Eisenberg-Berkowitz Information Problem-Solving Model (Smyth 2003, 28–29). All transcripts were gathered from one university library system. The results showed that "none of the models used in this analysis will serve to describe completely the scope and processes of reference and information services provided" (Smyth 2003, 30). It is unclear whether students actually gain information-gathering skills through the process of virtual reference systems. Beyond that, do students know they have achieved the skills or have an interest in such issues when conducting research? More research needs to be conducted to gain certainty of these issues.

The literature notes the lack of measurement of digital reference services (Johnson 2004, 237; Wasik 2003, 1). "We don't have a clue whether this [digital reference] is working, whether this satisfies people's information needs" (Burek Pierce 2002, 45). Much is written on the topic of digital/virtual reference, yet virtually no literature was found that measured the users' assessment of these services.

METHODOLOGY

The aim of the research undertaken for this chapter was to measure the effectiveness of virtual reference systems to one constituent group: academic students. Effective virtual reference systems (1) are convenient and provide ease of accessibility, (2) help students find the information they are seeking, (3) positively affect the return rate of students to the service, (4) provide basic information literacy knowledge that leads to students being able to use these skills in future searches of their own, and (5) are well marketed to students so that they understand the benefits of virtual reference systems and therefore use them. The survey instrument in this case focused on measuring the success of virtual reference systems by surveying student experiences with these systems.

This study compared individual library and consortia-based virtual reference systems, identifying pros and cons, and analyzing successes and failures. An additional task was to investigate other expert Web services and compare those systems with virtual reference databases.

INSTRUMENT

A survey was prepared and distributed to students using virtual reference systems at several colleges and universities to determine why they visited the site, if their quest for information was successful, and if they would use the service again. Responses were gathered about where those students began their research, what they found most appealing about the service, and what items they would change (Appendix A). These questions were formulated by the uncertainties illustrated in the literature review.

The survey instrument was designed to ensure that effectiveness of virtual reference systems could be measured by the content of the questions being asked. Therefore, several criteria were established to help define what is meant by effective virtual reference systems. The criteria are listed above. Next the questions were designed to mirror definitions of effective virtual reference systems listed earlier. An example may help to illustrate this point. This proposed that one criterion of effective virtual reference systems are that they are convenient and easy to use. Therefore, to measure the successfulness of the system, students were asked to rate how convenient and easy the service was to use.

Two questions were also developed to assess students' basic information literacy skills in accessing needed information effectively and efficiently. This is one of the standards (Standard Two) developed by the ACRL in its definition of an information literate student.

The ACRL defines an information-literate individual as being able to

1. determine the extent of information needed
2. access the needed information effectively and efficiently
3. evaluate information and its sources critically
4. incorporate selected information into one's knowledge base
5. use information effectively to accomplish a specific purpose
6. understand the economic, legal, and social issues surrounding the use of information, and access and use information ethically and legally (American Library Association 2000)

These questions on the survey were as follows: How confident are you about conducting a similar search again on your own effectively and efficiently accessing information? and How confident are you that you have gained new tools or skills for searching as a result of this service? Consistent with ACRL's Standard 2 of its definition of an information-literate person, these questions helped to assess whether students believed they were learning basic information literacy skills during virtual reference sessions. Teaching information literacy is a core mission of libraries and an important area of distinction between virtual and expert-based commercial services.

As the instrument was created using Flashlight, the nature of the tool allowed for privacy and integrity of survey information. The survey was completely anonymous, so students could feel comfortable giving their honest opinions of the service. The librarians conducting the virtual reference service provided access to the survey. Students only had access to the survey as the librarians gave it to them at the end of an online interaction. As the survey was only available by URL, it was easy to distribute, and only the researcher had access to write or review the results. The individual librarians played no other part in the survey process other than giving the student access to the survey.

SAMPLE

The objective of this survey was to incorporate findings from five academic libraries, which distributed the survey to those students for whom they provided virtual reference. Libraries were solicited for assistance through collegial relationships and through postings on four library Listservs for which more than 6,000 interested individuals participated from around the world.

The librarians and students that were part of the sample are from a variety of institutions, community college and university libraries. In this way, the sample of students participating in the study represented a spectrum of students using virtual reference services in academic libraries today.

RESULTS AND OUTCOMES

Comparison of Two Virtual Reference Systems

At first glance both of these systems (Docutek Virtual Reference Librarian and Live Assistance) are very similar in nature, providing chat reference options, pushing of URL to students, archiving of transcripts, and including survey and statistical features. The difference between the two lies in Docutek using co-browsing techniques, and LiveAssistance relying instead on the pushing of Web pages to students by the librarian. Co-browsing can be a daunting task at first, as both the user and librarian can change the search screen at any time. Therefore, it is best to decide up front who will lead the searches using this feature. At first thought, it may seem that the librarian should show a student how to do searches and lead them to various sites. There is also value in a student demonstrating searches, while the librarian uses the chat feature to convey search tips and advice for improving search skills. For libraries that would prefer to control search information, the selection of software without co-browsing may be a better choice. Docutek VRL further allows for the librarian to work with multiple patrons at a time, whereas LiveAssistance uses a queue system for those waiting in line. A look at these two virtual reference systems reveals that although the systems share similar reference capabilities, the library wishing to use such a system should choose based on its individual service needs, patrons, and policies.

Comparison of Three "Ask an Expert" Systems

Three "ask an expert" systems were examined for quality of response to an asked question, ease of use, and qualifications of "expert": Allexperts.com, WebMD.com experts, and AskJeeves.com. The query asked of all systems regarded weight gain for a certain medication.

Allexperts.com consisted of a directory by subject or search box to help users find an expert for the question. As the search was a medical question, the directory search was used to select the topic of Health/Fitness. From there a listing of further subtopics and links to experts in the field was available. A review of a few experts revealed their qualifications as having gone through a particular illness in the past and therefore having knowledge on the topic, those with nonadvanced degrees on the topic, and—interestingly—quite a few experts from other countries around the world. User ratings were available that could assist in selecting an expert. The response to the researcher's question was sent via e-mail in less than 24 hours; however, the response consisted of a URL to a diet and nutrition site, which was not a direct answer to the question posed.

The WebMD.com "ask an expert" area was actually a discussion forum with an individual doctor. Therefore, questions had to be posed publicly for anyone signed on to read, and the doctor would respond typically in 24–48 hours. The quality of the experts was high, but the responses of the doctors remained rather vague as they seemed leery of giving medical advice without enough knowledge of the patient. Most answers consisted of what research is known in the area and referrals to find a doctor in the user's area.

Finally, AskJeeves.com was examined using the same search question. As AskJeeves.com works through a database of links to Web pages and previous queries, no contact with a real expert is available. The results of the search question produced about 20 links to various Web pages. Interestingly, the first half of results were from sponsored sites, and the others were mostly to commercial sites to buy particular medications.

None of the expert sites examined allowed for synchronous exchange of information. As none of the responses answered the question asked, there was also no immediate way to converse with the expert to get more specific and relevant information. Examining these three expert sites illustrates the wide variety of expert sites that exist for users on the Web, some with more or less credentials of experts. Some answers were retrieved faster than others, yet all were relatively timely.

Survey Participation

Although 15 libraries were contacted through individual e-mails and requests for assistance were posted on four library Listservs, only 5 libraries agreed to participate in the virtual reference survey of their students using their service. Of the five libraries participating, three were universities and two were community colleges. The universities participating were from three different states, and of the community colleges one was from the same state as one of the universities, and one was from another state.

Several of the libraries that elected not to participate in the study shared their reasons for not doing so. These included a concern that there was not enough time to get approval from their institutional review boards to adequately participate, not wanting to submit their students to yet another survey, and feeling that their student base was higher academically than would be useful to the survey (i.e., more graduate than undergraduate students).

Of the schools that did participate, several were new to virtual reference, using virtual reference software on a trial basis with students, and/or had not yet surveyed student use of their service. One school was in a consortium for virtual reference across its state and reported answering many more questions from the public than its students via virtual reference. In addition, the students searching for answers electronically chose e-mail reference versus chat reference.

The survey ran for a month and a half toward the middle to end of the colleges' semesters. Perhaps the beginning of the semester would have yielded more use. All schools participating admitted to relatively low use of virtual reference in a given month. All of these factors contributed to the low survey response rate from those libraries that were willing to participate in the study.

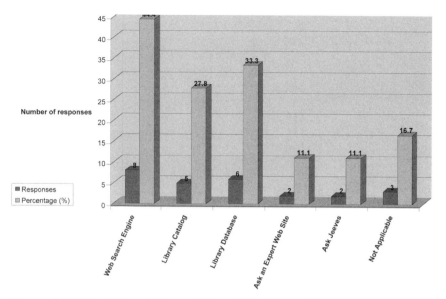

Figure 4.1   User's Descriptions of Where They Began Their Searches

Survey Results

There were 18 students who were willing to participate in the survey. Although this is not enough respondents to make definitive hypotheses, several trends are observable from the results. When asked about how students found out about the service, traditional methods of the library Web site, their instructor, and a librarian were noted. No one found the service from ads, flyers, or friends.

The majority of students as expected from the literature on the topic did not use virtual reference as the first resource for their search. Students reported using a variety of sources for their searches. While search engines were listed as most used for student searches, library catalogs and databases were also consistently used. A few students reported using Ask Jeeves and Ask an Expert Web site for help (see Figure 4.1).

Students selected a variety of reasons for why they chose to use the service. No one reason stood out over the others. Leading the results were not finding any information so far, looking for reliable research, and being curious about the service (see Figure 4.2).

Students participating in the survey overwhelmingly were using virtual reference for a class assignment. All but two participants indicated such. One respondent used the service for a job, and one used it for entertainment. When students were asked if they found the information they were looking for from the service,

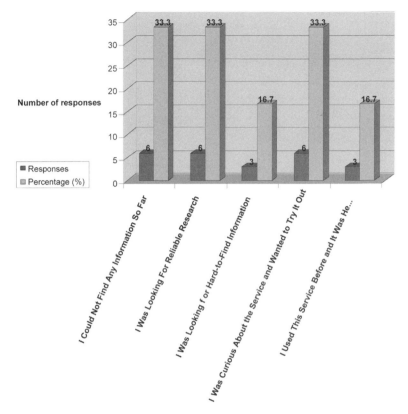

Figure 4.2 Reasons Listed for Using a Library Virtual Reference Service

all respondents but one answered yes, one neglecting to answer. Students appeared satisfied with the service offered to them.

Interestingly, although students indicated positive satisfaction with the service, the majority of respondents only noted that they might be willing to use this reference service again. Half the respondents still checked that they would use the service again only if they could not find information on the Internet. Positive for libraries, nearly 40 percent indicated that they would start their future searches with the virtual reference service (see Figure 4.3).

Students were asked how easy to use, accessible, and convenient they found the service to be. Approximately 72 percent (13 respondents) answered extremely easy to use, and two more found it very easy. One person answered somewhat, and two remarked it was not very easy to use. Some possible correlation to ease of use in noted in the last question on the survey asking what the student would like to see improved with the service. Three responses in that category referenced technical glitches the students encountered in the process of using the service.

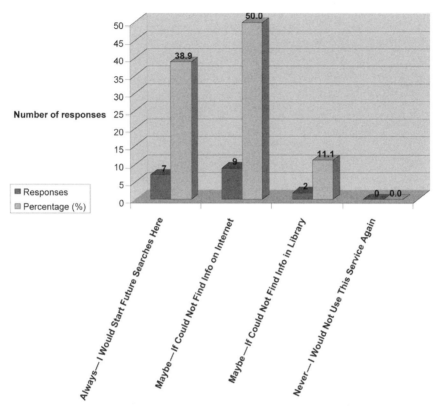

Figure 4.3   Proposed Return Rate for Library Virtual Reference Services

The two questions relating to information literacy skills gained through virtual reference service asked students to rate their confidence of accessing appropriate resources again on their own. Students responded positively in both categories, rating their confidence as extremely at 67 percent. Only one student rated future skills in these categories as not very high. A possible correlation exists again in the final question of the survey regarding suggestions for future improvements. One student responded as not being a "confident" computer user and would like clearer instructions for the service (see Figures 4.4 and 4.5).

The final two questions of the survey asked what students found to be the best part of using the reference service and what would they like to see improved with the service. Student responses indicated that they liked the synchronous interaction with the librarian, that it was fast, simple, and easy, and that the librarian was helpful. Other than the few suggestions indicated in the proposed correlations mentioned previously, the majority of students indicated there was nothing they would suggest for improvement of the virtual reference service.

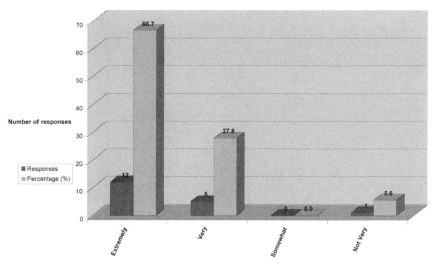

Figure 4.4 Confidence Level of Users Regarding Search Skills After Participation in the Library Reference Service

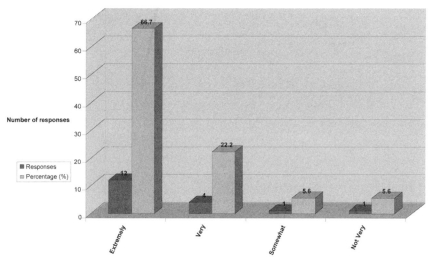

Figure 4.5 Confidence Level of Users Regarding Future Searching After Participation in the Library Virtual Reference Service

CONCLUSIONS AND RECOMMENDATIONS

This study reviewed pertinent literature in the field of virtual reference and expert-based systems, and examined student user comments on virtual reference services. Although several libraries supported this project, the level of student response was low. The study was certainly limited by the amount of time the researcher had available to complete the project; perhaps an entire semester instead of a month and a half to survey participants would have provided more sustained data. There may be additional information to be gathered based on the time of the academic semester for which students are completing work. Courses are different, with instructors assigning work at various intervals in the semester. Doing this study at the end of the semester could have provided a different set of tendencies than what might have been revealed earlier in the semester.

The biggest problem that occurred with identifying libraries that would participate in the study was their requirement to submit any survey to their institutional review board (IRB). Several additional libraries were willing to participate and even submitted the attached survey and request to their review boards but were told from their representatives that they needed more lead time on the submission and would not get a response in a period conducive to participation. This issue and my request for participation even sparked an additional debate on one of the library Listservs. One librarian started his own informal survey of respondents as to whether they had to submit brief virtual reference assessment surveys to their IRBs. The answer was that most do, as was corroborated by the small number of schools that participated in this study without IRB review.

One school reported several technological problems with the virtual reference service during the survey period. The reference desk fielded questions as they came in, and therefore the librarians opened up the software and left it that way during operating hours, waiting for questions to come in. However, the librarians did not know they were being timed out of the service. Students were still able to log in their questions, and virtual reference systems automatically respond to students with messages while the student is waiting for a librarian to receive their question. A typical message to the user might say, "Thank you for your question. A librarian will be with you shortly." The problem with this scenario is that several students reported waiting for a period of time for the librarian, and the librarian had no record of receiving the question from the student. Libraries should test and retest their services regularly to ensure that reference librarians fully understand what students are experiencing on the other end of their service. Technological problems can dissuade students from using the system, so much attention should be paid to this issue when implementing virtual reference.

Several observations can be made from this study of virtual reference and expert-based systems. First, individual libraries using virtual reference are likely to find low use of their systems by their students. Marketing may help to boost statistics, but this tendency was found in the literature (Ballesti and Russell 2003, 18) and supported by the survey completed in this project. Consortia-based virtual reference systems will likely have higher traffic via the service and require more regular assistance from librarians; however, the majority of the patrons asking the questions may not necessarily be students, or students of that individual institution. Depending on the type of virtual reference service a library uses, planning, research, and assessment can all contribute to a more effective experience for both staff and users. Library staff must institute new policies when starting up virtual reference, including hours and manpower assignments. Students need clear instructions for using this new type of service, and how it can be useful to them.

Some of the literature hinted at the fact that expert-based systems were competition to libraries (Bivens-Tatum 2001, 1; Coffman and McGlamery 2000, 69). At the completion of this study, it may be more accurate to simply say each service is different and has value. Expert systems generally do not have the quality of responses that reference systems can provide (Cloughley 2004, 22), but they are available in some cases instantaneously and much of the time are available at times that virtual reference systems are not. These are not hard and fast instances; for example, some expert systems use advanced degree experts, like doctors, for advice, and they may not be synchronous. Collaborative virtual reference systems are also providing assistance to patrons across time zones and locations, thereby increasing the opportunity for patrons to ask questions.

The point is that each system has benefits and drawbacks, and depending on the research need, one may be more useful at a particular instance. Traditionally, expert systems are good at providing short, factual answers, whereas reference services are better at providing resources and references to research type questions (Janes, Hill, and Rolfe 2001, 1106). What might ultimately be the best situation for academic students is the ability to distinguish the similarities and differences among these services and develop the skills necessary to determine where to go for their information need. One cannot say that one of these services is always the best place to go to ask an information question.

Students surveyed were overwhelmingly satisfied with the service, yet half were not sure if they would use it again. This brings up the question of whether virtual reference services derive from a knowledge need of users. A next step would be to survey librarians on why they have chosen to pay for a virtual reference system, and if they deem it to be successful. Students are satisfied with the level of knowledge that librarians impart during an online information exchange, but it is yet to be seen whether there is sustainability of these services when use continues to be low.

A critical next step in assessing student use of virtual reference systems would be a more comprehensive study as to why students do not use these services, when they are available at their libraries. It is unclear to what extent marketing draws students to these services, or what types of marketing appeal most to students. The survey results indicated that students who participated in the survey learned of the service through instructors, librarians, and the library Web page. No one indicated that advertising or marketing had a role in leading to the service. However, what is not known and would be beneficial is what types of marketing individual institutions are using to appeal to students and which methods are successful.

Finally, the last lesson learned from this project is that the need for surveying student experiences with virtual reference services is continual. "Ongoing evaluation allows reference staff to continually refine and improve their service—vitally important if the digital reference service is to successfully meet the information needs of its user community" (Wasik 2003, 2). As information skills of students change, as software services improve, as "ask an expert" services abound, and libraries incorporate lessons learned from their assessment of student use, these factors may well change how students view virtual reference and expert-based systems and where they turn for answers to their information needs.

APPENDIX A

Virtual Reference Student Assessment

Please complete this quick survey to help determine the strengths and weaknesses of virtual reference systems. The survey is anonymous and should take 3–5 minutes to complete. Thank you.

1. How did you find out about this virtual reference service?

   advertisement / flyer
   link on library Web site
   librarian referral
   instructor referral
   a friend

2. Is this the first resource you have used for your search?

   Yes
   No

3. If you did not begin your research using this service, what other resources did you try first? Check all that apply:

   Web search engine
   Library catalog
   Library database (journals)
   Ask an expert Web site
   Ask Jeeves
   Not applicable

4. Why did you decide to use this reference service? Check all that apply.

   I could not find any information so far
   I was looking for reliable research
   I was looking for hard to find information
   I was curious about the service and wanted to try it out
   I used this service before and it was helpful

5. Which type of project are you doing research for?

   Class
   Job

Club / Organization
Entertainment

6. Did you find the information you were looking for from this service?

Yes
No
The information was helpful, but did not satisfy what I was looking for

7. Would you use this reference service again?

Always—I would start my future searches here
Maybe—I would use this service if I could not find information on the
    Internet
Maybe—I would use this service again if I could not find information in
    my library
Never—I would not use this service again

Select from the following scale: (Questions 8–10)

Extremely Very   Somewhat   Not Very

8. How easy to use, accessible, and convenient did you find this reference
   service?
9. How confident are you about conducting a similar search again on your
   own effectively and efficiently accessing information?
10. How confident are you that you have gained new tools or skills for search-
    ing as a result of this service?
11. What did you find to be the best part of using this reference service?
12. What would you like to see improved with this reference service?

REFERENCES

American Library Association. 2000. "Information Literacy Competency Standards for Higher Education," 1–20. http://www.acrl.org/ala/acrl/acrlstandards/
informationliteracycompetency.htm. Accessed April 15, 2004.

Ballesti, R., and Russell, G. 2003. "Implementing Virtual Reference: Hollywood
Technology in Real Life," *Computers in Libraries*, 23(4), 14–18. Library and
Information Science database. Accessed January 15, 2004.

Bivens-Tatum, W. 2001. "Expert Services on the Web: the Commercial Competition for Libraries," *C&RL News*, 62(7). HWWilson database. Accessed
January 21, 2004.

Breeding, M. 2001. "Providing Virtual Reference Service: Libraries Are Finding
Ways to Expand Services to Remote Library Users," *Information Today*, 18(4),
42–43. Library and Information Science database. Accessed January 15, 2004.

Burek Pierce, J. 2002. "Digital Discomfort? 'Get Over It,' Says McClure," *American Libraries*, 33(5), 45. Library and Information Science database. Accessed
January 15, 2004.

Cloughley, K. 2004. Digital Reference Services: How Do the Library-Based Services Compare with the Expert Services?" *Library Review,* 53(1), 17–23. Emerald Library Database. Accessed February 20, 2004.

Coffman, S., and McGlamery, S. 2000. "The Librarian and Mr. Jeeves," *American Libraries,* 31(5), 66–69. Wilson OmniFile. Accessed February 19, 2004.

Curtis, S. C. 2000. "Listening to Generation X," *Journal of Educational Media and Library Sciences,* 38(2), 122–32. Library and Information Science database. Accessed January 21, 2004.

Dougherty, R.M. 2002. "Reference Around the Clock: Is It in Your Future?" *American Libraries,* 33(5), 44–45. Library and Information Science database. Accessed January 15, 2004.

Janes, J., Hill, C., and Rolfe, A. 2001. "Ask-an-Expert Services Analysis," *Journal of the American Society for Information Science and Technology,* 52(13), 1106–21. Computer Abstracts. Accessed February 20, 2004.

Johnson, C. M. 2004. "Online Chat Reference: Survey Results from Affiliates of Two Universities," *Reference and User Services Quarterly,* 43(3), 237–47.

Luther, J. 2003. "Trumping Google: Metasearching's Promise," *Library Journal,* 128 (16), 36–39. Library & Information Science database. Accessed January 21, 2004.

McCrea, R. 2004. "Evaluation of Two Library-Based and One Expert Reference Service on the Web," *Library Review,* 53 (1), 11–16. Emerald Library database. Accessed February 20, 2004.

McLaughlin, J. 2003. "Who's Better: Google or CU Librarians? Search Me," *Ithaca Journal,* http://www.ithacajournal.com/news/stories/20030920/local-news/297041.html. Accessed April 26, 2004.

Pack, T. 2000. "Human Search Engines: The Next Killer App?" *EContent,* 23(6), 16–22. Library and Information Science database. Accessed January 21, 2004.

Quint, B. 2002. "QuestionPoint Marks New Era in Virtual Reference," *Information Today,* 19 (7), 50,54. Library & Information Science database. Accessed January 15, 2004

Small, Helfer, D. 2003. "Virtual Reference in Libraries: Status and Issues," *Searcher,* 11 (2), 63–65. Library & Information Science database. Accessed January 15, 2004.

Smyth, J. 2003. "Virtual Reference Transcript Analysis: A Few Models, *Searcher,* 11 (3), 26–30. Library & Information Science database. Accessed January 15, 2004.

Soloway, E., and Wallace, R. 1997. "Does the Internet Support Student Inquiry? Don't Ask," *Communications of the ACM,* 40 (5), 11–16. Accessed February 20, 2004.

Tomaiuolo, N. G. 2000. "Aska and You May Receive: Commercial Reference Services on the Web," *Searcher,* 8 (5), 52–62. Wilson OmniFile. Accessed February 19, 2004.

Wasik, J. 2003. "Digital Reference Evaluation," *VRD.org.* http://www.vrd.org/AskA/digref_assess.shtml. Accessed April 6, 2004.

5   NEW DEMOGRAPHICS MEAN NEW SERVICES

Christine C. Godin

INTRODUCTION

For those of us who were entering college in the 1960s, the concept of the community college was still new. In my native Massachusetts, junior colleges were usually private institutions that served young women, training them to be administrative secretaries, early childhood educators, interior designers, and the like. The term "community college" referred to some emerging public institutions that offered basic undergraduate education as well as what we considered to be higher level vocational courses.

In other states, the terms junior college and community college were synonymous and often people just referred to the local institution as "the JuCo." The general perception was that the two-year institution, regardless of its official name, was a watered down version of real college, primarily serving students who could not make it otherwise.

Unfortunately, this perception has been perpetuated over the decades, in spite of the all-too-obvious truth—community colleges are serving an unprecedented number of students and those students are more diverse than ever. Women outnumber men; minorities often are the majority at many institutions. Indeed, some of the most enduring pioneers in the field began as schools for particular populations. An excellent example is the 100-year old St. Philip's College in San Antonio, Texas. What began as a sewing school for African-American girls is now a comprehensive institution that is not only historically black but also Hispanic-serving in its designation. The student population is actually quite varied in terms of age and ethnicity. The curriculum runs the gamut from the core academic courses to women's studies to upholstering and massage therapy.

Because of this very diversity in patrons and subject areas, the libraries in community colleges are presented with unique challenges not always found at other institutions of higher learning. Many students do require developmental help in reading, writing, and math. Often the student population will include local high school students taking advanced placement or dual-credit courses. In some parts of the country, there is a large immigrant population looking for programs in English as a second language. Accommodations must be made to offer equal access and to ensure that materials are available in a variety of formats to meet access and ability issues.

So what does this all mean to the library director at a community college? This chapter discusses the ramifications of the points already mentioned and how the community college library can or should respond.

THE WAY WE WERE

In 1940, of those aged 25 years or more, only 4 million had attended college for one to three years. By 2002, that number jumped, dramatically, to 46 million (Gaquin, DeBrandt, and Ryan 2003, 397). What accounts for this? Prior to World War II, the majority of college students were male and from the more privileged classes. The costs associated with attending college were prohibitive to most Americans. Financial aid was not widely available.

Following the war, the picture changed. Veterans were returning to college in record numbers with funds from the G.I. Bill of Rights. Women had taken jobs in industries previously thought closed to them. Higher education became more attractive to women as a means to gain independence or sometimes, simply, to meet eligible men with good potential. The result of these societal changes increased the demand for spaces in colleges. Many four-year institutions reverted to an open admissions policy, forcing the few community or junior colleges to refocus their efforts to maintain enrollments. The change in focus to vocational training and the strengthening of adult education was the answer—the number of two-year institutions changed from approximately 600 in 1960 to more than 1,400 by the early 1990s (Unger 1996, 239).

Gradually, the image of Joe College began to look less Ivy League and more diverse. The average age at many institutions began to rise; the gender makeup moved to a more balanced picture.

THE COLLEGE LIBRARY IN THE LATE TWENTIETH CENTURY

Like most academic libraries, community college libraries focused on the curricular needs of their particular community. Technology in the sense we know it today was almost nonexistent. Standard library offerings included books, periodicals, some audiovisual materials, a place to study, and reference services. The mission was to serve the students who were pursuing a two-year degree or certificate. Research was limited to larger university libraries. The biggest difference between these lower level academic libraries and the public library was probably in the development of the collections. For those institutions with highly vocational curricula (nursing, automotive technology, aircraft maintenance, hospitality management), the titles on the shelves were likely to be very technical and generally unavailable at a public library. Materials for the core curricula focused on lower level undergraduate offerings.

With the advent of automation, access to library holdings was transformed. Online catalogs, first in the form of microform readers or computer-produced book catalogs, gave way to real-time online databases that not only tracked items but could indicate their status at any given time. Libraries with more than one location could "see" what was available at another; interlibrary loan moved from a cumbersome, paper-based system utilizing the mails to a much faster service with improved turnaround times from request to delivery. Patrons could expect to complete research in much less time; patrons began to demand better service to accommodate them. With these new expectations, academic libraries became acutely aware of the dreaded paradigm shift.

WHO ARE OUR STUDENTS?

As noted previously, the demographics of the community college student body have evolved in terms of appearance, gender, and numbers. In addition, the overall ability of these students to begin and complete a degree or certificate program has become an issue. New York University's Joshua Smith tells us "the average age of the current national community college student is 29, with 63 percent attending part-time. This 'average' student is likely to be married with children, employed and have other adult responsibilities" (Smith 1998, 4). Although some community colleges may not mirror these figures, it is not too far from the truth for most two-year institutions. Other variables in addition to age and gender include race or ethnicity. Students from historically underrepresented groups are attending college in greater numbers each year. During the 1990s, minority participation in community colleges increased over minority participation in four-year institutions, with the gap widening into the 2000s. (Boulard 2003, 7). To what can we attribute the difference? A survey by the Education Commission of the States (2002, 1) found that most community colleges invest heavily in remedial education, a service needed by many disadvantaged (often low-income and/or minority) students. Universities usually don't emphasize this aspect of learning, leaving that task to the two-year colleges. Consequently, community colleges offer many more developmental courses than do their sister four-year colleges and universities. The trend is likely to continue. What does this mean for community college libraries?

DO YOU GIVE THEM WHAT THEY WANT OR WHAT THEY "NEED"?

That is the question! Certainly it's been an issue for many public libraries for years. Dwindling revenues, combined with citizen apathy, have caused many a public library director to address this issue. In Baltimore, Charles Robinson took a "give 'em what they want" attitude during his tenure as director at the Baltimore County Public Library. He was applauded and booed at the same time. (Pearl 1996, 138) Many a community college library director, along with the collection development staff, face the same predicament. Community college students (many of them from the MTV generation) want more audiovisual items to supplement the traditional textbook readings. Often, it is perceived that they prefer those items to actually reading the material. How often has the reference librarian heard, "Do you have any videos on [You Name It]?" Or perhaps the student wishes to view the popular film of a book or story that has been assigned. The ubiquitous videotapes of algebra topics are popular in most community college libraries. Often they are part of a package designed to go with the standard textbook. In another chapter of this book, the advent of telecourses is mentioned as part of the evolution of the popular distance learning movement. Many students perceived it would be "easier" to take the tapes home and watch them at their own pace, rather than locating a parking space and sitting in a class at a prescribed time. To be fair, more students have time demands that don't allow them to follow the traditional college curriculum. Consequently, the availability of alternate methods of delivery is very attractive. Perhaps we have unconsciously been providing what they want *as well as* what they need! This might explain the huge growth in the number of community colleges as well as the growth in enrollment. The obvious issues for their library programs focus on having the appropriate materials in the desired format(s) and available to as many as possible. How do we do this?

One of the biggest challenges for me as a director in a new institution was to build a collection of materials and services that would meet those needs and assure our college community that we are striving to continue to be part of the team for student success. In my last position I worked in an affluent and highly educated community. Many homes (approximately 65 percent in the early 1990s) had a computer. The local public school systems were outstanding. Support for and the use of the Johnson County (Kansas) public library was admirable. The community college demographics did not include a large number of minorities. In spite of all that, the number of developmental courses and services mushroomed over the years. In my present position at Northwest Vista College (San Antonio, Texas), I meet many students who are the first in their family to graduate from high school, never mind attend college. They often do not have a home computer. Some are arriving from schools that are considered low-performing. The college works hard to identify these students so that they can offer enough courses and services to help them achieve their goals. Examples of these services include Project Ganar (a Title V program to address low-performing students in the math skills), an extensive ESL program, and a mentoring program with a local middle school to prepare students to think about attending college. I think we are doing a great job in addressing the issues that are often obstacles for potential students.

The library is only one of the college areas that can work to reach those goals. By including a library tour in the general college orientation required for degree-seeking students, we have an ice-breaker that allows them to see us as a meeting place as well as the place to find help in their assignments. Keeping in mind that many of our students are not yet ready for college level courses, we have continued to develop our collections to reflect different levels of abilities and interests. Purchasing fiction titles for reading classes means looking at the high school reading lists for the state and consulting bibliographies of high-interest / low-ability materials. Adding audiovisual materials that will help those with a variety of learning styles is another way to ensure that we meet the needs of our students. Managing a mix of traditional print materials as well as a variety of online resources is a must for any contemporary community college library that wants to remain relevant to their users.

To sum it up, faculty and students *need* to have enough materials to support their curricular needs as well as recreational items to enhance their formal learning. What they *want* is usually the same thing, but with caveats as to format and accessibility. The latter has driven huge changes in how libraries provide information. Many faculty as well as students feel they don't have enough time for recreational reading but do arrive on Fridays to check out their video selections for the weekend.

WHO NEEDS THE LIBRARY ANYMORE? WE HAVE THE INTERNET!

Who hasn't heard that smarmy query? It could be a board member, an administrator, a student—even, alas, a faculty member. Television and movies often give the impression that anything is available on a computer, usually showing people hacking into systems that should be secure with relative ease. The advent of the Internet coming into homes and schools has certainly created an information explosion, but many people fall into the same trap they did with news from magazine and newspapers: "If it was printed, it must be true." Anyone who has done publicity for a nonprofit organization knows how information can be misprinted, omitted, or edited with little regard for accuracy. Now we encounter students (and friends and family as well!) who have read something "on the Internet" and assume it must be gospel.

What does this mean for the college library? Well, it certainly means we have an opportunity to demonstrate what we have to offer—a teaching moment, if you will. I sometimes show a student the results of a search in Google as well as one of our proprietary databases. That usually does the trick, especially if his or her professor has asked for peer-reviewed material or scholarly journal articles.

To many, the Internet is the be-all and end-all in information storage and accessibility. Often, students mistakenly believe that all information is now available, free of charge, over the Internet. For those of us working in libraries, we roll our eyes to the heavens and mutter that the library is often the place those same people gain access to the Internet. And, to complicate matters, they have no idea that their tax dollars are paying for those wonderful databases, the computers themselves, and the technology that makes it available. College administrators are often lulled into thinking along the same lines while they peruse the library budget each year.

The proliferation of information, good and bad, can be overwhelming to the college patrons. Since it all looks alike, we often find ourselves trying to explain the difference between the results in Google and those in Ebsco's Academic Search Premiere database. When indexed information appeared in various printed indices, it was easy to move from the green *Reader's Guide to Periodical Literature* to the tan or red or blue volumes on other tables that focused on social sciences or art or biology. A quick comparison of a popular magazine alongside a professional journal usually cleared up any confusion on the part of the student.

A popular game show host declared that "Librarians Rule!" This was never so true. Faculty and students are more dependent than ever on the guidance of librarians. And librarians are under the gun to stay in tune with the changes in technology so that they can continue to help patrons navigate the sometimes-uncharted territory of cyberspace.

HOW DOES THIS AFFECT OUR SERVICES?

The revolution in technology has driven many older, more traditional public services underground. When I was in college back in the Dark Ages of the 1960s, The photocopier was an enormous machine run by a person who took your work and your money and told you to come back later to pick it up. We still took notes; paying for photocopies was a luxury few of us could afford. Reserve materials were kept in the library so they were only accessible when the facility was actually open for business. Interlibrary loan was a tedious process of looking through the *National Union Catalog* to see who might hold the item in demand. Then a form was mailed to the various libraries, inquiring about a loan. It might be a month or more before anything was known as to the availability of the item. Resource sharing was an alien concept.

Today, we have coin-operated, self-service machines that make change. They are easily installed anywhere they are needed in the library. Reserve items aren't limited to print materials. Many automated library systems will support electronic "reserve rooms." Documents can be scanned and made available over the Internet to students for a particular class. Programs like WebCT or Blackboard are often used to augment in-class assignments or serve as the interface for online courses. Interlibrary loans are much speedier, thanks to real-time online requests and quick response times from loaning libraries. Articles can be scanned and sent by Ariel or fax machine. The advent of remote access, provided by a third-party authentication service or a proxy server in the library, has made a tremendous difference in how we provide access to material in periodicals. For our students, parts of the library are open 24/7 because they can access databases or electronic books from off campus. Community college students have many distractions and responsibilities that make it difficult to come to the physical library during standard operating hours.

For those patrons who cannot come to the physical library (the disabled, the working mother, the truly distant student), libraries need to find effective ways to communicate more efficiently. Telephone reference service is nothing new; email to a reference librarian has caught on with most academic libraries. Live chat reference service can be considered but staffing can be an issue. Some libraries have joined an informal consortium to share reference duty so that someone is always available.

Because so many of our resources depend on using a computer for access, students are expected to achieve some level of computer literacy to be successful. Librarians are often put in the position of assisting with PowerPoint presentations, setting margins in Word, or explaining how to set up an email account. The increased dependency on the profession for this kind of information has tremendous implications for reference service. Librarians must be comfortable using and demonstrating the use of various computer applications. Some institutions have extensive computer labs to which patrons can be referred. For most, however, the library has become a place to do the research *and* compose the paper or project.

Traditional services have been improved beyond belief and will continue to be refined in terms of speed and accuracy. Today's students have much different expectations of the library, and librarians must be prepared to meet those expectations. Services that address the needs of the working adult, students with children, students with learning disabilities, and services that take advantage of evolving technology are all in demand or will be in demand in the coming decades. Librarians must be able to deal with a patron who is never seen face to face. They must be prepared to present easy-to-follow instructions on the use of our resources to them. They must continue to recognize there will be students who have been on the other side of the digital divide.

After librarians have done all that, they must be able to evaluate how well they have done. By working with faculty on determining student success and retention in classes, they can get some idea of whether their points have come across. By checking the usage statistics on various databases and their own Web pages, librarians can see how much the library's efforts and resources are being utilized. By surveying students, they can determine how satisfied/dissatisfied they are with the library.

The results of those evaluative measures should drive the library's plans for the future.

BACK TO THE FUTURE

This chapter examines the changes in community college students and changes in technology; now we examine the changes libraries are expected to act on for the future. No longer will patrons be willing to wait weeks or even days for an item from another source. The boundaries between library systems, physical as well as ideological, have been broken down. Consortiums have allowed smaller institutions to increase their buying power as well as to develop a more efficacious transfer of materials. In Texas, the development of a statewide resource-sharing model known as TexShare has transformed the spectrum of offerings for many college libraries. Sharing the costs of online resources, including databases and electronic books, has made even the smallest college library more effective.

The student demand for services that seem non-library related are also increasing. Gone are the days of the Library Police who patrol for the errant patron daring to sip a drink or munch on a snack while studying. With the proliferation of large bookstores with comfy chairs and coffee shops, libraries have been forced to consider adding some of these amenities to attract and retain their users. We hope to add a cyber café in the next stage of our library's development. Offering wireless laptop service for those who merely want to surf the Internet or play games is a plus; we can then limit the use of the workstations in the actual library to research purposes only.

The change in student demographics requires that libraries be more prepared than ever to deal with issues of disability, underpreparedness, and diverse cultures. How libraries define the needs of their patrons and how they meet those needs (and wants!) will be the driving force behind their success or failure to serve.

REFERENCES

Boulard, Garry. 2003. "Diverse City," *Community College Week* 16 (August): 6–9.

Education Commission of the States. 2002. *State Policies on Community College Remedial Education: Finds From a National Survey.* Denver, CO: ECS.

Gaquin, Deirdre A., Katherine A DeBrandt, and Mary Meghan Ryan, Eds. 2003. *Education Statistics of the United States,* 4th ed. Lanham, MD: Bernan.

Pearl, Nancy. 1996. "Gave 'Em What They Wanted. LJ Interview with Charlie Robinson and Jean Barry Molz of the Baltimore County Public Library," *Library Journal* 121 (September 1): 136–38.

Smith, Joshua L. 1998. "Hrumph. Enough with the Half-Truths," *Community College Week* 10 (February): 4–5.

Unger, Harlow G., Ed. 1996. *Encyclopedia of American Education.* New York: Facts on File.

SUGGESTED READING

Baker, George, III, Ed. 2003. *A Handbook on the Community College in America: Its History, Mission, and Management*. Westport, CT: Greenwood Publishing Group, Inc.

Brint, S. and J. Karbabel. 1989. *The Diverted Dream: Community Colleges and the Promise of Educational Opportunity in America, 1900–1985*. New York: Oxford University Press.

Cohen, A.M., and F. B. Brawer. 1996. *The American Community College*, 3rd ed. San Francisco, CA: Jossey-Bass.

Montanelli, Dale S. and Patricia F. Stenstrom. 1999. *People Come First: User-Centered Academic Library Service*. Chicago: Association of College and Research Libraries.

Oblinger, Diana G. 2003. "Improving Education for the 'Next Generation,'" *Community College Week* 16 (October 13): 3+.

Ronan, Jana Smith. 2003. *Chat Reference: A Guide to Live Virtual Reference Services*. Westport, CT: Libraries Unlimited.

6 IF ONLINE EDUCATION IS A SHIFTING PLAYING FIELD, WHAT POSITION SHOULD COMMUNITY COLLEGE LIBRARIANS PLAY?

Linda Reeves and Celita DeArmond

GROWTH OF DISTANCE EDUCATION

Distance education has experienced phenomenal growth. In the 1997–98 academic year, the Education Department's National Center for Education Statistics estimated that 1.3 million students were enrolled in for-credit distance education courses. By the 2000–2001 academic year, the number had grown to 2.9 million (Kiernan 2003, A28). Increasingly, distance learners have their choice of more courses and programs, as more institutions are offering distance education courses. According to July 2003 U.S. Education Department survey results , 56 percent of two- and four-year institutions offered distance education courses in 2000–2001, compared to 44 percent in 1997–1998 (Kiernan 2003, A28). The survey, which ran from February 2002 through June 2002, showed two-year colleges leading the boom in distance education, with 90 percent of public two-year institutions offering distance education courses (Kiernan 2003, A28). Web-based technologies accelerated the growth of distance education, as educators realized that education no longer must be bound by time or place ("The Explosion of Distance Education" 2002, 2). Enrollment in online courses rose by 20 percent in 2003, and it is now estimated that 11 percent of college students will take at least one course online (Boser 2003, 58).

OBLIGATION TO PROVIDE LIBRARY SUPPORT

Academic libraries have an obligation to provide services to faculty and students participating in distance education programs. According to the *Guidelines for Distance Learning Library Services* (Association & College and Research Libraries [ACRL], 2000) institutions providing online courses must provide library services that are equivalent to the library services offered to on-campus students. The philosophy behind the Guidelines holds that

> Access to adequate library services and resources is essential for the
> attainment of superior academic skills in post- secondary education, regardless
> of where students, faculty, and programs are located. Members of the distance
> learning community are entitled to library services and resources equivalent to
> those provided for students and faculty in traditional campus settings. (ACRL
> 2000, 2)

With distance education students making up an increasingly large portion of their patron base, college libraries are looking for ways to provide services to this population. Many libraries are realizing the importance of having one person to coordinate the various kinds of library support to online students and are creating and filling positions for distance learning librarians. The *ACRL 2000 Academic Library Trends and Statistics* survey (ACRL 2000), which focused on distance education, revealed that academic libraries are, indeed, providing support for distance learning programs. Libraries at associate of arts institutions led the field at 90.3 percent participation, with bachelor's institutions at 50.6 percent, master's institutions at 76.1 percent, and doctoral-granting institutions at 83.2 percent (Thompson 2002, 339). Services must be provided to the distance learning population, but what kind of services, and how extensive should they be?

TYPE OF LIBRARY SUPPORT DEPENDS ON TYPE OF LIBRARY USER

As with other kinds of library services, library directors can have a better idea about what kinds of services to offer distance education patrons after determining the characteristics of this patron group. Does the institution provide distance education classes to students who are truly a considerable distance away? In other cities, other states, or other countries? Or are the distance learners actually local students who are taking online classes to have greater flexibility in their schedule? Information reported in the *2000 Academic Library Trends and Statistics* survey indicates that the distance learners at a great many colleges are indeed students who live close enough to make at least occasional trips to campus to take advantage of services. For example, 40 to 50 percent of all academic libraries report using on-campus orientation sessions to introduce distance learners to library services (Thompson 2002, 339). Survey questions asking how libraries deliver reference services to distance learners show a similar picture. On average, 57 percent of baccalaureate-, master's-, and doctoral-granting institutions use face-to-face contact to provide reference service to distance learners, and the figure for associate of arts institutions is even higher, at 71 percent (Thompson 2002, 340). As Thompson (2002) points out, these statistics suggest that the distance learners at most institutions are engaged in *distributed* learning rather than *distance* learning. That is, students may not be in a traditional classroom, but they are not too far away to be able to come to the campus library. However, it is likely that many of the students who enroll in online courses do so because other demands on their time make it difficult for them to come on campus.

In addition, even students enrolled in traditional, face-to-face courses on campus generally prefer using electronic library resources to using paper materials. In light of these trends, many colleges are opting to provide online library resources and services to all students, in recognition that the line between distance education students and local students is no longer clear. As Barron (2002, 28) points out, the restructuring of the academic environment to provide more Web-based applications has helped to blur the line between distributed learners and distant learners. The danger of not providing online library resources and services, Barron (2002, 28) warns, is that students will turn to the Web, both the free Web and the for-profit vendors of information such as XanEdu and Questia. If a majority of students start using these resources instead of library resources, academic libraries could quickly become obsolete.

THE NAME GAME: DISTANCE, DISTRIBUTED, OR ONLINE EDUCATION?

Barron (2002, 25) asks, "Is there a difference between distant and on-campus students anymore? Or is that distinction disappearing in our current state of academic 'wiredness'?" Barron describes the growth of *distributed education,* or instruction in which technology brings teacher and students together without meeting face to face. Increasingly, all students want the convenience and flexibility made possible by library services and materials that they can access online from off campus. As Barron points out,

> A student who is taking a class from a dorm room or an on-campus studio classroom still has a significant advantage over the student who is 70 (or 500) miles away, because he or she can usually walk across campus to the library if necessary. On the other hand, the restrictions on time, etc., that have led a person to choose an online or televised (distributed) course might also limit his or her access to the library every bit as much as physical distance. (Barron 2002, 26)

Libraries are looking for innovative and cost-effective ways to provide support to this new population of students who are distant from traditional on-campus library resources and services, either in geography or in schedule. Because of the variety of distance learning programs being offered today, the library support solutions that work at one institution may not work at another (Bryant 2001, 58).

A TALE OF TWO TEXAS COMMUNITY COLLEGES

The distance learning services offered at two community colleges in the Alamo Community College District in San Antonio, Texas, reflect some of the trends in providing library support of online education today.

Northwest Vista College (NVC) is the newest community college in the Alamo Community College District. It began offering classes on its new campus in 1998, and in 2000–2001 was listed as the fourth fastest-growing college of its size in the nation. It currently enrolls more than 8,000, including approximately 1,000 dual-credit high-school students. The main challenge the college has faced recently is finding classrooms for its growing student enrollment and office space for the faculty needed to teach them. In 2002 the college purchased fourteen portable buildings to provide more classrooms and office space, and in 2003 the college began offering classes at an off-site location. The college's growing online learning program has provided another alternative for the many students who want to enroll in classes at the college.

Northwest Vista College launched its online learning program in 1999 with five online courses and a total of 53 students. In the fall semester of 2003, a total of 1,669 students were enrolled in 95 online courses. Eighty-one courses were totally online, and 14 were hybrid courses, combining face-to-face and online learning. Data compiled by the Office of Institutional Research indicate that the students enrolling in online and hybrid courses at NVC tend to fit the definition of distributed learners rather than distance learners because most are local residents and many also take courses on campus. Many of these online learners have full-time day jobs, so they are distant in schedule rather than geography. They opt for online courses for the convenience available through this method of instruction delivery.

San Antonio College (SAC), founded in 1925, is the largest college in the Alamo Community College District, currently enrolling more than 20,000 students. San Antonio College has a traditional library with a well-rounded collection. The college also has a growing distance education program, which began in the 1980s with telecourses, now called videocourses. Since that time, off-campus initiatives in Kerrville, Seguin, and New Braunfels, Texas, were initiated, and in 1995, the first dual-credit initiative was offered for high school students. Internet courses soon followed and have been the fastest growing distance education effort at the college. During the fall semester of 1996, Internet courses had 9 enrollments, a number that has steadily grown to 4,757 enrollments by fall 2003 (Torres 2003). In fact, the enrollment statistics for off-campus locations has dropped from 2,429 to 863 enrollments in the past six years, indicating that students crave and are responding to the flexibility that Internet courses offer.

San Antonio College increases the number of Internet course offerings each semester, with 249 courses and 361 course sections listed as of fall 2003 (Torres 2003). Although the majority of students taking Internet courses are in-county residents, the college has also recently attracted Internet course students from out of state and through the Virtual College of Texas (VCT), a collaborative effort between Texas community college districts. In 2002, SAC responded to the growing need for library outreach services to these distance programs by creating a position for a distance learning librarian.

Access to Materials

The ACRL'S 2000 *Academic Library Trends and Statistics* survey, which focuses on distance education, indicates that academic libraries are employing a variety of methods to deliver materials to distance learners: email (46%), face-to-face (55%), fax-on-demand (51%), interactive Web pages (34%), and courier (45%) (Thompson 2002, 340). Having information about their colleges' distance learners has helped the librarians at NVC and SAC design appropriate kinds of services and support. In some ways, providing materials for online students was easier for NVC because the library opened when the electronic age was already in full swing. The library started out in the summer of 1998 in rented space in a church downtown with a handful of reference books, the library director, and her secretary. When the college began offering classes on their own campus in the fall of 1998, the library occupied a classroom. The library moved into its own space in the fall of 1999. The staff has now grown to include four full-time librarians and two part-time librarians in addition to the director. The collection includes around 9,000 circulating books, more than 1,600 reference books, and a popular audiovisual collection consisting of more than 3,250 videos and DVDs and more than 1,300 CDs.

The libraries at both SAC and NVC have made an effort to achieve a balance between print and electronic materials. As for periodicals, the trend has been toward purchasing electronic access over print materials. The libraries together subscribe to more than 100 proprietary databases, all but a couple of few are accessible from off campus. Access to databases is provided 24 hours a day, seven days a week through an authentication service. Off-campus access is simple; users do not need to configure their browser to a proxy server or memorize several different passwords. On the database page patrons are prompted to enter a single password that gives them off-campus access to virtually all of the databases.

Both the NVC and SAC libraries have a number of resources online, such as a library Web page, an online public access catalog, and off-campus access to subscription databases. Library staff also add links to free online reference sources and to authoritative Web sites in different subject areas.

Recently the Texas State Library has begun making available electronic books to patrons of academic libraries in Texas. In 2005, the number of full-text, searchable books available online reached 27,500. Students who are enrolled in Internet courses via the Virtual College of Texas have access to their primary institution's library resources since that is where they are officially registered. In addition, college students in Texas can obtain a TexShare card, which gives them borrowing privileges at many public libraries and most academic libraries throughout the state. The college where the student is enrolled is considered the sponsoring institution, but the student may also obtain TexShare cards from public libraries. Because the majority of NVC and SAC distance learning students tend to be local residents, and because TexShare provides access to print and electronic books, neither of the community college libraries mail materials to students' homes.

The SAC library does offer off-campus delivery of Interlibrary Loan articles via the Ariel document delivery system. If a patron supplies the Interlibrary Loan office with their email address on the online loan form, then a copy of that article can be scanned and uploaded to a secure Web server. The library then notifies the patron via email that their article is ready for online retrieval. The NVC library, which does not have SAC's vast collection of back issues of print journals, does not offer such a service, focusing instead on providing electronic access.

Reference Service

San Antonio College has an "Ask a Librarian" email service, which provides 24-hour turnaround time for answers to reference questions. Business for the email reference service at SAC is steady, with 51 reference replies sent during the first two months of fall 2003. Checking this email is divided amongst librarians who volunteer to check the inbox on their specified day of the week. A copy of each outgoing response is saved so that all librarians can evaluate responses to questions and generally get a feel for what kinds of questions come through the service. A Web form is used to gather information from the patron, including: name, email address, their status (i.e., faculty, student, staff, alumnus, other), geographic location, question, and reason for the question (i.e., class assignment description or personal need). Librarians at NVC answer reference questions sent through email, but because of its small staff size, it has not so far been able to offer a full-fledged email reference service.

However, NVC is experimenting with synchronous online reference service. In early 2003 the Alamo Community College District purchased access to Elluminate vClass for 100 concurrent users. Elluminate provides a classroom environment with a whiteboard that can serve as a chalkboard or as a screen on which to show PowerPoint presentations or PDF documents. Elluminate offers not only chat but also the ability to hold voice-over-Internet conversations among participants. The ability to perform co-browsing is especially useful for showing students how to navigate through the dizzying array of online databases and other resources. Moderators can send class members to a Web page or share their desktop to show students a process to follow.

Librarians at NVC began piloting the service in May 2003. A typical session involved chatting with students about their research assignment, showing a PowerPoint presentation about one or more databases appropriate for the topic, application sharing to demonstrate how students can access databases from off campus, and sending students to the library Web page to begin the research process. The librarian moderator used the chat feature to maintain communication with the student throughout the instruction session. In this way the moderator can immediately address any questions about the instruction being provided. So far, online reference service has been offered only to students in a few classes each semester. Students who have tried the service like it a lot but would prefer it to be available on a drop-in basis for more extended hours instead of by appointment. Further study must be done to determine whether the need is great enough to staff online reference service more extensively. Students who are able to come to campus for classes and to visit the physical library probably do not need online reference. Should the library provide online reference simply because that is how students would like to receive reference assistance? In contrast, students who are enrolled in online courses probably really need the service, because they are distant either in miles or in time constraints. A complicating factor is that online students are likely to need online reference service at night and on weekends, times when library staffing is ordinarily at a minimum. Therefore, making online reference open to all students and for more hours would probably have a significant impact on staffing. At any rate, it appears that Elluminate vClass holds great promise for providing both reference service and instruction to students who cannot easily come to campus.

Library Instruction

The librarians at both NVC and SACs knew they needed to do more than just make resources available to students on the library Web page; they also needed to provide instruction on how to access and use these resources. Every semester, NVC librarians use the library teaching lab to teach increasing numbers of library research classes to students whose instructor has requested a session. In September 2001, librarians taught 13 classes, whereas in September 2003, librarians taught 72 classes to 1,200 students in the library teaching lab. The staff, however, wanted to be able to provide library instruction to students in online courses, to students in classes whose instructors do not schedule library instruction sessions, and to students who do not realize that they need instruction in using the databases until they start working on their research paper—at 10 p.m. the night before it is due. It was determined that Web-based tutorials would work well at NVC, since this kind of instruction would be fairly easy to provide and easy for students to access. Because creating Web pages requires less manpower than providing real-time instruction, it was a good option for NVC's small staff. Furthermore, since so many students have Internet access now, whether at home, at work, or on campus, Web-based library instruction seemed a good way to reach a lot of students at their point of need.

Indeed, research done at other institutions indicates that students prefer Web instruction to other ways of delivering library instruction. At the University of

Maryland University College, where student enrollment is almost equally divided between on-campus and online courses, students rated Web-based tutorials and guides as being the most useful publications the college library offers (71.7%). In surveys done in 1996 and again in 2001, students reported that they wanted technology-based guides focusing on electronic resources and their use (Kelley and Orr 2003, 182). To address students' fondness for online research tools and online instruction about such tools, NVC librarians created tutorials on how to access and use the online catalog, the electronic books, and the most popular subscription databases.

San Antonio College also has a successful in-person instruction program, with 108 classes taught to 2,223 students in September 2003. The challenge will be translating that success over to the online environment. A move in this direction will take place in spring 2004 with the use of Elluminate vClass software. The plan is to first identify a core group of Internet courses that require a research assignment, then collaborate with the instructor of each course to tailor an Elluminate session and Web (library) research guide for their assignment. This core group will serve as a pilot program for offering synchronous, online formal library instruction. With the ability to record Elluminate sessions on the District Web server, students who are unable to make the synchronous instruction on a given date and time have the advantage of reviewing the entire recorded session through a Web link at their convenience.

Both libraries also have a Web page targeted specifically at distance learners. Certainly, an academic library should be a campus leader in information technology and have a well-designed Web site with links to useful online resources. As librarians begin offering new online services, they should take a critical look at their library Web pages and consider what kind of image they wish to project. In an era when many students are choosing the Internet over library resources, librarians should take this opportunity to redefine library resources and services, and what they are called. Lipow (2003, 11) cautions that transferring the model of traditional library features, such as the card catalog, into the online environment encourages users to assume that the same limitations and restrictions apply in the online environment. This may be a great time to abandon library jargon and describe library resources in terms that users might understand and find exciting.

This philosophy is reflected in the distance learning library Web pages of both NVC and SAC. The NVC librarians created an Off-Campus Services Web page to consolidate links to resources available from off campus (http://www.accd.edu/NorthwestVista/lrc/offcampus.htm). Links to online resources are paired with links to instructional material about them, and the resources are described in terms familiar to students. Under the heading "Searching for Books," for example, is a link to the online catalog and a tutorial about the online catalog. A link to the Net Library is followed by a tutorial on accessing electronic books. Students also find links to the library's online tutorials, a collection of useful academic Web sites, and information for contacting a reference librarian.

The SAC Library Distance Learning page (http://www.accd.edu/San Antonio College/lrc/librns/celita/distance/) presents links to resources in a question-and-answer format. Links are organized under questions such as "Looking for Books?" "Looking for Articles?" and "Need a Research Plan?" in order to help students find the right research path. A picture of the distance learning librarian is also included, with links to phone number, email, and chat research appointment information. Distance learners who may never physically visit the library appreciate a more personalized section of the library Web site that fits their specific needs and questions.

Collaboration

Planning for distance learning is a moving target that involves many people; therefore, true success resides in the ability to collaborate fully with library colleagues as well as faculty and staff from a variety of departments.

Distance learning librarians should share ideas and plans with their fellow librarians and especially elicit help with distance services from departments such as Interlibrary Loan and Reference. A more integrated approach to providing service ensures that one person is not trying to balance the entire weight of the program and ultimately helps cement the idea of distance service throughout the entire organization.

Distance librarians can also serve as liaisons between the library and other departments on campus, such as the distance education office. Establishing a working relationship with the administrators of distance education opens doors to opportunities for promotion and evaluation of library services. For example, SAC requires all Internet course instructors and developers to take a series of courses before they can be certified to teach online. Through relationships built with the Distance Education office and the Instructional Technology Center that provides instruction for these courses, the distance learning librarian at SAC is currently teaching one of these courses: The eLibrary: Research Strategies and Sources. Teaching this certification class has resulted in immediate wide exposure of distance learning library services to current and future Internet course faculty. In this eLibrary course, faculty learn how to integrate online library resources and information literacy concepts into their online courses, as well as brush up on their own research skills.

At NVC a librarian serves on the college Distance Education Committee to ensure that the library plays a role in the planning and provision of services. A project stemming from work on the Distance Education Committee was a pilot of online student services, including online academic advising as well as online reference. This pilot has resulted in ongoing collaborative relationships with people in various academic areas, including academic computing, instructional design, distance education administration, and academic advising, as well as several instructors of Internet courses. The pilot also provided the opportunity for individuals from different college departments to travel together and present their experiences at two conferences. Working collaboratively has allowed the participants to have a better understanding of the work done in other academic areas and thus to have a broader vision of the mission of the college as a whole. The network resulting from this ongoing collaboration has benefited each of the individuals by providing them with access to the special expertise of people working in other areas. An additional benefit that occurs when librarians work in collaboration with individuals from other academic areas is that people have a greater knowledge and appreciation of what librarians do and how they can make a contribution to the academic mission.

The Future

Based on data from the 2000 Survey, Thompson (2002, 340) concludes, "libraries will need to cope with potentially explosive growth in distributed learning as an educational model" and, as this trend continues, "libraries will need to continue to explore and 'push the envelope' to keep pace with the new paradigm of information delivery."

This dynamic population of distance learners will need to be reassessed at regular intervals to make sure that the library's level of service is meeting their needs. Librarians at NVC and SAC intend to keep their fingers on the pulse of the online learners that they serve, so that appropriate library resources and services are available to this growing population.

REFERENCES

Association of College & Research Libraries. 2000. ACRL Guidelines for Distance Learning Library Service. http://www.ala.org/ala/acrl/acrlstandards/guidelines-distance.htm. Accessed November 2004.

Association of College & Research Libraries. 2000. ACRL 2000 Academic Library Trends and Statistics. Center for Survey Research, University of Virginia. Barron, Brett Barclay. 2002. "Distant and Distributed Learners Are Two Sides of the Same Coin," Computers in Libraries 22 (Jan.): 24–28.

Boser, Ulrich. 2003. "Working on What Works Best," U.S. News & World Report (Oct. 20, 2003) 135 (13): 58–61.

Bryant, Eric. 2001. "Bridging the Gap," Library Journal 126 (16): 58–60.

"The Explosion of Distance Education." 2002. ASHE-ERIC Higher Education Report 29 (4): 1–12.

Kelley, Kimberly B. and Gloria J. Orr. 2003. "Trends in Distant Student Use of Electronic Resources: A Survey., College & Research Libraries 64 (3): 176–91.

Kiernan, Vincent. 2003. "A Survey Documents Growth in Distance Education in Late 1990s," Chronicle of Higher Education (Aug. 8, 2003) 49 (48): A28.

Lipow, Anne Grodzins. 2003. "The Librarian Has Left the Building—But to Where?" *Internet Reference Services Quarterly* 8 (1/2): 9–18.

Thompson, Hugh. 2002. "The Library's Role in Distance Education: Survey Results from ACRL's *2000 Academic Library Trends and Statistics.*" *College & Research Libraries News* 63 (5): 338–40.

Torres, Helen. Personal correspondence to Celita DeArmond. 15 November 2003.

SELECTED BIBLIOGRAPHY

Ariel, document delivery system by Infotrieve. http://www.infotrieve.com/ariel/index.html. Accessed January 2003.

Bar, Belinda, Jerome Conley, and Joanne Goode. 2003. "Chat Is Now: Administrative Issues," *Internet Reference Services Quarterly* 8 (1/2): 19–25.

Cichanowicz, Edana McCafferty. 2003. "Live Reference Chat from a Customer Service Perspective," *Internet Reference Services Quarterly* 8 (1/2): 27–32.

Dougherty, Richard M. 2002. "Reference Around the Clock: Is It in Your Future?" *American Libraries* 33 (5): 44–46.

Elluminate vClass 2003. http://www.elluminate.com/. Accessed November 2004.

Goodson, Carol. 2001. *Providing Library Services for Distance Education Students: A How-To-Do-It Manual.* New York: Neal-Schuman Publishers, Inc.

Ronan, Jana Smith. 2003. "Staffing a Real-Time Reference Service: The University of Florida Experience." *Internet Reference Services Quarterly* 8 (1/2): 33–47.

Torres, Helen. Director of Distance Education, San Antonio College. http://www.accd.edu/sac/distance/. Accessed 16 October 2003.

Virtual College of Texas, The Texas Association of Community Colleges. http://www.vct.org/. Accessed January 2003.

III

MARKETING AND
PROMOTING THE MESSAGE:
PLEASE COME IN; WE'RE FRIENDLY

7 IMPROVING COMMUNICATION SKILLS

John Stanley

Communication: We all communicate every day, but are we effective in our communication skills? What are communications?

First, there are your business communications—what your business looks like when strangers visit your library for the first time. You may be blind to what strangers see. They judge your business communications, not on how great the architecture looks, but on your housekeeping skills. Business communications reflect the image you are portraying to your patrons.

Remember, every business plays the image game, including your library. The key to success is to maintain visual consistency in the eyes of your patrons.

Take a walk down any shopping mall and look at the visual communications. Some corporate visual communications will be consistent within the store, around the nation and even globally. How do they achieve consistency? You will find they will do a regular visual audit and have a checklist to help them monitor their communications. It's the little things that make a big difference. The key to success in business communications is to ensure you have a checklist and that you implement it and act on it every single day that your library is open.

PEOPLE COMMUNICATE

In most of our minds, communication is about how one person effectively relates with another person, and this is the main emphasis in this chapter. Communication is more than words; it is a complicated procedure, relying on key elements in the communications game.

Improving communication skills in your library depends on the type of corporate culture you have within your library. I am sure we all have examples of libraries where, as visitors, we have enjoyed the experience and have also been to libraries where it has felt like the "library from hell."

All libraries basically provide the same service; it is just that some provide a more enjoyable experience than others. This experience is based on the library's internal culture. If it is a positive culture, then you, the visitor, will have a more enjoyable visit than at a library that has a negative corporate culture.

Therefore, the first step in improving communications is based on getting a positive leader and team together. This means your recruitment process is critical to your library's success.

RECRUIT TEAM MEMBERS BASED ON PERSONALITY

Great customer service teams in libraries are based on a team who have personality first, knowledge second. Knowledge can be learned—personality cannot!

Improving communication skills revolves around finding the right people in the first place. When recruiting, your aim should be to recruit for personality as first priority and then for technical knowledge as a secondary skill. The skills of the interviewer are therefore critical to the happiness and success of the library team.

But how do you recruit people with personality? You must conduct the interview in the right manner. The following tips may help:

- Start the interview by walking the candidate around the library with a colleague. This will be more relaxing for all concerned and give the team an opportunity to discover the real person you are about to formally interview.
- Ask what their hobbies and interests are. Remember, most people are motivated by friendship, achievement, or power. You need to find what motivates the candidate and ensure you are placing the right person in the right job position. A good way to find out what motivates a person is to ask what their hobbies and interests are.

For example:

A person who works or volunteers in a charity is likely to be friendship motivated.

A person who enjoys fishing is likely to be motivated by achievement.

A person who is involved with politics is bound to be motivated by power.

Place the wrong person in the wrong job and you will end up with an unhappy team member who may upset your patrons and also the team dynamics of your library.

As a general rule, "front of house" duties in a library are enjoyed by friendship-motivated individuals, whereas "back of house" duties in a library are enjoyed by achievement-motivated individuals. Most state library managers are power motivated.

You now have your ideal team; how do you communicate effectively with them?

IT'S NOT WHAT YOU SAY; IT'S THE WAY YOU SAY IT

Communication is divided into silent and verbal communications. We often put too much emphasis on what we say, when in fact it is the silent communications that are far more powerful.

When we meet a person for the first time, we judge people quickly, not based on what they say, but on what we perceive.

According to researchers in this field, we read people in the first 10 seconds of the meeting as follows:

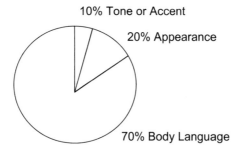

10% Tone or Accent

20% Appearance

70% Body Language

TONE OR ACCENT

Before you take in the content of a person's words, you are more likely to register the tone of their voice or whether that person has an accent. This is one reason many of us do not register a person's name when we are introduced to someone for the first time; we are subconsciously assessing him or her.

APPEARANCE

We all have our internal pictures in our brain of what a bank manager, car mechanic, nurse, or librarian should look like.

When we meet a person from one of these professions, we expect the appearance of the person in front of us to match our mental picture. Often we are surprised if the appearance does not match our picture of what we think they should look like.

The closer the person matches our mental picture, most likely the quicker we accept that person and trust their advice.

BODY LANGUAGE

Body language is the big one. We read body language most quickly, and it is body language that dominates our first impressions of the people we meet.

We can display positive body language or negative body language without being aware of it. A common problem is that we base positive or negative body language clues based on our own culture. However, what is perceived as positive in our culture may be perceived as negative in another culture. We need to be much more culturally aware and respect and accept cultures that differ from our own.

For example, when meeting a stranger, it is customary for a Caucasian person to aim to make eye contact with that person in order to create a positive first impression. In contrast, someone from Japan may look away as a sign of respect.

Let's look at the body language clues we send out when meeting patrons. In reviewing these, remember that perception is truth. It is what the receiver perceives as a message that is vital to good communications.

Positive Body Language	Negative Body Language
• Eye contact	• Not making eye contact
• Smile	• Frown
	• Stroking a beard, twiddling with hair, or rubbing one's ear when talking
• Arms open when talking standing up	• Arms folded when standing up talking
• Facing squarely toward the person you are talking to	• Crossing your legs when standing to turn your body away from the person you are talking to

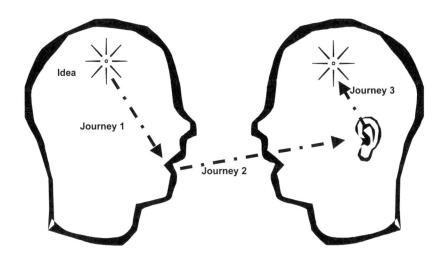

LISTENING SKILLS

We have two ears and one mouth and should use them in the same ratio. To be an effective librarian you must first be an effective listener. However, too many people do not actively listen to the other person during a conversation.

There are many barriers to listening along the communication journey. A thought starts in the brain and is then taken on a journey to the mouth; from the mouth the message takes a leap to the receiver's ear; and it then finally goes on its last journey, from their mouth to their brain. There are many hurdles the message must overcome along this journey.

Before looking at listening skills, let's concentrate on the journey of communications and the barriers or hurdles along the way.

First, on the first stage of the journey between your brain and your mouth, there are already numerous hurdles that must be overcome. These may include

- using jargon, that is words the other person does not understand;
- your prejudices, which can affect how you convey what you say;
- your perception of the other person's knowledge of the subject area;
- not adequately thinking through what you want to say before you begin to speak; and
- your knowledge level of the subject.

And this is before you have opened your mouth.

The message now continues its journey between your mouth and the receiver's ear. It now faces more hurdles, including

- distance,
- background noise,
- your accent,
- visual distractions,
- the temperature of the environment, and
- the amount of people you are communicating to.

Finally, it reaches the receiver's ear and now faces more challenges, which include

- whether the person you are speaking to is hearing impaired,
- their perception of you,
- their prejudices,
- their knowledge of the subject, and
- their understanding of the language.

And so the challenges continue.

If you think about it, it is quite amazing that general verbal communication is anywhere near as effective as it is and often relies on personal knowledge of the receiver and sender. Verbal communications face numerous obstacles, and it is not surprising we are often misunderstood or not understood at all.

But, back to listening. It is imperative to show the speaker that you are actively listening. In order to do this, you must give the appropriate cues. These include nodding in agreement, the occasional verbal agreement (remember, if you over-agree, the perception is you are not listening), make eye contact with the speaker, ask relevant questions, and maintain a positive body stance.

FINALLY, THERE ARE THE WORDS OF THE MESSAGE

Having reviewed all the other nonverbal cues, we can finally analyze how verbal communications can be improved.

An effective librarian is in the relationship industry. A librarian's role is to build lifetime library users in readiness for the knowledge economy and lifelong learning. Patrons become lifetime users, not because of the books or other products, but because of the positive relationships they have had with librarians. The effective librarian is liked and trusted, and is a good communicator.

The role of a librarian is explained in the following diagram:

A librarian is a host, consultant, and seller. Although money does not change hands, the role of an effective seller is to encourage the person to come back again—a key role in any library. A librarian's role is selling the benefits and services of the library to its patrons.

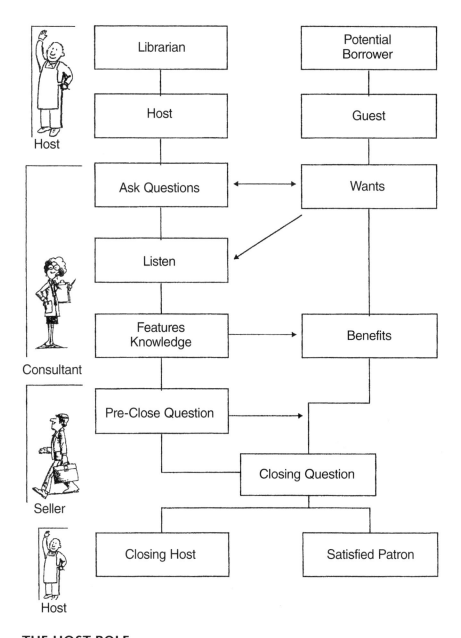

THE HOST ROLE

The role of a host is to make a guest feel welcome. Look on the library as you would your home and that visitors to your library are your personal guests.

A host makes eye contact, smiles, and whenever possible provides a verbal greeting to each guest. The greeting should be sincere.

The most effective host will also follow that greeting with a social sentence. That sentence will vary based on the situation, but examples could be as follows:

"How is your studying going?"
"When do your exams start?"
"Isn't it a lovely day?"
"Did you see the game yesterday?"

THE CONSULTANT'S ROLE

A consultant finds out what a patron needs and wants. A consultant's role is to start the conversation; therefore, the first sentence is the most important one. The way you construct your opening sentence dramatically affects the type of response you receive from the patron.

There are basically four techniques used in libraries by consultants.

1. Closed technique.
   This is the worst technique you can use but, alas, the most commonly used. Your objective is to start a conversation to find out the receiver's needs and wants. The closed technique, rather than opening up a conversation, closes the conversation down.
   Common closed openers include the following:

   "Can I help you?"
   "Are you alright?"

   You may wonder what is wrong with these. Research shows 70 percent of people say "no" to the first question and "yes" to the second question without even thinking about it. Their "no" or "yes" response closed the conversation down. The catch is they have actually come in for advice, but automatically reacted to the closed opener and shut down the interaction. For this reason, librarians who use closed techniques are the least effective in the role of consultant.

2. Open conversation techniques
   As the name suggests, an open technique opens up a conversation. An open conversation is where the librarian starts the consultancy conversation with one of the following words: how, what, when, why, where, who. One word can make a big difference in improving your communications skills.

   "Can I help you?"   = no (closed conversation down).
   "How can I help you?" = the majority of patrons will respond telling you their needs and wants (opening up an opportunity for good communication).

Once the communication has been opened, it is now possible to use your own technical knowledge to solve the patron's problems.

3. Leading conversation openers

   Personally, I am always wary of consultants who start a conversation with a leading opener. The aim is to get the receiver to agree, even if they do not. How do you do that? By using one of the following words at the end of your first sentence: isn't it, didn't it, couldn't it, hasn't it, and so on. For example:

   "The exams were easy, weren't they?"
   "Lovely day, isn't it?"
   "A great writer, isn't he?"

   These statements have to be used very carefully, otherwise you may find yourself getting into a situation where the receiver does not agree with you and it is then difficult to build trust with the patron.

4. Emotional openers

   Emotional consultants have an ability, not a skill. The previous three openers are skills that can be learned. Emotional openings are an innate ability some people have and others do not. If you try and train yourself in this ability, you may come across as being insincere and will lose the receiver's respect.

   An emotional opener is when you compliment the receiver at the start of the conversation. This must be sincere; when it is, it builds an empathy bridge between both parties.

   Emotional openers may include the following:

   "Your hair looks lovely today."
   "You look fantastic."
   "I do like that dress you are wearing."

   As you can see from these examples, if they are said sincerely, you have gained a friend. If they are insincere, you may gain an enemy. An effective consultant knows when and where to use the appropriate openers. An effective consultant rotates them to suit the situation; that is the fun of being a consultant.

SELLER

The final role in the library communication journey is the role of the seller. An effective seller sells something; then sells something in addition.

Patrons come into your library to obtain books, CDs, or DVDs, or to use the computers. Your role is not just to "sell" these but also to offer more advice, introduce them to new material, or just invite them back on the next visit—in other words, selling something (serving their words) and then selling something else (adding something to the experience).

All librarians are in the selling game, and patrons look forward to building an enjoyable, trusting relationship.

INTERNAL AND EXTERNAL PATRONS

In this article I concentrate on improving communication skills when dealing with external patrons.

But, remember you also have internal patrons, your team members. Team members are your patrons as well and should expect the same professionalism from you as you provide to external patrons.

How often do you have team meetings? Do you have daily "power" meetings to get the day started?

Teams that communicate regularly between themselves are often winning teams. Teams that never have team meetings are always without a doubt on the losing side.

Monthly and weekly meetings are essential, but rotate the chair so you do not have one person who continually dominates the meetings. Set an agenda prior to meetings and ensure everyone is aware of the agenda. After the meeting, follow up with a brief report.

Having a winning library revolves around having a winning team. Become the best library by improving your team's communication skills.

SELECTED BIBLIOGRAPHY

Stanley, John. 1999, 2003. *Just About Everything a Retail Manager Needs to Know.* Kalamunda, Western Australia: Lizard Publishing.

———. 2003. "Retail Technology Applications and Their Role in the Modern Library." In McCabe, Gerard and James Kennedy. 2003. *Planning the Modern Public Library Building.* Westport, CT: Libraries Unlimited.

8   SEEING THE LIBRARY IN THE BROADER CONTEXT ON CAMPUS: MARKETING OUR SERVICES

Rashelle Karp

INTRODUCTION

We all know that libraries are wonderful entities. Why is it, then, that librarians and libraries are so often taken for granted? Why is it that academic libraries and academic librarians are sometimes relegated to less than central positions at their institutions? Why does it sometimes seem that administrators and other faculty don't recognize the critical importance of our services? As an academic administrator, I will address these questions and provide some observations from an administrative viewpoint.

I would say that the reason that we are often overlooked or not given our due by our teaching faculty colleagues and university administrators is that we don't show them, in tangible ways, how our services benefit our students. My suggestions are organized around the ways we present our outcomes to the academic community and how we might adjust our communications about outcomes for better impact.

STATISTICS

The most obvious and easiest way to present ourselves to external audiences is through statistics. Four types of statistics come to mind immediately: door counts, circulation counts, titles and volumes added to our collections, and reference transactions and classes taught. I briefly describe each of these and provide some presentation options. The figures that are presented are for a theoretical library for purposes of this chapter.

Door Counts

In virtually all libraries, a major statistical category is the door count. We count every body that enters the library and compile these counts into monthly reports and annual reports. Then, we compare the numbers from year to year. Door counts are important. Consider the following:

- They are an indication of how much use the building is getting.
- They can be used to fortify proposals related to facilities improvements and library renovations.
- If the numbers are divided into hours of the day or night, they can be used to support proposals for additional staffing to cover nighttime hours or peak hours during the day.
- They can be used to explain why you don't have a librarian on duty during certain hours of the day or night, based on the number of people who use the library during this time.
- If the numbers are divided into hours of the day and specific time periods during a semester, they can be used to show a dean or president why you might need additional part time help during certain times in the semester, or why your librarians can't serve on committees or do research during certain weeks of the semester when papers seem to be due all over campus.
- They are easy to compile because most of us have automatic counters at the entrance to library. Some of us even have automatic counters for areas of the library. Counters for areas of the library can provide more discrete data such as how many people enter the library's computer lab and when, how many people enter the library's media center and when, or how many people enter the reference room and when. This information is great to have when we need to support an instructional support fee request for computer upgrades in the computer lab, or for additional reference librarians.

Here is one way of presenting door counts: "178,392 people entered the library from July 1, 2001, through June 31, 2002. 202,291 people entered the library from July 1, 2002, through June 31, 2003. 238,876 people entered the library from July 1, 2003 through June 31, 2004. The number of people using the library increased by 23,899 people, or 13 percent between 2002 and 2003, and another 36,585 people, or 18 percent between 2003 and 2004."

Although these numbers are correct and actually quite powerful, people's eyes tend to glaze over when they are read. Also, it is irritating to a busy administrator or faculty member to have to stop and give something undivided attention in order to understand it.

Figure 8.1 (Library Door Counts) shows what might be a better way to present this information. Even better might be a combination of text and picture as shown in Figure 8.2 (Library Door Counts).

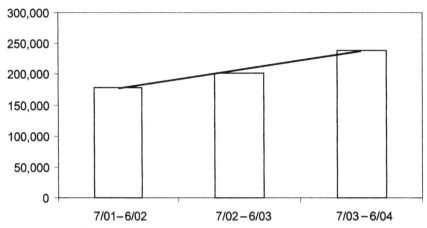

Figure 8.1 Library Door Counts (1)

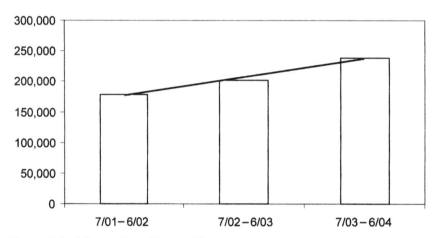

Figure 8.2 Library Door Counts (2)

Over the past three years, the number of people coming into the library has increased by more than 33 percent.

Circulation Counts

Virtually all libraries count the number of titles circulated—yearly, monthly, daily, hourly, by type of material (media, book, journal), by circulation method (reserves, in-house use, two-week loan, faculty loan), and in other categories that you have probably used at one time or another. Some libraries count the titles circulated by hour of the day, time of the semester, and other time-delimited periods. Circulation counts are also important. Consider the following:

- They can be used to show a president that people are using the resources in the library that cost so much.
- They can be used to support a request for additional collections money, based on increasing circulation counts.
- If circulation decreases, these figures can be used to support just about anything that the library wants them to—for example, the collection is so old because of lack of funding that no one wants to check out the materials, the teaching faculty aren't sending their students to the library to use the resources, the students don't know how to use the library because the institution doesn't have a required library skills class in the general education curriculum, circulation has decreased because the library had to cut hours due to staffing cuts.

Here is one way to present circulation statistics:

"Circulation of periodicals increased 23 percent from 124, 893 in 2002–2003 to 153,992 in 2003–2004. This follows increases of 28 percent from 2001–2002 to 2002–2003 (97,238 to 124,893) and 181 percent from 2000–2001 to 2001–2002 (34,602 to 97,238). Much of the total 345 percent increase in the circulation of periodicals since 2000 is due to the advent of electronic full-text journal access during the 2000–2001 academic year."

Figure 8.3 (Circulation of Periodicals) shows what might be a better way to present this information.

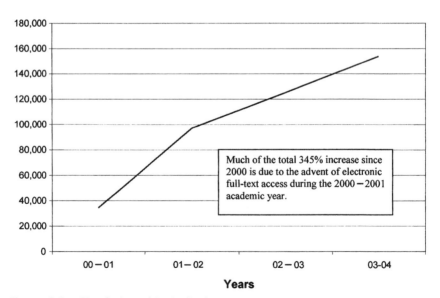

Figure 8.3   Circulation of Periodicals

Titles/Volumes Added

Another statistic that all libraries provide is the number of titles and volumes owned and the number of titles and volumes added to the library's collections each year. Sometimes we divide these numbers into months of the year, and sometimes we divide them by Library of Congress Classification or some other subject classification method. Sometimes we provide a listing of the titles that have been added each month by subject area, and sometimes we even provide an accounting of the amount of money spent in each subject area, along with percentages of the entire library budget.

Volumes and titles added are important. Consider the following:

- They show a dean, the faculty, and the president that the library is purchasing materials in the subject areas taught at the university.
- They can demonstrate that the library is using its budget responsibly by purchasing from library vendors and through consortia at prices that are well below retail.
- They can be used to show the volume of work being done by the librarians who have selected the materials, the librarians who are cataloging the items, and the staff who are processing the orders and the items.
- If there is a backlog in processing new materials, the numbers can be used to demonstrate that the volume is well beyond the level of staffing, or the numbers can be used to demonstrate how efficient a small staff is.
- It is questionable how valuable the number of volumes added to the library's collections is as a statistic. Although it does provide valuable information if the library is trying to support a request for additional space, the number of volumes added really doesn't mean much to an outsider. Because it is a larger number than the number of titles, it is a good gross number to use when describing the library for external audiences and in promotional materials for the institution (e.g., 325,000 volumes sounds better than 278,000 titles). But, its real value is minimal as far as its use in presenting the library to external audiences.

Figure 8.4 shows an attractive way that one library presented its volumes added by type of material.

Even more powerful than presenting single-purpose charts is the presentation of charts that show relationships. One example might be a presentation that shows the relationships among the number of titles added to a library, the size of collections in various Library of Congress Classification areas, and the circulation of those items. Tables 8.1 and 8.2 (Collection Use Reports) are adapted from reports provided by Brown University Libraries.

Note the first two columns in Table 8.1; you can see in column c that Mathematics is the largest collection in terms of size. Column e shows that the library continues to add titles at a very high rate (1,660 in 2001). Columns h and

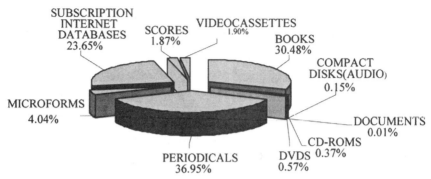

Figure 8.4 Volumes Added

Source: Dupont Ball Library, Stetson University. http://www.stetson.edu/departments/
library/annualreports.html. Accessed on March 5, 2004.

Table 8.1
Collection Use Reports, January–December 2001 Sciences Library: Sorted by
Collection Size

(b)	(c)	(d)	(e)	(f)	(g)	(h)	(i)	J	K
LC call number range & subject	Coll.Size	size	# Items	# Bibs	Orders	# Chk	chkout	Use	Use
	# Items	rank	Added	Cat'd	# Rec'd	Outs	rank	Ratio	Rank
QA1-69,80+ Mathematics	50,885	1	1,660	762	663	6,054	1	12%	11
QC Physics	23,866	2	1,087	428	346	3,162	2	13%	6
T-TJ,TL Technology & Engineering	22,953	3	770	393	272	1,545	6	7%	26
QN-QZ Physiology, Microbiology	16,433	4	788	188	157	2,078	3	13%	9
RC Internal Medicine	15,924	5	606	134	69	2,066	4	13%	7
QD Chemistry	13,649	6	689	38	33	1,101	8	8%	21
QE Geology	12,218	7	281	32	32	635	14	5%	29

Source: Adapted from Brown University Libraries. Developing and Managing the Brown
University Library Collections: Collection Data and Reports. http://www.brown.edu/
Facilities/University_Library/collections/colldev/data/sci_useration.html. Accessed
March 7, 2003.

i indicate that Mathematics materials had the highest checkouts during 2001.
However, if you look at column j, you see that its use ratio is only 12 percent.
So, although there were more Mathematics items checked out of the library than
any other subject, only 12 percent of the entire Mathematics collection was used.

Table 8.2

Collection Use Reports, January–December 2001 Sciences Library: Sorted by Use Ratio (number of checkouts/collection size)

(b)	(c)	(d)	(e)	(f)	(g)	(h)	(i)	(j)	(k)
LC call number range & subject	Coll.Size	size	# Items	# Bibs	Orders	# Chk	chkout	use	use
	# Items	rank	Added	Cat'd	# Rec'd	Outs	rank	ratio	rank
C-F History, etc.	708	37	20	2	4	311	19	44%	1
S-SZ Agriculture	2,815	22	55	21	17	730	12	26%	2
BF Psychology	9,721	9	279	126	147	1,807	5	19%	3
RE-RL Medical Specialities	4,966	19	140	36	21	756	11	15%	4
RA-RB Public Health, Pathology	6,926	13	333	121	53	1,041	9	15%	5
QC Physics	23,866	2	1,087	428	346	3,162	2	13%	6
QA1-69,80+ Mathematics	50,885	1	1,660	762	663	6,054	1	12%	11

Source: Adapted from Brown University Libraries. Developing and Managing the Brown University Library Collections: Collection Data and Reports. http://www. brown.edu/Facilities/University_Library/collections/colldev/data/sci_useration.html. Accessed March 7, 2003.

Also, if you look at column d, you see that mathematics is first in terms of its size, but column k shows that it is only eleventh in terms of use.

Table 8.2 shows the same data, only sorted by each collection area's use ratio. Here, note that although History is ranked 37th in terms of size within the science library collections, it has a very high rate of checkout, and its use ratio is much higher than Mathematics at 44 percent.

Think about the possibilities of using charts like these to present and analyze a library's data. If the library were to add cost into these charts, the library could show that the overall expenditures in specific subject areas are in line with the use that the area was getting. Or the library could begin to determine how to make better use of its collections money by decreasing expenditures in areas where the use ratio is low. Some libraries, especially those at smaller institutions, might consider adding data on circulation per full-time equivalent (FTE) student. If a library's online system does not allow differentiation between student and faculty circulation, this can be noted and the circulation would then be presented as circulation per faculty and FTE student.

Another possibility to consider is providing circulation totals divided by type of circulation such as reserve use or interlibrary loan. Providing this type of circulation data avoids potential underreporting if the library's circulation totals are being provided through an online system that only counts checkouts. For example, although mathematics materials are checked out at what looks like a relatively low rate in Table 8.2, they might be showing high in-house use, reserve use, or interlibrary loan use. An example from one library director is from the areas of linguistics and semantics. Although these two areas showed very low circulation in the library's online circulation system, shelvers found books from these disciplines all over the tables and carrels every morning when they came into work. If in-house use is not added into circulation counts, underreporting is likely.

The most powerful data is data that compares input statistics to outcomes statistics.

Reference Transactions and Classes Taught

Most libraries count the number of reference transactions that are completed at the reference desk. Most libraries also count the number of library instruction classes and students that are taught (both in the library and in classrooms across the campus). These types of counts are important. Consider the following:

- They show the level of activity for librarians at the reference desk providing point-of-use service and, thus, the need for librarians to work at the public reference desk.
- They show the number of individuals who are taught by librarians in more traditional classes over the course of a year or a semester.
- Categorizing reference transactions by discipline or type of resource can show a direct link to academic programs and resource expenditures (e.g., number of "research in psychology" classes taught, number of reference transactions involving electronic databases, number of reference transactions on subjects related to mathematics, biology, or other discipline).
- Analyzing reference transactions in terms of time spent, pedagogies used, and end-user results can provide helpful trend information. It can also provide useful data for a librarian's promotion file, especially for categories related to teaching effectiveness.
- Counting reference transactions and students taught can support staffing requests.

Table 8.3 (Reference Transactions per Full-Time Reference Librarian) is an example of how a library might present data that conforms to decision-making processes on the campus. This example has been modified from a model presented in the annual reports from the University of Hawaii West Oahu Library.

Suppose that these were figures from an existing library. Beginning with the first line for 2003–2004, note that the total number of reference transactions dur-

Table 8.3
Reference Transactions per Full-Time Reference Librarian (Fall/Spring, 2001–2004)

Year	a Total Reference Transactions	b Total Reference Librarians	c Transactions per Reference Librarian per year (a / b)*	d Total reference desk hours per Reference Librarian per year (18 hours per week– 32 weeks)**	e Number of Reference Transactions per hour per reference librarian (c / d)
2003-2004	30,000	5	6,000.00	576	10.42
2002-2003	27,936	5	5,587.20	576	9.70
2001-2002	21,371	5	4,274.20	576	7.42

* 2001–2002 = 21,371 transactions by 5 FTE librarians (21,371 / 5= 4,274)
* 2002–2003 = 27,936 transactions by 5 FTE librarian (27,936 / 5 = 5,587)
* 2003–2004 = 30,000 transactions by 5 FTE librarians (30,000 / 5 = 6,000)

**Reference transactions per librarian per hour is equal to: 18 hours per week x 32 week or 576. 6,000 divided by 576 = 10.42 reference transactions per hour per librarian. 5,587 divided by 576 = 9.70 reference transactions per hour per librarian. 4,274 divide by 576 = 7.42 reference transactions per hour per librarian.

ing that year was 30,000 (a) and that these transactions were completed by five reference librarians (b). This equates to 6,000 reference transactions completed per reference librarian each year, in a total of 576 hours worked at the reference desk per year (c). Finally, note that these numbers translate into 10.42 reference transactions completed per hour by each reference librarian (d). It would be pretty powerful for a library to say that it completes 6,000 reference transactions for every one full-time reference librarian during a year. This type of data becomes even more powerful when it is carried a bit further. For example, let's say that this was data from a college library. Let's say that our reference librarians are scheduled to work the reference desk about 18 hours each week. If our semesters are 16 weeks long, this equals a total of 32 weeks during the academic year, or 576 hours per year of scheduled librarian time. If we divide the number of hours for one librarian by the number of reference transactions, we find that a librarian completed 10.42 reference transactions per hour in 2003–2004, up from 7.42 completed reference transactions per hour in 2001–2002. This data provides a benchmark from which to begin tracking faculty productivity, a concept that is used throughout the world of higher education. When a reference librarian is answering more than 10 reference questions an hour, the integrity of the reference process and the quality of the service provided to a student may begin to suffer. Tracking this kind of data, and identifying the point at which service begins to suffer, provides a way to begin looking at other options for library instruction that might be more efficient, or that might cut down on the number of point-of-use reference transactions.

Some ideas that are in the literature include the following:

- Teaching credit-bearing library instruction classes. In addition, if the librarians teach credit-bearing classes, this has the added benefit of allowing the libraries to show that they are generating credit hours for their institution. Credit-hour production is often a number used in state systems to evaluate programs.
- Teaching a series of co-curricular general library use workshops that are scheduled at the beginning of each semester. By working with faculty to design the workshops, and by providing the schedules ahead of time, library faculty can work with teaching faculty who can add these co-curricular workshops to their syllabi.
- Teaching co-curricular discipline-specific library use workshops for each degree program on campus. These workshops could be designed in conjunction with the faculty teaching in a degree program so that the workshops would cover what needs to be covered, and in a time frame that meets the degree program's requirements.

The nice part of these types of models is that the instruction is offered on set schedules (not on-demand), designed in collaboration with teaching faculty, and can be required at strategic points in student's matriculation.

Budget Projection Data

So far, all the numbers mentioned are those that libraries provide after the fact. The ways that I've suggested for presenting these numbers allow us to evaluate what we do in terms that administrators can understand. However, we also need to be concerned with providing budget projections so that library allocations can be made on the basis of predictive data. Some libraries are involved in collection evaluation using the WLN Conspectus approach. (Recall that this is an approach developed by the Washington [now Western] Library Network to assess whether the library's collections are meeting the needs of its constituen-

Table 8.4
Collections Data

Subject	Median Gap between Collection & Goal Levels	Titles Held as of 1/2000	Additional # of Titles to Reach Goal Levels	One-Time cost to Reach Goal Levels	# of Titles (per year) to Maintain Goal Levels	Average cost (per Year) To Maintain Goal Levels
Anthropology	-2	5,155	773	$44,764	170	$9,485
Art history	-1	20,934	2,093	$101,636	850	$41,276
Biology	-2	11,324	1,699	$145,502	340	$29,118
Chemistry	0	4,055	203	$17,385	170	$14,559
Computer Science	-1	5,090	509	$43,591	170	$14,559
Economics	-2	58,409	8,761	$3,990,746	1,190	$68,913
Education	-2	19,817	2,973	$172,166	680	$39,379
Geography	-1	4,651	465	$39,823	170	$14,559
Health, fitness, medicine	-1	13,610	1,361	$116,656	510	$43,676
History	-2	81,040	12,156	$590,295	3,060	$148,594
Journalism	-1	2,167	217	$12,566	85	$4,992
Law	0	5,833	292	$16,910	170	$9,845
Language, linguistics	-1	33,378	3,338	$162,093	1,190	$57,786
Literature	-1	43,161	4,316	$209,585	1,700	$82,552
Mathematics	-1	11,492	1,149	$98,400	510	$43,676
Music	0	18,062	903	$43,850	680	$33,021
Performing arts	-1	8,078	808	$39,236	340	$16,510
Philosophy & religion	-1	27,158	2,716	$131,889	1,020	$49,531
Physics	-1	6,251	625	$53,525	170	$14,559
Politics & government	-1	28,057	2,806	$162,495	1,020	$59,068
Psychology	-1	7,479	748	$43,317	255	$14,767
Sociology	-1	29,419	2,942	$170,371	1,020	$59,068
Technology	0	9,054	453	$38,795	340	$29,118
Total		453,674	52,306	$6,445,498	15,810	$898,901

Source: Adapted from American University, Washington, D.C. University Library Annual Report May 1, 2001–April 30, 2002. http://www.library.american.edu/about/policies/annual_report_2001-2002.pdf. Accessed March 5, 2004.
Average costs for books in Arts and Humanities, Social Sciences, and Sci/Tech/Med come from Blackwell's Book Services. Approval Cost Program Coverage and Cost Study 2002/2003. http: //www.Blackwell.com/pdf/cc0203.pdg. Accessed March 5, 2004.

cies.) It involves assessing the current level of a library's collections according to criteria set through the WLN approach, comparing this level to the level that our constituencies indicate is necessary, and then setting goals for reaching appropriate collection levels and maintaining those levels. Other libraries use guidelines from American Library Association standards or state-imposed formulae.

Table 8.4 (Collections Data) is one way that this data might be presented to an administrator.

Looking at the first line in Table 8.4 for Anthropology, you can see that there is a substantial gap between the level of the library's collections and the level that the library and teaching faculty felt was necessary for the library's collections (–2). In the third and fourth columns, note that the library needs to purchase an additional 773 titles in order to reach the agreed-upon collection level and how much these additional titles will cost. The last two columns show the number of titles that must be purchased each year after the goal level is reached in order to maintain the level and how much this will cost.

Information presented in this manner is understandable because it begins with collection numbers that are based on a recognized process of collaboration among librarians and teaching faculty, and it then equates the collection numbers with actual dollars. This type of presentation might be an excellent way to negotiate annual budgets and incremental increases. For example, the school might spread out the remedial budgets over several years but provide the maintenance budgets every year. It might be decided that only some of the disciplines would receive remedial budgets, but maintenance budgets would always be provided. Best case scenario: The institution embarks on a capital campaign to endow the library collections. The point of this is that it allows the library to stop approaching administrators with unsubstantiated requests for money—for example: "We should have 6 percent of the institution's total budget"; "We are falling seriously behind in our collections and will not be able to keep up if we don't get additional money"; "Our book budget is only $85,000, which is not enough." Armed with data, librarians can talk to administrators with hard data that is directly linked to the instructional programs at the school. This is very powerful.

Thus far, this chapter focuses on how to present numbers to external audiences so that librarians can make their points more forcefully, and, it is hoped, with better results.

When presenting numbers, remembering the following is helpful:

1. Present numbers as part of a theme. For example, if the library is trying to increase or decrease its hours, equate the door counts to the proposed hours of increase or decrease.
2. Become familiar with the way that your Division of Finance and Administration presents numbers. Examine the way that numbers are presented in your school's Fact Book. Look at the way that numbers are presented to the institution's trustees. This will show you what the administrators on your campus are accustomed to and the formats that they trust. Once you know this, then you should try to present your numbers in similar formats and using similar language.
3. Present numbers as pictures or brief sound bites but always provide the details for further examination.
4. Use the summary language and chart conventions that your administrators are already accustomed to seeing. Busy administrators and faculty don't have time to read and digest numbers that are buried in text. They want to be able to get the message quickly. If they want to have actual numbers, they will go to the details of the pictures. But, the holistic, or gestalt, approach is a better starting point.

112

5. Make sure that library numbers equate to numerical outcomes that the administration and faculty on your campus pay attention to. For example, does your dean or president look at credit hour production as a measure of productivity and as a means of determining whether a department should get additional faculty? Does your dean or president use student faculty ratios to determine resource allocations? What kinds of learning outcomes are your provost and faculty most comfortable with? How do your administrators and faculty view survey data? How is data on grade point averages (GPAs) used on your campus? Who is concerned with data on student retention and how is it used?

If you don't present your data in ways that align with the decision-making processes on your campus, your data will be overlooked or, worst case scenario, not even considered.

INVOLVEMENT ON CAMPUS AND LIBRARIAN CREDENTIALS

There is another part to the way that librarians present ourselves to the academic community: through the activities that they are involved in on campus and through their credentials. It is very important that we integrate the library and the library faculty into the regular institutional processes.

The Doctorate

One of the things that cause librarians to lack credibility when we approach the teaching faculty is our lack of the doctoral degree. It is correct that the Master in Library Science is considered, within the profession, to be both the entry level and the terminal degree for practicing librarians. However, in higher education, regardless of what a faculty member is hired to do, the doctorate is considered the terminal degree. In some state systems, the JD and MFA degrees are considered to be equivalent to the doctorate for purposes of faculty appointment and promotion. The MLS is not. When we don't hold the approved research or applied research degree, we are not on the same level as the teaching faculty who do. We are seen as what one recent program review consultant termed "mid-level worker bees" with tremendous expertise but, nonetheless, not at the same level as the faculty. It is true that we don't need a doctorate in order to be tremendous academic librarians. However, in order to be tremendous faculty, we do. Many of you are probably thinking that to do our jobs well, a more important degree in addition to the MLS is another master's degree in a subject area. Many academic library job advertisements ask for this. It is correct that a second disciplinary master's degree provides relevant background in a subject field that is undeniably valuable for our jobs as collection developers and reference specialists. 'When we go the teaching faculty with our master's degree (or degrees), they perceive us as excellent master's degree professionals—very qualified to assist them because we have a degree in research and using the library—but still only qualified at the "worker bee" master's level. This makes it very hard for us to work with them on an equal footing because we are not perceived as co-equals.

What is the solution? One obvious solution is for academic librarians to earn doctorates. If we want to explore the field of librarianship, we can get a professional doctorate in library science such as the DLS that is offered at Simmons library school in Massachusetts, or we can get a research doctorate at schools such as University of Pittsburgh and Drexel. Some of us will really balk at the thought of getting a doctorate in library science, which will prepare us to do something we are not planning to do—teach future librarians or administer libraries. If this is something that is totally unpalatable, there is another option: Earn a doctorate in a disciplinary field. This type of degree not only prepares us to work in libraries as collection developers and reference specialists (the same way that a second master's degree does), but it also prepares us to teach in a discipline represented by degree programs at our institutions. What better way to get teaching faculty to recognize the contributions of librarians than to have the requisite credentials to teach alongside them in their own disciplinary programs? What better way to develop partnerships with the teaching faculty than to discuss their discipline with them, as one doctorate to another? What better way to gain credibility by advancing through the promotion ranks to full professor? The doctorate is one of the keys to success in much of academe.

But it is hard to get a doctorate, especially when working full time. What substitutes would help? This brings up yet another important way in which we present ourselves to the university community: research and publication.

Research and Publication

Most faculty members are expected to do research and publish the results in peer-reviewed journals or in books. Promotion beyond associate professor often depends greatly on a faculty member's record of research and publication. In some situations research doesn't necessarily have to be published in peer-reviewed, tier-one journals. This is because an institution might have a unique and admirable focus on teaching. But, research must be performed, and it needs to be published in respected journals. Who better to do research than librarians, who spend their lives helping others find, evaluate, and apply the results of research? The possibilities are endless for librarians. We have read the research produced by others, we know how to evaluate it, we know which journals are respected in every field, and we know how to teach these skills to others. Here are some avenues for publication that might be most fruitful for librarians:

- Featured reviews in top-tier reviewing journals
- Co-authored publications with disciplinary faculty
- Bibliographic essays for books published by academic publishers
- "Best of" lists for disciplinary journals

- Guides to the literature of larger and smaller disciplines
- Results of library research related to the impact of library services on student GPA, retention, and overall academic performance
- Webliographies
- Online tutorials for database and library use
- Core collection recommendations
- Finding aids for research topics
- Research toolkits to accompany academic textbooks

A few caveats, though. Traditionally, research and publication in the sciences is the most respected kind of research, especially during reviews of faculty promotion files. Second comes empirical research in the social sciences. Faculty members who have earned a doctorate understand research that is empirical, utilizes the scientific model, and results in peer-reviewed publication. Less understood is the kind of research and publication that results in creation—for example, a painting, acting in a play, performing in a musical, a sculpture, a juried art show. Even less understood is research and publication that results in organization of other people's research—for example, a bibliographic essay, a guide to the literature, Webliographies. This leads to an extremely important element of presenting ourselves to external audiences.

We must show others that our research and publication is credible. We need to educate the campus community about the importance of guides to the literature, reviews of reference materials and academic texts, lists of recommended titles in specific subject areas, lists of collection recommendations, and online tutorials. Our research and publication contributes to the public good in many ways, and these need to be explained to our external constituencies. Unlike other faculty, whose disciplines are generally understood, the discipline of librarianship is often not well understood. Or, because we all have used libraries, it is often perceived as less rigorous. Here are some ways to show our peers that our discipline is valuable and our research credible:

1. Publish a one-page newsletter. This could be monthly or weekly, depending upon how much time the librarians have to devote to it. It is better to publish a little bit less often and do so consistently than it is to publish more often and not consistently. Monthly is usually a good publication schedule. The types of things that should go into a newsletter are pieces of information that are interesting and helpful for a wide audience, entertaining, and that encourage faculty and students to use the library. Here are some suggestions:

   - Highlight a particular academic program by talking about what is new in the program and then linking these pieces of information to the library.
   - Highlight new resources that are particularly useful for a broad audience.

- Introduce a different librarian in each issue. Talk about their areas of expertise, areas of research and publication, and liaison responsibilities.
- Introduce a different library service in each issue. Talk about how the service affects student and faculty research, explain how to access the service, and give some examples of how someone used the service with positive results.
- Highlight assessment activities in which the library has engaged.
- Provide a question or series of questions for students, to be answered through library research. Each month, reward the people who answered the previous "quiz" correctly, and publish the answers. Rewards can be as simple as giving them a longer loan period for the semester, forgiving any library fines that they may have, increasing the number of free prints or photocopies that they can make in the library, increasing their interlibrary loan limit, or providing one hour of individualized library research instruction from a librarian on a topic of their choice.
- Provide a question for faculty that must be answered through library research. Publish the answers and the winning faculty member each month. Reward the faculty member with prizes such as one hour of bibliographic research done by their library liaison, $100 worth of books in their discipline to be purchased by the library for the library collections, or a specialized library instruction unit for a class of their choice.
- Highlight a different database in each issue. Talk about what it contains, who should use it, and then provide a link to the library's online instructional unit that teaches how to use the database.
- Provide an interesting tidbit about the field of librarianship that people don't usually consider. For example, librarians work to battle censorship. They also work to battle commercial publishing monopolies that lead to a focus on mainstream publishing and eliminate publication of cutting-edge texts. For example, if the commercial publishing system of today had been in effect 100 years ago, we would never have published works by famous authors such as James Joyce. And, if the current system of electronic indexing had been in effect, we would never have found Einstein's work on relativity because it was published in a journal so small that it probably would not have been indexed electronically. You can also talk about the publishing cycle and how long it takes to get published in journals—thus the delay in dissemination of new information that is valuable to us all (e.g., new medical procedures, new drugs).

2. Publish with teaching faculty. We can use our specific skills in the area of bibliographic research to co-publish with other faculty. A librarian can provide the literature search and summary, and the partnering faculty member can provide the disciplinary subject matter.
3. Use our ability to reach students across the campus to perform research with other faculty. We have tremendous capacity to survey students, talk

one-on-one with students, and summarize the results of these conversations. We should use this ability to help faculty do their research when it involves students.

4. Highlight our work in annual reports from the library. A good way to do this is to use formats suggested by a vita or by our local promotion processes. Figure 8.5 is an impressive example of a library publications list from American University Library (Washington, D.C.). The list is quick to read, and the sheer number of publications is bound to be impressive to faculty and administrators.

STUDENT OUTCOMES ASSESSMENT

So far, this chapter discusses ways to present ourselves to the academic community that focus on outcomes in terms of financial productivity and efficiency, credit hour productivity, and faculty productivity. The last, but the most important, is the way that we present ourselves in terms of how we contribute to student learning outcomes.

This is probably the most difficult presentation to prepare, because it involves research that many of us, including the teaching faculty with whom we work, are not used to doing. However, the fact is that the ultimate measure used by administrators and faculty is whether our students have become more successful as a result of their experiences in college. Many programs use measures of success such as the number of students who got jobs in their field, the number of employers who say that our students are well prepared for their jobs after graduation, and the number of alumni who say that they were well prepared by their academic education. All of our programs use grades in classes as one way of showing that students have learned the material presented in a class. Some of our programs even use less traditional methods of measuring student learning outcomes—for example, portfolio assessment, journaling, sophomore review boards, and performance juries for music and art majors. The point is that every program must provide evidence that students are learning and that this learning is benefiting the students. Libraries are not exempt. But, since using the library is a tool to an end—being able to perform better in classes—librarians need to use student learning outcomes assessments that go beyond traditional tests to see if material presented is learned.

Using the previously mentioned mantra—"Library outcomes data must align with outcomes data that is important to the institution"—I suggest the following. Try to show that library services and library instruction lead to one or more of the following:

- Higher GPA
- Better ratio of earned hours to attempted hours
- Better semester to semester persistence

AMERICAN UNIVERSITY LIBRARY
LIBRARY PUBLICATIONS AND ELECTRONIC RESOURCE GUIDES
2001-2002

New publications

Gateway Publication (Eagle insert)
BiblioNet, library newsletter (Fall, Spring, and Special issues)
Bi-weekly library column in *American Weekly*
Library Team Training Manual (looseleaf, internal)
Library Publication Manual (looseleaf, internal)
Supervisor's Manual (looseleaf, internal)
Books and Videos for Understanding September 11 (Bibliography)

New Web Pages and Pathfinders

Revised the entire library Web site. Approximately 1,000 pages.
New Sections of the website:
  o Subject guides to the print collection
  o Information and online study guide pathfinder for standardized admissions tests and TOEFL
  o Information for Students section of the website
  o Information for Faculty section of the website
  o Help section for **technical** troubleshooting when connecting to databases
  o Help sections of the website including the following new information literacy pages:
    Using the Library
    Using the World Wide Web in Research Papers
    What Kind of Source Do I Need?
    Basic Database Syntax
    Multiple Concept Searching
    Databases in Print
    Web Searching Tips
    Reference Sources
    Finding Periodicals
    Finding Newspapers
    Finding Images
    Understanding Call Numbers

New Web Pathfinders

Practical and Moral Support for Graduate Students Writing Theses and Dissertations
    www.library.american.edu/e_ref/grad_survival.html
Women in Art Subject Page www.library.american.edu/subject/art/women.html
Librarian Office Hours Flyer and Page
www.library.american.edu/about/services/instruction/officehours.html
Information Literacy Program Page
www.library.american.edu/about/services/instruction/forum.html
What Kind of Source Do I Need? Help Page www.library.american.edu/Help/research/sources.html
Using the World Wide Web in Research Papers
www.library.american.edu/Help/research/web_evaluate.html
Databases in Print Help Page www.library.american.edu/Help/research/printindex.html
September 11 www.library.american.edu/subject/september_11/internet.html

New Course Specific Research Guides (on e-reserve pages)

Spring 2002

Advanced Reporting, COMM 425
Domestic Violence, JLS 526
Foreign Policy and the Press, COMM 546
International Comparative communication Policy, SIS 645
International Economics
World Wide Web Evaluation, samples

Figure 8.5 American University Library Publications and Electronic Resource Guides 2001–2002

Source: http://www.library.american.edu/about/policies/annual_report_2001-2002.pdg. Accessed March 5, 2004.

Fall 2001
Boolean Operators
College Writing (2 courses)
Communication and Society
Competition in an Interdependent World Economy
Dance History
Humphrey Fellows Library Workshop 2001
Introduction to International Relations Research
Introduction to Justice Research
Language Acquisition
Linking to Electronic Resources at American University Library
Psychological Research

New brochures and information guides
Book Reviews
Film Reviews
Stocks
Value Line Investment Survey information guide
Washington DC

New Policy Information Sheets
Copyright Policy slip
Guidelines for Use of the Library by High School and Community Groups
Guidelines for Use of the Library by Groups from Other Educational Programs

Mediagraphies (available in print or on the Web) n= new; u=updated
Advertisng, marketing and public relations -n
African-American history, culture, and current issues-u
AIDS-n
Animation-u
Area studies: Africa - n
Area studies: Israel/Palestine - n
Authors and poets on video and audiotape - n
Biology - u
DVDs - u
Education - n
Environmental issues - u
Feature films - u
Films on Film-makers/Film-makers on film - n
Food - n
Gay, lesbian, and transgender issues - u
Islam - u
Justice, law and society - n
Shakespeare - n
Vietnam War - n

Updated brochures and information guides
Accounting and Taxation
ALADIN Databases
Alphabetic list of Indexes
American Politics
Art History Brochure
Circulation policy
Citation Style Guides
Company and Industry
Copy Center
Disability brochure
Finance
Financial Aid

Figure 8.5 (continued)

Grants & Grantwriting
International Business
International Financial Statistics Information Sheet
Library Facts, fall and spring updates, also placed on the Web
Library Welcome Sheet
Library Class Schedule, handout and page
Literature
Journalism
Marketing and Advertising
*my*ALADIN
Periodicals handout
Real Estate
Sociology
Teaching English as a Second Language (TESOL) brochure
Women in Religion
World Development Indicators Information Sheet

Pathfinders updated:
Advanced Reporting Course Page http://www.library.american.edu/course/research/comm-425.html
Call Numbers www.library.american.edu/Help/research/callnumbers.html
College Writing www.library.american.edu/subject/cw/badland.html
Communication www.library.american.edu/subject/com/internet.html
Film studies: Internet sites www.library.american.edu/subject/film/internet.html
Film studies: Library research primer www.library.american.edu/subject/film/film_research.html
Finding Newspapers http://www.library.american.edu/Help/research/newspaper.html
Finding Images http://www.library.american.edu/Help/research/images.html
Foreign Policy and the Press Page http://www.library.american.edu/course/research/comm-546.html
Law and Legal www.library.american.edu/subject/law/internet.html
Linking to Full Text Resources Sample Page
www.library.american.edu/course/research/prestest.html
Literature www.library.american.edu/subject/lit/internet.html
Quick Stats - an index to freely-available statistics online -
www.library.american.edu/e_ref/statistics.html
Using the Library www.library.american.edu/Help/research/process.html
World Wide Web Evaluation Exercise www.library.american.edu/course/research/wwwexer.html

Library entries updated in:
AU Student Handbook for 2002-03
Unofficial Student Guide
Student Handbook and *Parent Handbook*
American University Catalog
Information for International Students

Retrieved from World Wide Web on March 5, 2004 at
http://www.library.american.edu/about/policies/annual_report_2001-2002.pdf

Figure 8.5   (continued)

- Better overall retention
- Higher graduation rates
- Decreased time to degree
- Increased quality of work in a specific class
- Better grades in a specific class
- Lower drop rates for a specific class

Finally, here are some specific research programs that might be undertaken:

If your library is teaching a credit-bearing class:

Match students taking your classes with a control group of comparable students who are not taking your classes. You will need to be sure that your control group reflects the profile of the students taking your class in terms of things like prior GPA, primary language or ethnicity, attempted hours during the semester that the class is being offered, and perhaps even SAT scores or high school rank. Then track these students over several semesters on semester GPA, attempted hours that were completed, persistence to the next semester, and overall retention at the institution. If you find statistically significant differences among the students, you may be able to show that "Students who successfully complete Library 101 have significantly higher GPAs and complete significantly more attempted hours than students who do not complete Library 101."

If your library uses an infusion method for library instruction where library units are infused into specific classes or programs:

Infuse library units at strategic points within a program or a class that is taught within a program. Use pre- and post-test results to determine if the infused library unit results in improvement of library skills, increased quality of disciplinary work within the class or program, lowered drop rates for classes, increased retention at the institution, higher GPA, lowered time to degree or program completion, or other areas of interest. You just might be able to show that "the papers produced by students in psychology classes with infused library units were significantly higher quality than those produced by students in psychology classes without infused library units." You might be able to show that the GPA of students who took classes with infused library units were significantly higher than those of students who did not complete library-infused classes. Or, you might even be able to show that students who completed library-infused classes had higher retention rates than students who did not.

If you provide library workshops for students covering various library skills areas:

Examine the demographic data of the students who take the workshops, and compare these students' success rates to students with similar demographic profiles who do not take the library workshops. You might be able to state that completion of library workshops significantly improves student GPA.

Unfortunately, my search of the literature didn't yield many examples of these types of assessment. However, I did find some promising reports from the Glendale Community College Library in Glendale California (www.glendale.edu/library). The lack of library literature on student learning outcomes assessment doesn't necessarily mean that it is not being done, but it does reinforce my comments earlier about the need for librarians to publish. If important and groundbreaking research in libraries does not get published, no one knows about it, and no one can use the results from one library to grow a field of research for everyone's benefit.

CONCLUSION

It is my hope that as a profession, we will all:

- Use numbers in ways that focus on outcomes.
- Use numbers that conform to institutional templates.
- Earn advanced degrees.
- Do research and publish the results.
- Embark on consistent and effective promotional activities.
- Assess student learning outcomes.

Finally, it is my hope that we will all perform, promote, and use the results of serious research on the positive and tangible outcomes from libraries.

9 MARKETING THE LEARNING RESOURCE CENTER AT KANKAKEE COMMUNITY COLLEGE: A CASE STUDY

Donna J. Smith

Kankakee Community College (KCC) is a small, rural community college in Kankakee County, population just over 104,000, in central Illinois. In FY2002, KCC had 3,000 students (about 1,800 full-time) in the credit division, almost 3,000 students in continuing education, and another 5,000 persons served annually through special noncredit programs. KCC serves the 130,000 residents of Community College District 520, which includes all of Kankakee and Iroquois counties and portions of Ford, Grundy, Livingston, and Will counties. The counties served cover more than 1,800 square miles. KCC's main campus is located on 178 scenic acres on the southern edge of the city of Kankakee, about 60 miles south of Chicago. Situated on the tree-lined banks of the Kankakee River and surrounded by the Kankakee Conservation Area and rich farmland, the KCC campus provides an ideal environment for learning.

In October 2000 when I arrived at KCC, the Learning Resource Center (LRC) had been without a librarian for three years. Day-to-day activities such as circulation, interlibrary loan, cataloging, and acquisitions all worked well. Strategic activities surrounding collection development, budgeting, and marketing had been deferred until a librarian was found. The book budget had been decreased to the point where the 1982 LRC self study showed a higher book budget than in FY2001. Collection analysis showed a collection of 47,856 total items, of which 60 percent had not circulated in more than 20 years. The collection was extremely aged. Fifty-six percent of the titles were published prior to 1980; an additional 31 percent were published in the 1980s.

As part of a transition period, priorities for the LRC were determined. The number-one priority was improving the collection; this also translated into a need to improve the budget. The second priority was increasing both student and faculty LRC use. Marketing was a key component of success for both priorities.

COLLECTION IMPROVEMENTS

A five-year collection development plan was established. Utilizing a year's worth of course schedules and an organization chart, approximately 60 subjects (e.g., history, biology, computer science) were divided into the five instructional areas (Business, Health, Humanities/Social Science, Math/Science, and Technology). A sixth category—Other—was created to encompass collection needs for the library, athletic division, faculty development, and so on. Program review schedules were consulted to determine an order of importance for development. Each year, approximately 13 subject areas are collected in depth. Each of the other 52 subject areas is collected very lightly, with about six books per topic. As a specific example, in FY2002, the subjects of Business, Medical Laboratory Assistant, Paramedic, Radiography, Respiratory Therapy, Geography, Philosophy, Sociology, Data Processing, Law and Criminal Justice, Construction Management, Electricity (with Industrial Electrical Technology), and Literacy for adults and the family were reviewed and collected.

Beginning Marketing

Marketing began once the five-year plan was drafted. I met with each division program coordinator to discuss the overall plan. Working together, we developed a process for review. In-house newsletter articles are published in August and April to encourage all areas to make purchase suggestions. Once a month, between October and April, several activities occur. The LRC staff members use automated system reports to identify items that have not circulated in 20 years and were published prior to 1980. Items related to the subject under review are moved to a special "review" area. The program coordinator is sent an email containing the subject area being reviewed within a division along with names of faculty who might be involved with the review and purchase of new materials. Once the program coordinator reviews the list, each faculty member is sent a letter explaining the request to review old materials, the request for syllabi in the subject area, and the promise of a list of titles with positive reviews in the subject area. Faculty members are encouraged to submit titles or choose 25–30 titles from the list provided.

The division program coordinators were supportive of a project that ensured that each area they coordinated would have a materials review once every five years. In addition, at least a few titles would be purchased for all of their subject areas every year. Gaining division support of the collection plan was an essential first step for justifying budget increases.

Statistics for the collection development plan show the success of this effort for its first two years:

- 4,600+ titles pulled
- 3,858 weeded from the collection
- 79 marked "core"
- 165 put in storage for one year
- 82 checked for updates
- 130 returned to circulation
- 27 subjects reviewed
- 23 of 27 subjects reviewed had faculty do both reviews and selection
- 51 percent uncirculated items down from 60 percent

The biggest drawback of this effort is the time involved. I am the only librarian with an MLS degree and do the majority of the selection work. BooksInPrint.com (with reviews) helps tremendously with building lists of positively reviewed items. In addition to the selection effort, the faculty involvement requires time on my part. In the 23 subjects with faculty reviews, I contacted all 23 faculty members and arranged for a half-hour initial meeting (in the review area). In the four areas that didn't have faculty review, I did not make the time to personally talk with or meet with the faculty.

The pluses of this marketing effort are the positive effect on faculty relations, the less dated look of the LRC, and a way to justify the book budget. Faculty time to review the materials was lower than expected. Bookmarks labeled with "pull," "store," "core material," and so on were added to the books as students pulled titles. A faculty member looks at a title, marks the bookmark, and leaves the book in the review area. LRC staff sort the books by the bookmark disposition. After a while, we shortened the process so that books to be discarded were 'turned down' and only titles to be kept stayed upright with the bookmark checked and the call number viewable. The largest number of items pulled was 400 titles for sociology. It took the faculty member about four hours to review all 400 titles.

BUDGET IMPROVEMENTS

The second marketing step in the collection improvement area was to "sell" the book budget. (Online resources and periodicals are separate line items and are not included in this discussion.) The defense of the book budget increase was very business oriented including reference to community college standards, statistics regarding the age of the LRC collection, and statistics regarding the lack of circulation and comments by members of a visiting accreditation team from 1994. The focal point of the statistics drew attention to industry standard costs for reference and nonreference books plus previous costs of standing orders. Money was requested in four areas of book purchase: standing orders, reference books, nonreviewed subjects, and reviewed subjects. Definitions and reasonable requests for a quantity of titles were made in each area. (The librarian defined *reasonable*.)

The justifications and numbers for the original budget increase are shown in the following:

1. Standing orders consist of annual titles such as *World Almanac, Book of Facts, College Blue Book*, and Peterson's Guides.

   Budget request: 80 titles @ $125 per title $10,000

2. Reference books—The reference collection consists of 2,755 items (including the 80 standing orders). This category covers replacements for old reference books, irregular reference books, and new topics in reference books like *Grove's Dictionary of Music and Musicians* (published once every 20 years; $4,000), general encyclopedias, dictionaries, and subject-specific items.

   Budget request: 40 titles @ $200 per title $ 8,000

   Our curriculum teaches around 344 different classes in 65 different subject areas (e.g., health, business, accounting, computer science, drafting)

3. Purchase six new titles per subject not being reviewed per year (e.g., business could buy six books to increase the knowledge areas of Accounting, General Business, Marketing, Economics, etc) This would mean 6 titles X 52 subject areas = 312 titles

   Budget request: 312 titles @ $40 per title $12,480

4. Consciously rebuild the collection over a five-year cycle. Once every five years, review a subject area of the curriculum by (a) deselecting worn, obsolete, or inaccurate material, (b) replacing editions of materials, and (c) selecting print or nonprint items appropriate to support the current curriculum in that subject area. This allows a complete review of all LRC materials every five years. In the 2001–2002 budget year, the development plan includes subject reviews of the reference and main collections in the 13 areas of Law and Criminal Justice, Construction Management, Electricity (including Industrial Electrical Technology), Data Processing, Business, Sociology, Geography, Philosophy, Medical Laboratory Assistant, Paramedic, Radiography, Respiratory Therapy, and Adult Literacy. The order of subject areas review was determined by (a) program reviews and (b) division director input. The five-year cyclical reviews, along with the

annual six-title purchase, keep the collection current with the curriculum. Regular review is particularly important in the health, technology, and science areas.

Budget request: 13 areas, 30 titles @ $40 per title $15,600

Verbal defense of the budget pointed out the fact that 56 percent+ of the materials in the LRC were published before most of our students were born. The division program coordinators support of the plan was referenced. Adding very specific details regarding quantities, costs, and subjects provided a clear and complete business rationale for the budget increase. Although the total budget increase was not funded, the book budget was increased 25 percent between FY2001 and FY2002.

Ongoing marketing efforts in the book budget have been tied to organizational goals. In FY2003, a special category for "new programs" was added. In FY2004, a category for "faculty development" was added. The book budget has increased slightly each year. As the collection development plan has been implemented, statistics are added to the book budget request referencing the total collection size, number of materials reviewed/weeded by faculty, number of purchases in the special review areas, and the decreasing uncirculated items statistics. So far, the book budget has not been decreased as a result of budget cuts. I like to think this is a result of the modest increase requests (about 3 percent per year), continued reference to the collection development five-year plan, division/faculty support of collection development activities, and continued marketing of plan results.

INCREASED LRC USE

The second LRC priority developed was to increase LRC use through both increased student use and increased faculty use. No method of tracking patron use of the LRC was in place in FY2001. Shortly after my start at KCC, a head count was implemented. Once an hour on the half hour, a staff member or student counted patrons in the LRC. I considered the FY2001 counts as practice to build the process for FY2002. There were many hours of many days with zero patrons in the LRC. In FY2002, the head count was around 35,500.

I saw the LRC space as open with a great view of the river. There were three floors that were often empty. Given the age of the collection, this was not surprising. More amazing to me was the lack of computer use. The LRC had 9 general research PCs plus two computer labs with an additional 18 PCs. The KCC policy in FY2001, however, was to grant Internet login accounts only to those classes that requested access. The general student population could log in as "student" to work with word processing packages as needed.

Student use of the LRC is the area where the least marketing activity has occurred. The initial intent was to publish regular articles in the student newsletter.

However, the newsletter is published on an erratic schedule and most issues do not contain LRC articles. Instead of direct marketing to students, a LRC use survey was implemented. The survey obtains information regarding reasons for using the LRC, research needs met, research needs not met, and electronic database use. Indirectly, this survey pointed out to both students and faculty the availability of on- and off-campus resources. The survey results provided information regarding simple LRC changes that could be implemented and marketed to students. As an example, students complained of a lack of group study areas on campus. The LRC began advertising an already existing space as a small group meeting room. A second minor change was to shift some months of display case and bulletin board use to highlighting ethnic customs, biographies, heritages, and histories.

Two other changes related directly to the student use of the LRC. First, KCC changed its policy regarding student Internet accounts. All students were provided with email and network accounts in FY2002. Second, a two-credit, eight-week Library Research Skills course was extensively modified. The course was originally designed to teach students physical resources in the LRC. Neither the Internet nor electronic search tools and strategies were covered. The course had not been seriously revised in more than 10 years. Students completed assignments in less than an hour each week. In January 2002, the course content switched to an Information Literacy curriculum in which resources from books, article databases, and the Internet were used to support a student-determined research topic. Rather than eight weeks on campus, students could complete six of the eight weeks off-campus by utilizing Internet access to KCC resources. The trade-off was that each week would take two to four hours of work to complete. The change in content was then marketed to KCC Advisors and Humanities faculty. In addition, an online version of the course was developed to increase student access. Initial enrollment in the research course dropped due to the increased time required by the information literacy focus. Due to positive student evaluations and continued marketing, however, current enrollment surpasses those of the old course.

In FY2001, faculty visited the LRC primarily to request videos for class use. With the exception of English I, which requires an orientation, few classes utilized the LRC for research assignments. Faculty use of the LRC was the second issue addressed following the implementation of a headcount. The easiest marketing change was to print a monthly new book list in *Update*, the faculty/staff weekly newsletter. The first article emphasized the LRC new bookshelf where new purchases are kept for four months. I was amazed by the positive response to the new book list. Faculty members enjoy seeing both titles they recommend and titles in their area selected by the LRC.

Update was also used a second time each month to highlight different electronic resources in the LRC. Databases available off-campus were addressed first. The response to these articles led to future marketing efforts at division meetings. Once a term, I attended division meetings to demonstrate electronic resources and discuss possible LRC assignments. The database demonstrations were most useful in the Humanities division since the off-campus databases were primarily general undergraduate resources. Discussion of information and research opportunities was less successful in division meetings and more successful in the Learning Resources Committee meetings. The Learning Resources Committee consisted of 10 faculty and staff members from all divisions. This group had livelier discussions on LRC resources and the use of such resources in possible assignments. The committee members then took information regarding research opportunities back to their divisions. The advocacy of the committee members made more of an impact to faculty in the area of assignments than my general presentations to divisions.

As a final marketing effort directly to faculty, I worked with groups organizing high school counselor and principal sessions, and annual faculty in-service and part-time faculty training sessions. A list of LRC services, including research orientations, was presented to the counselors and principals of District 520 High Schools. For the first LRC presentations, faculty members were presented with both the services handout and instructions on accessing research databases within their office or off-campus with passwords. These traditions continue. Four area high schools bring research classes to the LRC annually. KCC faculty orientations have grown from 55 to more than 80 in three years. The earlier orientations were primarily from English I and KCC orientation classes. Now, additional subject specific information literacy presentations are made to history, government, speech, literature, psychology, and business classes.

Marketing to faculty has had a positive effect on both in-house library use and electronic database use. In-library use statistics have changed from many hours with zero patrons to almost no hours with zero patrons. Within the first eight months of FY2004, the LRC surpassed the 35,500 patrons mark. An automated patron counter has been purchased because staff members become so busy with patrons that counts cannot be made. FY2003 electronic database statistics showed increases in both number of articles obtains and the number of patrons being "blocked" from limited license databases. The statistics on refused patrons were then used to increase electronic resource budgets on two products so both unlimited and off-campus use could be obtained. Marketing of the increased user limits and off-campus use of specialty databases in FY2004 has already led to increased orientations in English II and Sociology classes.

GENERAL MARKETING PLAN

1. *Update* (faculty/staff newsletter)
   a. Monthly article on new books
   b. Publicize grants as received
   c. Monthly article on AV/book purchase suggestions, databases, or electronic access to specific resources such as the *Chronicle of Higher Education* and *the Chicago Tribune*

2. *Cavalier Canvas* (student newsletter)
   a. Identify publication schedule
   b. Publish articles in each issue
3. News releases
   a. Suggest news releases to the Marketing Department on LRC activities including grant receipts, special displays related to grants, awards received, offices held and new purchases
4. Collection Development Plan
   a. Send division coordinators reminders of subjects being reviewed
   b. Have materials for review moved to a review area
   c. Request names of faculty teaching in each subject
   d. Contact faculty
   e. Schedule time for the review
   f. Send a thank you
5. Meetings
   a. Present LRC update during fall/spring faculty in-service training
   b. Present LRC update at the part-time faculty orientation
   c. Meet with divisions annually on Collection Development and databases
   d. Meet with Learning Resources Committee twice annually
   e. Develop flyers/attend principals' meeting for District 520 high schools
   f. Develop flyers/attend counselors' meeting for District 520 high schools
   g. Develop flyers/create Librarian's Day meeting for District 520 high schools
   h. Attend Kankakee Area Librarian's Association—promote local libraries when possible
   i. Attend statewide group meetings
   j. Suggest KCC as a host location
   k. Publicize committee and officer positions in *Update*
6. Grants
   a. Publicize within KCC and with news releases
   b. Receipts of grants
   c. Grant updates
   d. Final grant activities
   e. Northern Illinois Anglers Association (annual grant)
   f. Send appropriate letters
   g. Crease and send an annual listing of collection contents
   h. Create an annual display of new purchases for the 4th of July
   i. Send a special invitation to members to view the display

I once heard marketing described as "blowing your own horn. "To me, marketing is the opportunity to educate others in the services and opportunities available through information in general and KCC's LRC in specific. Marketing isn't blowing my horn as much as relaying pride in my staff, in administration's support of the LRC, and in the resources available through the LRC. Marketing can be mentioning a specialty database at a staff meeting, producing an article on new books, creating a display around a certificate program, or promoting information access in an orientation. Almost every contact made with a faculty or student can be thought of as marketing. The marketing plan was created to remind me of important tasks. The hardest part of the marketing plan is remembering that it is a living document. For instance, the plan does not (yet) include a reminder to submit a faculty research assignment to the innovative awards committee each year. What has worked? Any part of the plan involving human contact has worked. The collection development and faculty/staff newsletter activities have worked. Creating wider recognition of KCC's LRC throughout the state via meetings and committee assignments has worked. Supporting grants such as the NIAA grant has worked. What has not worked? Publishing regularly in the student newsletter and remembering to suggest press releases to the Marketing Department have not worked. What are the problems with marketing? The largest problem has been the success of marketing activities. The great part of the marketing success is increased student use, increased faculty orientations, changes to information resource projects in courses, increased budget, and an improved collection. The tough part of the marketing success is the lack of staff increase, which means less time to complete needed activities. As an example, only 5 of 12 faculty subject areas were contacted personally as part of the FY2004 collection development plan and only 5 of 12 areas had faculty input on the review. This compares with 23 of 27 areas with faculty review during the previous two years. What is the next step? Marketing will continue. A new goal will be determining a marketing strategy that will sell administration on the need for a reference librarian.

SELECTED BIBLIOGRAPHY

Association of College and Research Libraries. 1994. "Standards for Community, Junior, and Technical College Learning Resource Programs," *C&RL News* (55): 572–585.

Association of College and Research Libraries. "Standards for Libraries in Higher Education," *C&RL News* (65): 530–543. Available at http://www.ala.org/ala/acrl/acrlstandards/standardscommunity.htm>. Accessed 18 August 2005.

Bowker Annual: Library and Book Trade Almanac. 2003. New York: R. R. Bowker.

Junion-Metz, Gail. 2003. "Sell Yourself." *School Library Journal* (October): 40.

Schrock, Kathy. 2003. "The ABC's of Marketing," *School Library Journal* (November): 36.

IV

WORKING AND SHARING TOGETHER: JOINING FORCES FOR THE COMMON GOOD

10 JOINT-USE LIBRARIES: ISSUES AND MODELS

Lyn "Mimi" Collins and William Duncan

Library managers consider many critical issues in developing and evaluating programs of service, but the consideration of a joint-use library stands out as requiring special expertise in planning and particularly in collaboration. Although anecdotal evidence may suggest more attempts than successes, there are several models for the successful development of joint-use libraries. We review some of the key issues to be considered and describe some of the models, emphasizing the combination of community college libraries with those of other agencies.

Combining libraries for joint use takes many forms. The most common combinations for joint-use libraries are school–public; community college–public; university–public; university–community college; and university–community college–public. The combined libraries may be cooperative ventures with the partner agencies operating independently within shared facilities, or they may be consolidated libraries operated by joint governance. This chapter addresses consolidated libraries, or those in which partners combine services within the same building rather than operate independently in separate parts of the building.

One of the first applications of combining community college libraries with other agencies occurred in South Australia in the late 1970s (Amey 1987, 113). State-administered Technical and Further Education (TAFE) colleges were combined with public libraries in designated rural areas as part of a statewide public library service outreach plan. Much of the early literature of the 1970s and 1980s, however, reflects a predominance of school–public library combinations, with little on community college joint-use libraries.

In general, contemporary literature of the 1990s and 2000s reflects a broader application of combining libraries, including a great deal of emerging literature on joint-use community college libraries. A Google search for *"joint use" library "community college"*, for example, yields nearly 4,000 results. The move from school–public toward community college–public combinations, in particular, allows a comfortable fit for general adult and community college populations that may build lifelong learning habits among college students and even increase community college enrollments by exposing public customers to the college community.

The initiative for developing joint-use libraries may come from governing agencies, rather than staff members in the affected libraries, and may be driven by funding issues. In California, for example, a public library bond act was passed in 2000 that gives state funding priority for construction of new public libraries to those with joint-use agreements with school districts (Berger 2000, 3). Although current literature reflects the interest of governments in combining libraries as a means of reducing duplication of services and saving money, the evidence suggests that facilities costs may be reduced but that operational cost savings may not be as great as expected, and staff increases rather than reductions may be recommended as hours and services may expand in response to increased use.

A joint-use library demonstrates the ultimate resource sharing program. As with early efforts in multitype library resource sharing, however, joint use represents a number of ownership issues—not only of physical resources such as equipment, collections, and database subscriptions, but of human resources such as traditional loyalties to one agency or another. In the recent case of the much-touted merger of San Jose State University and San Jose Public Library, for example, faculty opposition spawned Save Our University Library (SOUL), an advocacy group that actively demonstrated against the proposed joint-use library. A visit to SJLibrary.org, however, demonstrates a user-friendly interface, with links for SJSU students and faculty, kids, teens, and seniors and adults. Dornseif (2001, 103) says it all: "Joint-use libraries are successful when the patrons of each partner believe that the library functions well for them."

ISSUES

Because early joint-use libraries were predominantly school–public combinations, issues largely reflected concerns for the different missions of school and public libraries, particularly the school's greater emphasis on structured learning rather than self-directed or recreational activities, and concerns for the different program and service interests of children and adults. A school location may be unappealing or inconvenient for adults, and the availability of adult library collections and unfiltered Internet access may pose problems for younger students. School–public library concerns receive less attention in community college–university–public library combinations largely because the community college mission, as compared with that of the K–12 schools, is a closer match to the mission of the public or university library and the customers have more common interests in programs and services. Issues in combining the community college with a public or university library tend to reflect more on governance, staffing, and operations.

Governance and Management

Governance may consist of a governing board or an advisory committee with members representing all of the partners. A governing board reviews policy functions such as budget, planning, and program evaluation. Depending on size, the board might designate subcommittees for specific functions. An advisory committee ensures balance of the respective partners' interests in best serving their customers.

Three management models are most common in community college library combinations: (1) a director reports to a joint governing board and all staff members report to the director; (2) one partner contracts with another to provide a director and staff members; and (3) each partner employs a co-director and staff members, in which case salaries and benefits may vary among employees. In the last two models, a joint advisory committee should be in place to ensure balance of interests among the partners. The first two models, with all staff members part of the same system, seem to operate most smoothly in many cases.

Professional and Support Staff

Professional staff in a joint-use library must represent all of the partners—that is, school, academic, public, or special libraries, as appropriate. Professional specialists are instrumental in providing good service in a combined library. At the same time, there is frequent reference in the literature to the critical importance of cooperation and commitment to the combined mission. "Mine" and "yours" must become "ours" if combined libraries are to provide the best service to end users.

Staff assignments and reporting structures require a clear line of authority and clearly defined responsibilities for each position. The professional and support staff of each partner should be cross-trained; for example, public librarians should be prepared to assist with academic research papers and academic librarians should be prepared to assist with public service programs for adults and children. A community college–public library combination is particularly well suited to offering the partners' respective customers a seamless continuum of information literacy and lifelong learning experiences.

Operations

Building design, parking, utilities, maintenance, and the like will be among the first issues addressed. Joint-use libraries are most frequently new structures or remodeled and expanded structures, making facilities issues part of the earliest planning concerns when agencies are considering combining libraries.

Some of the issues that will be addressed over time include joint use of electronic equipment and resources and print and audiovisual collections; choice of integrated library systems and classification systems; hours of operation, policies and procedures, and library cards. As the joint-use library evolves, these and other operational decisions may be adjusted to better fit customer needs and the smooth operation of the combined library.

Funding operations in a joint-use library may be as simple as a formula based on numbers of registered users, on space needs, or on similar measurable factors. Regular review of the funding structure should be part of the evaluation process. In any case, the operational cost for each partner may only be somewhat less than that for a single-agency library.

Guidelines and Checklists

Florida community colleges were among the first and most prolific developers of joint-use community college libraries in the United States. Broward Community College, for example, opened its first joint-use library 20 years ago and has since opened four others. Based on several years of experience, the Florida community colleges developed a comprehensive report outlining practical advantages and disadvantages of joint-use libraries, as well as issues of agreements, operations, and facilities (Florida Community College System 1996).

The support of key players from end users to administrators is critical to success, from planning through implementation, evaluation, and modification. In one of the most comprehensive recent examinations of joint-use libraries, Bundy (2003, 141–43) offers a planning checklist and lists key factors for the success of a joint-use library (Bundy 2003, 138–39).

Responsibilities of each partner must be clearly defined, even though it is likely that these responsibilities will change over time. Lines of communication must be defined and kept open in a combined library even more than in more traditional settings. Everyone must be prepared for not only consensus but compromise; each partner will be giving up some control in moving from a single-agency to a joint-use operation, no matter what the final structure. Frontline librarians for each partner are central to designing a workable partnership that is responsive to both end users and governing agents.

The Agreement

Throughout the literature, it is emphasized that issues in combining libraries are best addressed by a solid long-term agreement between the partners, including processes for conflict resolution and for dissolving the partnership. As part of the ongoing evaluation process, agreements must be revisited regularly to ensure balance, protect the integrity of the partnership, and reflect the needs of the end users. The Florida Community College System (1996, C1–C5) offers a report that includes a comprehensive sample agreement. The Florida model addresses the joint mission; goals and objectives; administration of the joint-use library; organizational structure of public and technical services; hours of operation; acquisition of property; replacement and disposal of property; property accountability or ownership; merger of collections, personnel, and special services; expenses for books and other collections, grants and gifts, personnel, building maintenance, security, and utilities; payment procedures; accounting methodology; special allocations or grants; review and modification of the agreement; and termination of the agreement, plus a list of additional items for consideration.

In designing the agreement, it must be remembered that the mission of each joint-use library is different from the missions of the individual partners and that each joint-use library will have its own unique mission.

Joint-use library agreements tend to be between two agencies, but if more are involved, separate agreements should be made with each partner. Agreements between Indian River Community College (IRCC) and Florida Atlantic University, and IRCC and St. Lucie County are published in Roshaven and Widman (2001, 77–87).

It may take three to four years to go from the first suggestion to combine libraries to the actual signing of an agreement. Attempts that fail initially may succeed at a later time. The agreement is the key to opening the joint-use library, but sufficient time and commitment must be devoted to the effort.

Ongoing Communication and Collaboration

It is strongly evident from the literature that a joint-use library is not the sum of its parts. Rather, each combined library is a unique entity and, more than a single-agency library, always in development. Once the building location has been chosen, parking has been agreed upon, and construction or extensive remodeling has begun, it comes down to daily operations. Much of the success of a joint-use library depends on the personal commitment of key staff members; even a change in staff may make it necessary to renegotiate some issues. There is much to be learned as participants grow with the experience of operating a joint-use library. Those community college libraries that have existed for a few years have depended on constant communication among the partners and have made adjustments and changes in operations as the partnerships developed. When partners are part of larger agencies, as is the case with an academic satellite campus or a public library branch, lines of communication must remain strong not only within the joint-use library but with and between the parent agencies.

MODELS

The model joint-use libraries described next reflect combinations between community colleges and city and county agencies as well as those between community colleges and other educational institutions. These models are representative of the diversity of community college library partnerships. As evidenced by this selection, there is no shrink-wrapped solution; rather, a great deal of commitment on the part of each joint-use library's planners results in made-to-order combinations.

One of the longest-operating community college joint library programs has been successful in Florida since 1983, when Broward Community College (BCC)—South Campus joined with Broward County Library System. Broward Community College now has four joint-use libraries with the county and one with Florida Atlantic University—Broward. BCC joint libraries with the county are located at North Campus, South Campus, Downtown Center, and Pines Center. Pines Center also serves a charter high school. At each site, online databases are provided by the county, and learning assistance for college students is provided by BCC.

The BCC joint-use library with Florida Atlantic University—Broward opened in 1994. The University/College Library, located on the community college's Central Campus, operates with both a governing board and an advisory committee. Funding is 60 percent community college and 40 percent university based. As the new library was being designed and built, an outside consultant worked with administrators, librarians, and faculty members to develop an organizational structure and an interagency agreement. The consultant strongly recommended that university staff members become community college employees, noting that conflict between the two groups could be eased by having everyone report to the same administrator (Woods 2001, 45–46).

In Bothell, Washington, near Seattle, state officials decided in 1994 that two new institutions, the University of Washington—Bothell (UWB) and Cascadia Community College (CCC), should be joint occupants of the same facility, largely because land was at a premium in that congested area. The Campus Library offers some shared services, but the building fascia and furnishings are slightly different to set off areas specific to either UWB or CCC (Fugate 2001, 60). Operating with an agreement, Campus Library is essentially two libraries under one roof. Funding comes to about 60 percent by the university and 40 percent by the community college, based roughly on numbers of students.

The Brevard Community College—Cocoa Campus Library reopened in 1995 as a joint-use library for Brevard Community College and the University of Central Florida. The Cocoa Campus Library includes the Florida Solar Energy Center's special collection, which is housed on a separate floor, and a Grants and Nonprofit Resource Center in collaboration with the Space Coast Grants Professional Network.

Since 1995, three agencies in a new community between Orlando and West Palm Beach, Florida, have operated the St. Lucie West Library. Florida Atlantic University (FAU), Indian River Community College (IRCC), and St. Lucie County Library System use a self-managed team to operate the three-way library under two agreements. These agreements, between IRCC and FAU and between IRCC and St. Lucie, are appended to Roshaven and Widman (2001, 77–87). The county contracts with the community college for staffing, collections, and adult services; FAU librarians are the only staff members not supervised by IRCC.

The facility is jointly owned and maintained by the university and the college. Collection development is divided between the two academic agencies. St. Lucie West Library currently uses all three agencies' integrated library systems and directs customers to their own agency's electronic databases.

Harmony Library in Fort Collins, Colorado, opened in 1998 as a joint-use library for Front Range Community College (FRCC)—Larimer Campus and Fort Collins Public Library following the failure of an earlier attempt at combining libraries (Dornseif 2001, 104). FRCC and the City of Fort Collins made an agreement to construct and operate the joint-use library. Although Harmony Library is managed jointly by the campus librarian and the public library branch manager and many of the operations are independent, the materials of both agencies are shelved together. Subscription databases are also shared and available to all customers. The college agreed to convert from Library of Congress to Dewey Decimal classification, to migrate its bibliographic records to the city's integrated library system, and to follow the public library's policies and procedures, with some exceptions. Harmony Library has an advisory committee representing both partners. According to the agreement, FRCC paid 60 percent of construction costs based on space needs, and the city pays 60 percent of operations costs based on anticipated use.

New in 2002, Tippecanoe County/Ivy Tech Library was built by the county on college land. As with other joint-use libraries, this configuration was proposed to save construction costs while giving each agency expanded library space. The college contracts with the county for some services and provides academic staff, maintenance, utilities, and security. The county's databases are shared with the college.

Model Operating Joint-Use Libraries: Library Home Pages Accessed June 2004

Brevard Community College—Cocoa, Florida
   http://web2010.brevard.cc.fl.us/library/content/CocoaLibrary.html
   The Brevard Community College—Cocoa Campus Library is a joint-use facility with the University of Central Florida—Brevard Campus and the Florida Solar Energy Center.

Broward Community College 1—Davie, Florida
   http://ucl.broward.edu/
   The University/College Library (U/CL) located on the Broward Community College—Central Campus is a joint use facility of Broward Community College and Florida Atlantic University.

Broward Community College 2—Fort Lauderdale area, Florida
   http://www.broward.edu/libraries/
   The libraries on Broward Community College's North and South campuses and the Downtown and Pines Centers are operated as a joint facility with the county library system.

Cascadia Community College—Bothell, Washington
  http://www.cascadia.ctc.edu/campusinformation/library.asp
  http://www.bothell.washington.edu/library/
  Cascadia Community College and the University of Washington—Bothell share the Campus Library as a unit of the University of Washington Libraries.

Front Range Community College —Fort Collins, Colorado
  http://www.frontrange.edu/pub_index.cfm?cid = 2134
  Harmony Library is one of two joint-use libraries operated by Front Range Community College and is a partnership with the City of Fort Collins and the FRCC Larimer campus.

Indian River Community College—Ft. Pierce, Florida
  http://www.ircc.cc.fl.us/learnres/libsrv/aboutlib/slw.html
  St. Lucie West Library is operated jointly by Indian River Community College, Florida Atlantic University, and St. Lucie County Library.

Ivy Tech State College—Lafayette, Indiana
  http://www.ivytech.edu/library/lafayette/
  http://www.tcpl.lib.in.us/branch/index.htm
  This joint effort between Ivy Tech State College and the Tippecanoe County Public Library serves as the first branch of the public library and as the main library of Ivy Tech State College—Lafayette.

Model Planned Joint-Use Libraries: Pages Accessed June 2004
Several community college joint-use libraries are still in the planning stages. Among these, the three listed here will be triple-agency rather than dual-agency combinations, which may indicate a growing trend in cooperative ventures:

Diablo Valley College—Pleasant Hill, California
  College library: http://www.dvc.edu/library/index.htm
  Planning is underway for a new campus center and a Contra Costa County-City of San Ramon-Diablo Valley College joint-use library in a new development in the Dougherty Valley.

Los Rios Community College District—Sacramento, California
  Project information: http://www.saclibrary.org/new_projects/project_info_nn.html
  A joint-use library partnership is planned among the Sacramento Public Library, Natomas Unified School District, and Los Rios Community College District.

Metropolitan Community College—Omaha, Nebraska
  College library: http://www.mccneb.edu/library/

The City of Omaha, Metropolitan Community College, and Omaha Public Library have approved an agreement to build a joint-use public and academic library in South Omaha.

SUMMARY

The number of community college libraries that have combined with libraries of other agencies into single joint-use facilities is beginning to grow rather rapidly. From early examples in the late 1970s, when South Australia added public services to community college libraries in remote areas, to the Florida projects of the late 1980s and the 1990s, to plans for triple-agency community libraries in the 2000s, it is evident that community college library managers can expect to see increasing emphasis on joint-use libraries.

Issues involved in planning, implementing, operating, evaluating, and modifying joint-use libraries touch every aspect of library management. In any attempt to develop a joint-use library, the key players must represent managers and end users from every affected agency, and must be prepared to communicate extensively with all stakeholders, to give up ownership in specific areas for the greater good of a joint mission, and to be personally committed to the success of the venture.

Read the literature, visit the sites, and talk with the people on the floor, both staff members and customers. Although the initial catalysts for entering into the process of combining libraries will vary in every case, the end result of joining a community college library with another agency or agencies must be customer satisfaction.

REFERENCES

Amey, L. J., ed. 1987. *Combining Libraries: The Canadian and Australian Experience*. Metuchen: Scarecrow.

Berger, Christopher. 2000. *Public and School Libraries: Issues and Options of Joint Use Facilities and Cooperative Use Agreements*. Sacramento: California State Library.

Bundy, Alan. 2003. "Joint-Use Libraries: The Ultimate Form of Cooperation." In G. McCabe and J. Kennedy, eds. *Planning the Modern Public Library Building*. Westport, CT: Libraries Unlimited. Available: http://www.library.unisa.edu.au/about/papers/jointuse.htm

Dornseif, Karen A. 2001. "Joint-Use Libraries: Balancing Autonomy and Cooperation." In W. Miller and R. Pellen, eds. *Joint-Use Libraries*. New York: Haworth. Co-published simultaneously as *Resource Sharing & Information Networks*, Volume 15, Numbers 1/2 2001.

Florida Community College System. Standing Committee on Joint-Use Libraries. 1996. *Establishing Joint-Use Libraries*. Tallahassee: College Center for Library Automation. Available: http://www.ccla.lib.fl.us/docs/reports/joint_use.pdf

Fugate, Cynthia. 2001. "Common Ground: Making Library Services Work at a Collocated Campus." In W. Miller and R. Pellen, eds. *Joint-Use Libraries.* New York: Haworth. Co-published simultaneously as *Resource Sharing & Information Networks*, Volume 15, Numbers 1/2 2001.

Roshaven, Patricia, and Rudy Widman. 2001. "A Joint University, College and Public Library." In W. Miller and R. Pellen, eds. *Joint-Use Libraries.* New York: Haworth. Co-published simultaneously as *Resource Sharing & Information Networks*, Volume 15, Numbers 1/2 2001.

Woods, Julia A. 2001. "Joint-Use Libraries: The Broward Community College Central Campus Experience." In W. Miller and R. Pellen, eds. *Joint-Use Libraries.* New York: Haworth. Co-published simultaneously as *Resource Sharing & Information Networks*, Volume 15, Numbers 1/2 2001.

SELECTIVE BIBLIOGRAPHY

Dilevko, Juris, and Lisa Gottlieb. 2004. *The Evolution of Library and Museum Partnerships: Historical Antecedents and Contemporary Manifestations.* Westport, CT: Libraries Unlimited.

11 COOPERATIVE MANAGEMENT ISSUES IN A MULTITYPE LIBRARY CONSORTIUM

Sharon D. Jenkins

INTRODUCTION TO THE CONSORTIUM

This chapter is a discussion of managerial issues, technological, and logistical, arising from a cooperative arrangement among a group of libraries in rural southeastern New Mexico, one of whose founding members is a junior college library. This group, the Estacado Library and Information Network (ELIN) currently comprises seven libraries—five public and two academic. All of them are state-funded institutions except one of the public and one of the academic libraries. The libraries share an integrated automation system supported by funds channeled through the private, nonprofit entity, ELIN.

This is not an exhaustive list of all challenges encountered by all consortium members over the lifetime of the entity. Instead, I discuss some of the major challenges that have directly and indirectly affected the operations of the junior college library. However, since New Mexico Junior College (NMJC) hosts the majority of the technological infrastructure on its campus, as well as providing all technical support for the consortium, most events and situations that touch the consortium tend to have an effect on the junior college's library. For this reason, during any discussion of issues it should be assumed that the effect described is from the perspective of the junior college library, unless otherwise stated. A short discussion of the current situation and possible implications for readers of this work follows. I conclude with a selected bibliography of some resources readers might find useful.

ELIN was designed to provide the citizens of Lea County, New Mexico, with a variety of services; full Internet access (at much faster speeds than would be available from their homes for several years), email, 24/7 access to shared information resources, desktop applications software (e.g., word processing, spreadsheets), and a combined automated catalog.

To put the consortium operation into the proper perspective, it's useful to have some information on the background of this entity as well as an understanding of the players involved. In 1995 a proposal to hire an outside consultant to explore options for a consortium in Lea County, New Mexico, was submitted to and subsequently funded by a local foundation. The consultant was selected and began to facilitate the planning process. An additional proposal to construct the network itself was subsequently submitted to and funded by the same foundation. The original consortium consisted of five institutions (see Table 11.1): the Hobbs Public Library (HPL), the Lovington Public Library (LPL), Pannell Library at NMJC, Scarborough Memorial Library at the College of the Southwest (CSW), and the Woolworth Community Library in Jal (WCL). The latter two entities are both privately supported. At the time of its conception (1994–1995), the consortium members collectively had a total materials budget of $351,500, a full-time equivalent (FTE) of 40, a circulation of 377,070, and approximately 260,700 cataloged titles. Whereas HPL, NMJC, and WCL were each using different integrated automated systems, LPL and CSW had not yet automated their collections.

Although LPL was not automated, some records were kept in electronic format, thereby justifying a small automation budget (see Table 11.2). It also maintains a substantial collection of genealogical resources.

As it is both a school library and a community library, WCL is a joint-use facility. Its budget for automation was—and is—provided by its foundation and was not readily available for inclusion here. There is a satellite branch across the street from the main library in Jal. The NMJC Library was (and continues to be) a federal and state depository library and maintains a collection of legal reference material. CSW supports a small branch campus in Carlsbad, New Mexico.

It was determined that ELIN would consist of a centralized consortium built around a complex telecommunications infrastructure called a virtual private net-

Table 11.1

Members and Statistics of the Consortium

	CSW	HPL	LPL	NMJC	WCL	TOTAL
Size of Facilty (1,000 SQ. FT.)	16.1	40	14	24	15.2	109.3
Total Circulation (1,000 PATRONS)	4.68	179.8	107.4	26.23	28.89	377.07
# of Cataloged Titles(1,000 ITEMS)	31.5	79.6	53.7	69.9	26	260.7
Staff (FTE)	3	15	6	12	4	40
Materials Budget (THOUSAND $)	46.2	89.3	40.3	131	44.7	351.5

Table 11.2

Automation Budget for Consortium Members

Name Parent Entity	Student FTE or Population of Town	Automation Budget
City of Lovington	*9,860	$4,400
City of Hobbs	*26,208	$16,200
City of Jal	*2,234	10,000
New Mexico Junior College	1,600**	$18,500
College of the Southwest	564**	$0

*City Population Estimates—U.S. Bureau of the Census 1994.
**FTE just prior to ELIN implementation.

work (VPN) with the NMJC campus providing technical support and physical space for its servers, and CSW would act as its fiscal agent. The VPN is a means by which authorized individuals have secure access to an organization's intranet (internal network) by means of an extranet (external network). The various component pieces of this are discussed subsequently. In addition to the decision to centralize resources, an automated system was selected and the technological resources were acquired and installed. Approximately two years after the system was implemented, two new members were brought into the consortium, the Carlsbad Public Library (located in an adjacent county) and the Tatum Public Library, both of which are publicly funded city libraries in the southeastern corner of the state. Carlsbad had its records in electronic format; Tatum did not. With the addition of these two libraries, the consortium added 13.75 FTE staff members and 58,000 records to its holdings.

With that brief introduction to the ELIN consortium and its members paving the way, we launch into a more specific discussion of the challenges encountered at each stage. Implementing any new system naturally lends itself to many exciting learning opportunities, both for staff and for patrons. Many of these issues would have to be dealt with regardless of geographic location, size of institution, or patron and employee knowledge and experience with technology. Some, however, would seem to be unique to this situation. Specifically, the fact that the local junior college provides all technical support for the consortium rather than the local four-year institution is a novel situation. In addition, the blending of privately and publicly funded entities together to form a new, private nonprofit entity (ELIN) seems to present a unique learning opportunity and model for other library groups.

DISCUSSION OF ISSUES

The issues facing the consortium can be loosely divided into three phases: preimplementation, implementation, and postimplementation. The preimplementation phase lasted generally from the conceptualization, sometime in 1993–1994 through fall 1999. Implementation continued from fall 1999 through the summer 2000 when the consortium began its ongoing postimplementation phase. In addition, there are, for lack of a better term, free-floating issues to contend with that seem to be ongoing.

One free-floating challenge is that the level of expertise in several areas is quite variable from one library to the other; as is the level of computer literacy among the staff and the patron population. At the junior college, staff is encouraged to upgrade skills by being offered variable work schedules to accommodate classes. Online tutorials as well as live face-to-face instruction should all be part of the available continuing education formula at any location considering implementing a new system.

Another free-floating challenge may be due mostly to, borrowing a phrase from the real estate market, "location, location, location." The member libraries are all located within a rural area whose economic base does not include vendors with any experience or knowledge of the needs of the library community. There was difficulty even locating them initially. Some of the work proved to be unreliable and/or inconsistent. There was also the attendant problem of a shortage of competent technologically savvy personnel. To help locate knowledgeable and experienced consultants and vendors, the consortium turned to its regional bibliographic service provider, AMIGOS. The AMIGOS Bibliographic Council submitted a bid to do the groundwork in support of the formation of the consortium. The bid was accepted and an AMIGOS consulting team produced the reports included with the initial grant proposal that subsequently funded the ELIN consortium. These services are available from almost all the regional bibliographic service providers, so any library with similar needs would be advised to check with their local regional provider first before proceeding with a project.

Preimplementation Phase

The preimplementation phase is limited to formation of the consortium, vendor vagaries, contractor support, the VPN configuration, personnel, and training.

This first challenge came about with the forming of the consortium itself. Since public and private institutions had never had occasion or need to share funds, special legislation had to be passed at the state level to allow this partnership to take place. The lesson here would be to obtain the goodwill and interest of local legislators and the wholehearted support of college administration and its board of trustees. They were fundamental in proposing the legislation and lobbying for its passage. All parties involved were continually updated and educated about library affairs, to impart a sense of ownership among them all in the library. Out of this came the new 501(c) (3) entity called ELIN. Governance and management issues were dealt with through a written Operational Agreement with the junior college stating that NMJC would provide the operational home for the consortium and through signed letters of support from all other parent bodies of the library members.

The next issue could be called vendor vagaries. As stated previously, three of the libraries were already fully automated. The problem was that each had a different automated system. Each set of staff adapted to dealing with its own vendors' vagaries, however quirky—they were inured to them. Each library had been used to a DOS-based system, and the new automation system was Windows based. This a multitype library consortium, so finding a vendor that satisfactorily dealt with academic concerns and public library concerns was no mean feat. Again, the members worked closely with the consultant to produce a request for proposal (RFP) that accurately described the situation and consortia needs. Sufficient time should be allocated to deal with receiving the RFP and interviewing the vendors. (As these issues are adequately covered in other works, there is no need for further coverage here.) After a new vendor was chosen, the librarians were tasked with learning how to most effectively communicate with them. The one chosen by ELIN, for example, would not deal directly with the consultant; they would only communicate with the client (consortia members). This was not clear before the start of the process, since it had not occurred to anyone to ask about it.

One other issue that manifested itself during the latter part of the preimplementation phase: as mentioned previously, the lack of competent technologically savvy personnel. A contract was let to do the initial configuration of computers on their delivery at each library. The contract had to eventually be rescinded and the contractor fired so another one could be hired to complete the installation. (The contractor went on vacation during the time the computers were due to be installed.) Perhaps insufficient diligence on the part of both the contractor and the ELIN management council led to a basic misunderstanding about the scope and time frame of the work. An electrical contractor was employed simply to deal with the maze of wires all the new hardware brought with it. We realized something needed to be done after weeks of threading pathways through an ever more narrow aisle cluttered with electrical cords—and the system was not even operational yet! Hiring an electrical contractor to consolidate some, tether others, and eliminate a few, ensured that the finished product would not only be esthetically pleasing but technologically sound, safe, and compliant with all current regulatory statutes.

Next was the problem of the actual network architecture and its VPN. The network uses a thin client/server model; this is a distribution model that allows applications to run fully from the server. The fledgling digital subscriber line (DSL) service was utilized to transmit data over the regular phone lines—not without the judicious use of firewalls, of course. These component parts require continual monitoring and regular upgrading to ensure that the system run as seamlessly and painlessly as possible. Having a thin client server model enabled ELIN to:

- Have one centralized application server
- Offer remote access to local network resources
- Have dial-up access to local network as a backup
- Let local organizations dial directly with no Internet service provider (ISP) costs
- Allowed for application delivery over low bandwidth lines

Since the consortium has centralized technical support, a way to monitor these systems from the central site (currently at NMJC) was devised. Remote system administration tools were acquired. The central tech support personnel can monitor any PC or server and its LAN from the NMJC campus.

Other issues revolved around personnel. Over the lifetime of the preimplementation phase, staff at all the libraries fluctuated. The total library staff at NMJC went from 12 to a low of 8. There was a change in the NMJC director midway through preimplementation. Other member libraries experienced similar personnel fluctuations. Fortunately, the momentum of the project was not lost, nor was continuity jeopardized. This was accomplished through careful record-keeping of each interaction with the automation vendor and backup documentation by the consortium consultant. Besides keeping all other staff generally informed about the progress of the implementation project, each library had involved at least one other staff member in addition to the director in the entire process.

Finally, training was provided prior to going live with the new system. The problem was that the gap between staff training on the system and staff actually working with the system was too large; it was more than three months before the system went live. There was no provision for practicing new skills (while unlearning the old system) during the interim. Training was held in November, and the go-live date was to have been two to three weeks later. This hiatus stretched into three months. Having a practice system with dummy data to use would have been most helpful and could probably have been negotiated as part of the contract.

Implementation Phase

The hardware having been set up and configured, software installed, the system parameters defined, and the staff trained, the next phase began, Implementation. During the implementation phase the integrated library system was brought online at all five libraries and a closer relationship with one of the technology consultants evolved. Issues during this phase include new details, inoperable or varying features, ISP challenges, consortium policies, and patron expectations.

The first of these issues involved making a concerted effort to not become overwhelmed by all the new details that go along with bringing up a new system. Formal training had taken place more than three months previously, and much of that new information had been forgotten. Complicating matters at the junior college library was the fact that, for the first time, the rest of the campus was operating from an entirely separate network. Email communications were continually being missed and/or misdirected—a problem that has not entirely gone away, it must be noted. Due to the variation in how the other ELIN libraries are connected to each other and the network and how the junior college library is connected, problems would often occur in the system that would not affect Pannell Library—and vice versa. The junior college library building also contains an open computer lab for students to use to prepare class assignments that is entirely separate from the computers used to access consortium resources. The decision was made not to load software other than the browser on any of the machines on the ELIN network. This is a marked difference in how all the other libraries have chosen to configure their machines. The ELIN-networked PCs are often needed to teach library skills classes or give other, less formal instruction. These PCs are kept for instructional and research purposes only. We have found that though there was initial grumbling about this, it has become widely accepted by students and faculty. The library network is Web accessible from all other computers on campus with Internet access though so there is not really a hindrance to use.

The most error-prone part of the system was the ability to offer remote access to users 24/7. Again, this continues to be an ongoing challenge. Remote access was inconsistent or nonexistent for many users throughout the service area. If access was possible, then authentication and authorization problems occurred. Neither we nor the patrons were ever sure what was going to be available and when. We devised a standard explanation and troubleshooting regimen so that whichever staff member was on duty when problems occurred was able to provide some support for the patron, at least until more technologically knowledgeable help could be obtained.

The second part of this notion of inoperable or inconsistently operable features centers on the ISP for the consortium. LeaCo is the Lea County Electrical Cooperative. The main complaint was their seeming inability to notify either the consortium members or the campus computer personnel when they had problems and/or planned some system maintenance task. The network would inexplicably become inoperable, then just as inexplicably, come back on line. Inconsistent support from LeaCo was also a perennial problem, both for the libraries and for the computer services division at the college. These were discussed in several meetings over the past five years but only recently were they truly addressed in a useful way. At this point the consortium board of trustees became involved. Meetings with the ISP (LeaCo) were held and attended by representatives from the ELIN management council, the consortium board, and NMJC computing services. A procedure for notifying consortium members was outlined and implemented. Communication continues to be the best insurance against many problems that arise.

The next issue members still find themselves dealing with is a difference in the idea of what constitutes service to patrons. This service is reflected in the kinds of policies each library creates and maintains. We have found that generally the junior college library is less restrictive in its application of policy than either the other academic library or the public libraries. The NMJC library does not need to collect the same level of personal information on each patron as the public library would when a patron card is issued. Our patrons are, for the most part, students or college employees, and we already have access to all of their personal information. It should be noted that although the population is similar throughout the county, patrons come to each library for different purposes. This means that despite the ideological differences about provision of service, delivery of those services to patrons has been remarkably smooth systemwide. The problems that have arisen have mainly been traced back to insufficient communication.

Finally, we come to patron and staff expectations. At the junior college, the old automated system was antiquated, convoluted, and difficult to use. Getting reports from it necessitated scheduling time with computer services personnel. With the acquisition of the new system, staff could prepare their own reports whenever they needed them. The new system was eagerly awaited and enthusiastically embraced at NMJC. The level of technical expertise among patrons at the time of implementation was fairly rudimentary, leading to low usage and a good deal of frustration on the part of students. A lot was expected of the new automated system by all parties and in the main, these expectations were met. The key to successfully meeting staff and patron expectations was a continual emphasis on promoting and developing realistic goals. Repetition of what the system could and could not do led to a tempering of unrealistic goals and aided eventual successful adoption with what was delivered. The gap between what was expected and what was actually delivered turned out to be very small, resulting in overall satisfaction.

Postimplementation Phase

During our postimplementation phase two events occurred that would shape the future direction of the consortium. First, and most significant, has been the introduction of two more libraries into the consortium. The second event has been the transition from the consortium being grant supported to complete financial self-sufficiency. Other issues that need to be addressed during the current phase are consortiumwide policies and determining a future direction for the consortium.

At the end of the implementation phase an invitation was made to libraries in communities in the surrounding area to join the consortium. Ultimately, two chose to do so. A new grant proposal was submitted to the original foundation to expand the consortium. This proposal was subsequently funded, and both libraries began the transition from autonomy to a consortium arrangement with ELIN. Tatum is the northernmost community in Lea County and had a population of 683 souls immediately prior to the start of the project. Carlsbad is the largest city in neighboring Eddy County and had a population of 25,625 according to Census 2000 data. The Tatum Public Library (TPL) was not automated, and we determined that since its collection was limited to about 2,500 titles, it was feasible for the other consortium members to perform the retro-conversion in-house rather than outsource it, saving us money and familiarizing the rest of the group with this library, its staff, and holdings. The coordination of all technical services groups was needed. Staff performed these operations during normal work hours, while still accomplishing their regular duties.

Having more experienced staff, NMJC and HPL performed the initial steps of locating records in Online Computer Library Center (OCLC) to import into the system. The other libraries checked records after downloads and performed maintenance on them. The original estimate about the number of items in the TPL collection turned out to be less than half of what was finally processed by the consortium staff. Had this been an outsourced, contract situation, execution of this task might have been prohibitively expensive. Training of the new staff was done by both the automation vendor and the local library staff.

The Carlsbad Public Library (CPL) already had an integrated library automation system and a collection of more than 55,000 items, so the task was simply to prepare these items for inclusion in the consortium's database. Figure 11.1 shows graphically the change in consortium holdings after these two libraries were brought in during fiscal year 2001–2002.

The other major development has been the transition to full financial independence. The parent institutions made definite commitments to the ongoing support of the consortium and have indeed fulfilled those commitments. The ELIN management council, made up of the library directors and the director of computer services at NMJC dedicate several meetings each spring to crafting a consortium budget for the upcoming fiscal year. Each library is then assessed a certain portion

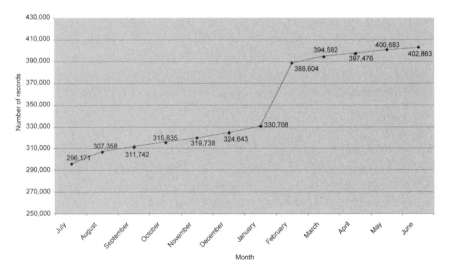

Figure 11.1 Items in Catalog, Fiscal Year 2001–2002

of that budget based on number of ports in use at the library. The only change has been that now NMJC acts as both the fiscal agent for the consortium and its operational home. This means that the library has a separate operational budget dedicated to consortium support. The management of this budget was transferred to computer support services in the past two years. However, all transactions and requests for payment—except those for computing support salary and incidental compensation for their personnel—are routed through the library for approval.

One other issue that promises to be problematic is documentation of policies and procedures or, rather, the lack thereof. Personnel change; in fact, five of the seven libraries have different directors than they began with almost 10 years ago. Currently there has been enough continuity in staff that the collective memory of the organization remains relatively intact. Staff members remember, more or less, how this or that procedure was done, or a poll of opinions is done to gather memories about what decision was made and why on a given situation. However, the further away from initial implementation of the interlibrary system the consortium gets, the less reliable this method will become. A record of system operations has been produced monthly by the junior college library and a set of ELIN management council minutes is produced by the current chair of that group. A separate technical services committee was formed to better address specialized concerns. This group meets each quarter and also maintains a set of minutes. Unfortunately, unwritten rules abound and seem to proliferate at a scandalous rate. With more than 450, 000 records to maintain and close to 60 staff members using the same interlibrary system, the consortium requires consistency in its operations and collection management. This final graphic (see Figure 11.2) shows the current level of collection growth during the past fiscal year, 2003–2004.

The junior college library is spearheading a move to document other decisions in a formal consortium policy manual that would include all decisions made collectively that affect consortium operations. In addition, copies of the monthly

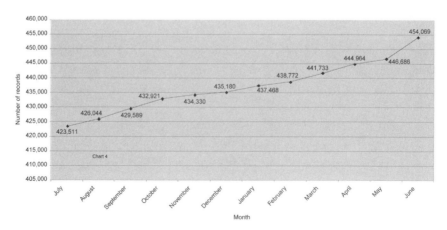

Figure 11.2 Items in Catalog, Fiscal Year 2003–2004

operations reports have been catalogued and included in the circulating collection at the junior college. Progress has been slow but acknowledgment of the problem and a willingness to address it is universal in the group. Maintaining this progress, however slow, is the task of the NMJC library group.

A final task during the postimplementation phase has been determining a future direction for the consortium. To that end, the ELIN board of directors, consisting of the chief executive officers of the parent bodies for each library, called several special planning meetings. These meetings produced inventories of what does and does not work for the consortium as well as its strengths, weaknesses, opportunities, and threats. It was determined that one of the opportunities involved growth through the addition of new libraries. The management council was tasked with making the initial approaches about membership to at least two other area libraries. The names of several possibilities were discussed and inquiries were made. Coincidently, one of the prospective institutions made contact with the junior college library expressing an interest in membership. The consortium was asked to provide estimates of possible costs to the new library for becoming part of the consortium. This would again involve a first-time automation project for the members. The group's vast prior experience in this area will prove to be a definite plus should this library decide to join ELIN. This projected cost estimate was provided by the NMJC library, and we are waiting for a decision from the parent institution of that library.

A Promising Future

This chapter is a discussion of some of the issues a junior college library in a multitype library consortium has been confronted with over the past several years. I present the life cycle of the interlibrary system, along with the details of unique and cost-effective network architecture. The hope is that staffs in junior college libraries will understand that they may inherit, assume, or be given leadership roles within organizations that normally would not be available. They need to prepare themselves in anticipation of these opportunities, however, through continuing education opportunities, by attending workshops at professional organizations, and by resisting the temptation to give up decision-making responsibilities to consultants and contractors or even its own computer support group. The staff members at the NMJC library were receptive to assuming these additional tasks, and they were prepared to undertake them, both technologically and attitudinally. The coincidence of proximity to the operations center home and the enthusiastic support of its administration put the NMJC library staff in an ideal position to grow with the consortium—and it has.

The ELIN consortium continues to thrive in southeastern New Mexico. Its management group meets regularly and is engaged in ongoing discussions about additional services to be offered by the consortium. The junior college library has taken advantage of recent financial windfalls (passage of general obligation bonds at the state level) to purchase access to several new databases that are not available through the consortium. Each library maintains its own identity and collection development strategies while maintaining its position in the consortium.

The Selected Bibliography that follows is a list of reference materials I found useful in preparation of this work.

SELECTED BIBLIOGRAPHY

Bosseau, Don L., Susan K. Martin, and Arnold Hirshon. 1999. "Visions: Libraries, Consortia, and Change Management," *The Journal of Academic Librarianship*, 25 (2), 124–26.

Evans, Edward G. 2002. "Management Issues of Co-operative Ventures and Consortia in the USA, Part 1," *Library Management*, 23 (4/5), 213–26.

———. 2002. "Management Issues of Consortia, Part 2," *Library Management*, 23 (6/7), 275–86.

Nfila, Reason Baathuli, and Darko-Ampem, Kwasi. 2002. "Developments in Academic Library Consortia from the 1960's through to 2000: A Review of the Literature," *Library Management*, 23 (4/5), 203–12.

Shoaf, Eric. 1999. "The Effects of Consortia Membership on Library Planning and Budgeting," *Library Administration & Management* 13 (4), 196–201.

12 ALPHABET SOUP: WHAT DOES IT SPELL?

Mary M. Carr

INTRODUCTION

Every profession has its own language punctuated with abbreviations and initialisms. Librarians are no exception. This chapter provides an overview of the many and varied library and library-related organizations and associations, each with its own set of initials, which together form an alphabet soup. Before addressing the specific groups, it is beneficial to discuss the reasons to learn about the associations behind the initials. Only then is it possible to decide which organizations to join and in which to be active. By doing so, you will discover the myriad of opportunities these affiliations provide.

The landscape of libraries, their form and shape, as it were, continues to change, oftentimes at a dizzying rate. Change seems to be one of the few constants. Yet, for all the changes that are occurring and will occur, at the very core a library's central mission remains the same. Librarians everywhere in the United States and the world remain committed to the organization and dissemination of information. However, the form and shape of information and thus of libraries continues to change. Some changes are prompted by the many and varied ways information is stored and disseminated; other changes are a direct result of societal and technological shifts. How librarians access the information, from what location, and in which format may change. Yet librarians are ready and willing to help people find the right information for the right person just at the right time. Finding new and appropriate ways to navigate information and solve people's information needs is the way for libraries to flourish.

Living with constant change is both exhilarating and exhausting. If a librarian is working alone, especially if one is isolated or develops solutions and standards based only on one's institution's, city's, or region's data, the librarian will find him- or herself in a lonely place. And, more to the point, the solutions developed will not be designed with the experience and wisdom of others who have had, or are having, similar needs for new solutions. That is where associations and organizations come into play. Whether the problem is educational, technological, or sociological, associations provide a network of professionals who are all working on similar issues in similar time frames. The associations provide a ready group of advocates, whether the issue is the first amendment, professional stature, or resource allocation.

The jargon, acronyms, and initialisms of association-speak are confusing, and the overlapping and expansive missions of library-related associations daunting. However, the rewards of joining, contributing, networking, and advocating more than make up for the effort it takes to learn about the organizations and join those that meet your professional needs.

PROFESSIONAL ASSOCIATIONS—NOTHING NEW UNDER THE SUN

Associations of like professionals date back to the guilds that grew up in Europe's Middle Ages. Professionals, then and now, have a need to find others who live and breathe in the same milieu. The guilds came together to further the interests of the profession. Modern associations and organizations do much the same work.

Associations provide professionals working in specific career fields with resources for career development and employment, as well as opportunities for networking and advocacy. These organizations typically provide students about to enter the field with career information, graduate school information, and possibly employment listings for entry-level positions. Professionals who are already established in the field can find continuing education, networking with colleagues, job placement assistance, support for issues and concerns that arise in the workplace, advocacy for issues that affect the profession, and idea exchanges.

Guilds regulated standards of quality in merchandise made and sold by their members, and penalties were invoked for inferior merchandise. Today, professional library associations do much the same for our knowledge-based "industry." The associations write standards, position papers, and advocacy materials. These standards and stances are available to all professionals to help shape the way library service is delivered to the students, faculty, staff, and communities we serve.

The guilds were also a place where informal and formal networking took place. So too it is with library associations. Whether professionals attend conferences, read the associations' publications, or receive email updates, they have the chance to find out what is happening in other libraries, with library service providers, with the legislature as it pertains to libraries and library services, and help students and new professionals as they enter the field. The association also provides an opportunity for a call to arms when there is a threat to the core values of the association. There are other parallels with guilds of old, but suffice it to say that guilds, like professional organizations, looked out for the welfare and continued existence of the profession and the professionals in the field.

By the close of the twentieth century, the American Library Association (ALA) estimated that there are more than 117,000 libraries of all types were in the United States (*ALA Library Fact Sheet 1*). The ALA proudly claims more than 64,000 members nationwide. These institutions and the librarians that work therein have the opportunity to cooperate and collaborate for the good of libraries and people they serve.

KEY ISSUES FACING THE PROFESSION TODAY

Dr. Bill Nelson, Library Director at Augusta State University, who chairs the American Library Association ACRL Standards Task Force, identified seven key issues facing today's profession in an interview by Scott Cohen (2003):

1. *Graying of the Profession and Recruitment*—The large number of librarians nearing retirement must be replaced with new recruits to the profession. This must be a top priority for all librarians and library organizations.
2. *Staff Training*—Professional development for librarians and staff development for paraprofessionals is a continuing need in order to meet the challenges of technology and to train new recruits.
3. *Low Salaries*—Library salaries are generally low for the degrees, training, and expertise required. This makes recruitment even more difficult.
4. *Library Funding*—Adequate library funding is a challenge in good economic times and a critical problem when institutional budgets are lean.
5. *Collection Development*—Libraries are faced with escalating costs for electronic resources while simultaneously facing the necessity to maintain print collections.
6. *Advocacy*—There is a continuing need to advocate for the library within the institution. Librarians must develop more expertise in outreach. Leading and/or actively participating in a campus information literacy initiative is one way librarians can serve and influence the institution while being an advocate for libraries.
7. *Planning and Assessment*—Higher education institutions are expected to be accountable—to parents, to funding bodies, and to regulatory and accrediting bodies. The institution and the library must continually plan, assess outcomes, and produce a revised plan based on the assessment. Budget allocations should be based on planning priorities. Ideally, this would produce continuous improvement, which will please all constituents.

All types of higher education libraries are addressing these seven areas of concern. Library professionals should choose from these and other issues, and begin to put their time and talent toward formulating solutions to further the success of libraries and those they serve. To summarize, Peggy Sullivan, librarian extraordinaire and former executive director of the American Library Association, once said the reason to join and participate in associations is "divine discontent." It is a blessing that some in the library profession dream that there are issues and causes within our profession that could be better but for our participation and contributions. The divine discontent is the power to make a difference.

ACADEMIC EXPECTATIONS AND CONTRIBUTIONS

A professional librarian's work is marked by his or her contributions beyond the specifics of a particular job description or environment. As a librarian's career begins to build from its early stages, the librarian circle of influence expands to different parts of the home institution, where committee work or other tasks need to be accomplished, and then out into the professional world on local, regional, national, and international levels. The contributions can be made in time, money, energy, and attention.

Since opportunities to contribute and organizations needing support far outnumber the hours in a day or days in a week, it is the professionals' responsibility to be intentional about their specific activities and contributions. It is important to plan in advance to nurture your professional momentum, build deliberately, and consider the strategic impact of specific activities. What are your professional priorities? What are your talents? Careful consideration will ensure that you can demonstrate professional commitment in areas of interest. Professionals can contribute by writing, speaking, teaching, mentoring, facilitating, creating, and just plain working hard. You should consider the strategic impact of specific activities and consider if this is where you wish to focus your efforts.

SERVANT LEADERSHIP

Leadership of all sorts is needed within associations and within professions. Librarianship is certainly no exception. Considering the work that needs to be done, servant leadership best suits association work and typifies the purpose for professional organizations.. This style of leadership was first identified by Robert K. Greenleaf (1970). He defined servant-leadership as a practical philosophy that supports people who choose to serve first and then lead as a way of expanding service to individuals and institutions. Servant-leaders may or may not hold formal leadership positions. Servant-leadership encourages collaboration, trust, foresight, listening, and the ethical use of power and empowerment. As Greenleaf states:

> The servant-leader is servant first.... . It begins with the natural feeling that
> one wants to serve, to serve first. Then conscious choice brings one to aspire to
> lead. He or she is sharply different from the person who is leader first, perhaps

because of the need to assuage an unusual power drive or to acquire material possessions. For such it will be a later choice to serve—after leadership is established. The leader-first and the servant-first are two extreme types. Between them there are shadings and blends that are part of the infinite variety of human nature.

The difference manifests itself in the care taken by the servant-first to make sure that other people's highest priority needs are being served. The best test, and difficult to administer, is: do those served grow as persons; do they, while being served, become healthier, wiser, freer, more autonomous, more likely themselves to become servants? And, what is the effect on the least privileged in society; will they benefit, or, at least, will they not be further deprived? (Greenleaf 1973, 7)

Max De Pree furthered this concept. In his book *Leadership Is an Art* (1990, 11), De Pree states: "The first responsibility of a leader is to define reality. The last is to say thank you. In between the two, the leader must become a servant and a debtor. That sums up the progress of an artful leader." Using Greenleaf's and De Pree's approach, you will put the needs of others, whom you serve and in the profession, ahead of your own, and what you find, is by doing so, your needs as a professional will also be served.

LEARNING RESOURCE CENTERS: A PERFECTLY MARVELOUS COMMUNITY COLLEGE IDEA

Of the 130,000 libraries (including some very small not counted by ALA) in the United States, there are approximately 1,293 libraries in "less than four-year" settings (Fourie and Dowell 2002, 41). These libraries employ 1,040 active ALA members. Although libraries are more similar than different, there is something to be said for close cooperation and collaboration with libraries that operate in the same setting. This is particularly true of community college librarians, whose environment varies somewhat from other academic librarians. Most community college librarians work within learning resources centers. Besides libraries, the centers often include media services, instructional technology, learning centers, interactive classrooms, and perhaps a myriad of other services. The concept of a learning resources center, which offered integrated services in support of teaching and learning, originated in the community college movement and has lasted in the community college environment.

Therefore, it is important to get to know and work with colleagues in community colleges whose working environments are similar. There are several groups that provide that opportunity. One is the National Council for Learning Resources (NCLR), an affiliate council of the American Association of Community Colleges (AACC). The other is the Community and Junior College Library Section (CJCLS) of the ALA's Association of College and Research Libraries.

NATIONAL COUNCIL FOR LEARNING RESOURCES

http://ol.scc.spokane.edu/nclr

The AACC mission is simple. The AACC (www.aacc.nche.edu), the voice of community colleges, states that its mission is building a nation of leaders by advancing America's community colleges. It looks to all college functions to assist in accomplishing that mission. Thus, over the years, the AACC adopted various position statements pertaining to many functional areas of the college, each emphasizing the ways in which that function or service could improve the community colleges' educational offerings. However, no AACC position statement mentioned, let alone stressed, the centrality of library services to teaching and learning. In the 1990s, members of the NCLR, as an affiliate council, decided it was time to change that, to come forward with a statement about the contribution that libraries and learning resources programs make to teaching and learning. It took several years, and the contributions of many in the NCLR, to develop a statement that was finally presented to the AACC Board. The NCLR membership advocated their position strongly and effectively. As a result, on November 8, 2002, the AACC Position Statement on Library and Learning Resource Center Programs was adopted.

AACC Position Statement on Library and Learning Resource Center Programs

Community colleges are comprehensive institutions that provide a full array of educational programs. Library programs, as part of that full array, are indispensable to the teaching/learning mission of the community college. In today's world, libraries are not just a place, because many library resources and services are online and accessible from anywhere. Community colleges continue to need libraries as a physical space, as long as students need assistance to conquer the digital or information divide and there is a need to house and provide access to materials not available electronically. Whether the term used is Library, Learning Resource Center, or Instructional Resource Center, it describes a set of programs and services that provide an organized universe of knowledge to users. Library programs have long served a vital role in the mission of the community college. In fact, the concept of the learning resource center—one of creatively merging access to traditional library services with media and instructional support—had its genesis in the community college. From the beginning, library programs have promoted dynamic and efficient access to knowledge for all learners. Indeed, the management of these varied learning resources using limited budgets, consortial arrangements, and internal and external partnerships has added complexity, technical sophistication, and greater economic responsibility to librarians who staff these centers.

The term librarian describes a professional member of the academic community with, at a minimum, an appropriate master's degree in the disciplines of library science and information management. Librarianship is uniquely structured and systematized by its professional members to serve the constantly changing knowledge management needs of students, faculty, and the local community. The library profession has long shown exceptional and immediate responsiveness to managing access to widely diverse knowledge resources. Today more than ever, librarians are educators and teachers of information literacy for faculty and students, as well as the local and worldwide community. A growing percentage of information resources are digital (online indexes, full-text databases, websites, e-books and e-journals). Yet this new format will not replace the large number of useful knowledge resources that will continue to be in print (e.g. books, newspapers, periodicals and other documents), or to be available in magnetic and optical media (e.g. tapes, CDs, DVDs). In collaboration and partnership with other faculty, librarians teach members of the community the information literacy skills necessary to access and to evaluate critically the myriad of available resources.

Learning resources programs that provide information literacy skills are essential to the development of the independent lifelong learner. Tenets of information literacy include the ability to:

- Determine the nature and extent of information needed
- Access and use needed information effectively and efficiently
- Evaluate information and its sources critically, and incorporate selected information into one's knowledge base and value system
- Use information effectively to accomplish a specific purpose
- Understand many of the economic, legal, and social issues surrounding the use of information.

Libraries and librarians help to establish the foundation on which all lifelong learners can build. An information-literate person has the ability to be a knowledgeable, active participant in the workforce, the community and the democratic society in which we live.

For these reasons, the Board reaffirms the vital role of library and learning resource center programs and librarians to formal education, information literacy and to lifelong learning as a core value.

Approved by the AACC Board of Directors November 8, 2002

COMMUNITY AND JUNIOR COLLEGE LIBRARIES SECTION, AMERICAN LIBRARY ASSOCIATION

http://www.ala.org/ala/acrl/aboutacrl/acrlsections/commjr/cjcls1.htm

The purpose of American Library Association's Community and Junior College Libraries Section (CJCLS) of the Association of College and Research Libraries (ACRL) is to contribute to library service and librarianship through those activities that relate to libraries and learning resources centers and services and that support the educational programs in community and junior colleges and equivalent institutions.

At the time of this writing, I am privileged to be completing a term as chair of the NCLR and am chair-elect of CJCLS. By my commitment of time and energy, I have made a statement that these two associations are important to the future of community college learning resources programs. During my tenure as chair, the AACC adopted the statement on the importance of libraries and learning resources programs, and at the time of this writing, the NCLR and the Information Technology Council of AACC is preparing a similar statement on the importance of library and student support services for remote learning.

LOCAL ASSOCIATIONS: AN EXAMPLE FROM THE INLAND NORTHWEST

Inland Northwest Council of Libraries (INCOL)

http://www.library.ewu.edu/incol/

INCOL's mission is to engage in cooperative activities, which enable member institutions [from the Inland Northwest] to improve library services to their constituencies. INCOL membership includes libraries from Washington and Idaho. INCOL is incorporated as a nonprofit agency in the State of Washington. It has articles of incorporation, bylaws and a treasury. (I use INCOL as an example because I've participated in INCOL and its activities for more than 20 years.) Other such organizations exist in other areas of the country.

STATE AND REGIONAL ASSOCIATIONS

I have been president of two state associations, the Washington Library Association and the Idaho Library Association. While president of the Washington Library Association, I was working in Idaho. As it turned out, by the time I rose to president of the Idaho Library Association, I was working in Washington. I probably hold a record of sorts for the only person to be president of two library associations, neither time while working in that state. Nonetheless, my experience with state associations is considerable, and this, along with local opportunities, is a place to start contributing. It's been my experience you only need to lift your hand or raise your voice, asking for volunteer opportunities. The members of the associations are more than happy to share the workload, which is generally greater than the available volunteer hours.

What follows is a list of the state and regional associations and their URLs, along with their mission and goals. Contact your state association if you are not already a member. Ask how to join and what you can do. If you are already a member, find a niche, a place where you can learn and contribute.

Alabama Library Association

http://allanet.org/

The Alabama Library Association (ALLA) is a nonprofit corporation formed to encourage and promote the welfare of libraries and professional interests of librarians in the State of Alabama.

Library Association of Alberta

http://www.laa.ab.ca/

The Library Association of Alberta strengthens the library community in Alberta by effectively providing responsive member services, advocating for libraries and cooperating with partners.

Alberta Association of Library Technicians

http://www.aalt.org/

Alberta Association of Library Technicians (AALT) is an organization dedicated to fostering and enhancing the professional image of Library Technicians. AALT was formed in 1974 to help promote a wider understanding and acceptance of the Library Technician's status in Alberta and to assist in the implementation of recognized provincial education standards.

Alaska Library Association

http://www.akla.org

AKLA is a nonprofit professional organization for the employees, volunteers and advocates at academic, public, school and special libraries of all sizes in Alaska, and library products and services vendors.

The goal of the organization is to promote vibrant libraries which deliver outstanding services to their users, and to provide professional development opportunities.

Arizona Library Association

http://www.azla.org

The mission of the Arizona Library Association shall be to promote library service and librarianship in libraries of all types in the state Arizona.

Arkansas Library Association

http://www.arlib.org

The Arkansas Library Association's mission is to further the professional development of all library staff members; to foster communication and cooperation among librarians, trustees and friends of libraries; to increase the visibility of libraries among the general public and funding agencies; to serve as an advocate for librarians and libraries.

California Library Association

http://www.cla-net.org/

The California Library Association provides leadership for the development, promotion and improvement of library services, librarianship and the library community.

Colorado Association of Libraries

http://cal-webs.org/

The purposes of the Association are to improve library services to the people of Colorado, to foster professional development of its members, and to encourage the effective utilization of information literacy in all libraries.

Connecticut Library Association

http://www.lib.uconn.edu/cla

Connecticut's professional organization of over 1,000 librarians, library staff, friends, and trustees working together:

- To improve library service to Connecticut
- To advance the interests of librarians, library staff, and librarianship
- To increase public awareness of libraries and library services

Delaware Library Association

http://www.dla.lib.de.us/

The goal of the Delaware Library Association is to promote the profession of librarianship and provide library information and media services to the people of Delaware by developing a unified library association.

Florida Library Association

http://www.flalib.org/

The Florida Library Association (FLA) develops programs and undertakes activities to earn it a leadership position for all areas of librarianship. To do this, the Association works with other professional organizations and professions that are relevant to librarianship; provides increasing opportunities for librarians and support staff in Florida to advance their skills so that they can maintain their effectiveness in the new information age; works closely with the information industry, facilitating productive links with the library community; and continues its role as legislative advocate for excellence in all types of library service within the state of Florida and beyond.

Foothills Library Association

http://www.fla.org/

The objective of the FLA is to bring together individuals within the Calgary [Alberta] library community to share and promote the concerns of the library and information professions.

Georgia Library Association

http://wwwlib.gsu.edu/gla/

The Georgia Library Association is dedicated to:

- Developing an understanding of the place that libraries should take in advancing the educational, cultural, and economic life of the state
- Promoting the expansion and improvement of library service
- Fostering activities towards these ends.

Hawaii Library Association

http://www2.hawaii.edu/hla/

The Mission of the Hawaii Library Association is to promote library service and librarianship in Hawaii in cooperation and affiliation with the American Library Association and other groups having allied objectives.

Idaho Library Association

http://www.idaholibraries.org/

The purpose of this Association shall be to advance the common library interest; to promote the organization and development of better library service in the State of Idaho; and to foster a friendly relationship among all those interested in library service.

Illinois Library Association

http://www.ila.org/

The Illinois Library Association shall be a not-for-profit educational organization, the purpose of which shall be to improve and develop library service and librarianship throughout the state of Illinois.

Indiana Library Federation

http://www.ilfonline.org/

The Federation is devoted to fostering the professional growth of its members and the promotion of all libraries in Indiana. It accomplishes its goals through statewide continuing education, public awareness, and library advocacy.

Iowa Library Association

http://www.iren.net/acrl/

The Iowa Library Association promotes the development of the libraries that all Iowans depend on for information and life-long learning. The Association provides leadership, education, and support to enable its members to meet the challenges of providing quality library services to all Iowans.

Kansas Library Association

http://skyways.lib.ks.us/kansas/KLA/

The Kansas Library Association is a non-profit, educational organization with 501-C(4) tax exempt IRS classification. The K.L.A. operates to promote library and information service to the state of Kansas, librarianship, and cooperation among all types of libraries and organizations concerned with library and information service.

Kentucky Library Association

http://www.kylibasn.org/

The Mission of the Kentucky Library Association (KLA) is to provide leadership for the development, promotion and improvement of library and information services and the profession of librarianship in order to enhance and ensure access to information for all.

Louisiana Library Association

http://www.llaonline.org/

This corporation is organized and it shall be operated exclusively to promote the library interests of the State of Louisiana, including keeping members of the profession informed of developments in the library field, promoting interest in books about Louisiana and encouraging their production, recruiting desirable people to the library profession, and the encouragement and promotion of scholarship in the field of library science.

Maine Library Association

http://mainelibraries.org/

The object of this Association is to promote and enhance the value of libraries and librarianship, to foster cooperation among those who work in and for libraries, and to provide leadership in ensuring that the global information network is accessible to all citizens via their libraries. The Council may adopt and publicize positions on issues and legislation affecting libraries.

Maryland Library Association

http://www.mdlib.org/

Maryland Library Association provides leadership for those who are committed to libraries by providing opportunities for professional development and communication and by advocating principles and issues related to librarianship and library service. MLA was founded in 1923 to promote library service in the state. Among members are library staff and trustees, library school students, libraries, and friends of libraries representing the full spectrum of librarianship in Maryland.

Massachusetts Library Association

http://www.masslib.org/

The Massachusetts Library Association advocates for libraries, librarians, and library staff, defends intellectual freedom and provides a forum for leadership, communication, professional development and networking to keep libraries vital.

Michigan Library Association

http://www.mla.lib.mi.us/

The Michigan Library Association is a professional organization dedicated to the support of its members, to the advancement of librarianship, and to the promotion of quality library service for citizens of all ages of the State of Michigan.

Minnesota Library Association

http://mnlibraryassociation.org/

The Minnesota Library Association (MLA) is a statewide organization representing all libraries and library workers. Its members strive to improve library services and resources.

Mississippi Library Association

http://www.misslib.org/

The mission of the Mississippi Library Association is to provide professional leadership for the development, promotion, and improvement of library and information services and the profession of librarianship in order to enhance learning and ensure access to information for all.

Missouri Library Association

http://www.molib.org/

The Missouri Library Association is a non-profit, educational organization operating to promote library service, the profession of librarianship, and cooperation among all types of libraries and organizations concerned with library service in the State of Missouri. Founded in 1900, MLA is proudly beginning a second century of service.

Montana Library Association

http://www.mtlib.org/

The mission of the Montana Library Association is to develop, promote, and improve library and information services and the profession of librarianship in order to enhance learning and ensure access to information for all.

Mountain Plains Library Association

http://www.usd.edu/mpla

The mission of the Mountain Plains Library Association is to further the development of librarians, library employees, and trustees and to promote quality library service in the states of the Mountain Plains Region, i.e., Arizona, Colorado, Kansas, Montana, Nebraska, Nevada, New Mexico, North Dakota, Oklahoma, South Dakota, Utah and Wyoming.

Nebraska Library Association

http://www.nol.org/home/NLA/

The Nebraska Library Association supports and promotes all libraries, library media centers, and library services in the state. Its foremost concerns are the professional development of its members, library advocacy, and open access to information for all citizens.

Nevada Library Association

http://www.nevadalibraries.org/

The purpose of NLA shall be to promote library service of the highest quality for all present and potential users of libraries in Nevada. NLA is organized and operated for educational and literary purposes, no part of the net earnings of which may be used to benefit any private individual or member.

New England Library Association

http://www.nelib.org/

The mission of the New England Library Association is to promote excellence in library services to the people of New England and to advance the leadership role of its members in developing and ensuring that excellence.

New Hampshire Library Association

http://www.state.nh.us/nhla/

It shall be the objective of the Association to promote good library service from all types of libraries to all people of the State and to cooperate with other groups of similar interest.

New Jersey Library Association

http://www.njla.org/

[The NJLA:]

1. advocates for the advancement of library services for the residents of New Jersey,
2. provides continuing education & networking opportunities for librarians,
3. supports the principles of intellectual freedom &
4. promotes access to library materials for all.

New Mexico Library Association

http://www.nmla.org

[The New Mexico Library Association goals:]

- Provide leadership to initiate, maintain, and enhance library legislation and act on political issues affecting library interests
- Foster an awareness of and support the activities of the New Mexico Library Foundation
- Provide and support educational opportunities for library personnel
- Provide and communicate the role and value of libraries and librarians
- Plan, direct, and evaluate the growth and effectiveness of the organization
- Support and assist planning efforts for networking in New Mexico

New York Library Association

http://www.nyla.org/

The mission of the New York Library Association (NYLA) is to lead in the development, promotion and improvement of library and information services and the profession of librarianship in order to enhance learning, quality of life, and equal opportunity for all New Yorkers.

North Carolina Library Association

http://www.nclaonline.org/

An affiliate of the American Library Association and the Southeastern Library Association, the North Carolina Library Association is the only statewide organization concerned with the total library community in North Carolina. Our purpose is to promote libraries, library and information services, librarianship, intellectual freedom and literacy.

North Dakota Library Association

http://ndsl.lib.state.nd.us/ndla/

The purpose of this organization is to exercise professional leadership and to promote library services and librarianship.

Ohio Library Council

http://www.olc.org/

To serve as an advocate for public libraries and to provide opportunities for education and growth for library trustees, library Friends, library staff, and library related personnel.

Oklahoma Library Association

http://www.oklibs.org/

The purpose of the Oklahoma Library Association is to strengthen libraries, library services, and the librarianship in Oklahoma.

Oregon Library Association

http://www.olaweb.org/

The object of the Oregon Library Association shall be to promote and advance library service through public and professional education and cooperation.

Pacific Northwest Library Association

http://www.pnla.org/

The Pacific Northwest Library Association (PNLA) is an organization of people who work in, with, and for libraries. PNLA provides opportunities in communication, education and leadership that transcend political boundaries. PNLA will have the support of its community. PNLA will meet continuing education needs of the region. PNLA will develop stronger library networks and networking in the region. States and provinces included in PNLA are: Alberta, Alaska, British Columbia, Idaho, Montana, and Washington.

Pennsylvania Library Association

http://www.palibraries.org/

The association represents the profession in Harrisburg and provides opportunities for professional growth, leadership development, and continuing education for librarians.

Rhode Island Library Association

http://www.uri.edu/library/rila/rila.html

The Rhode Island Library Association is a professional association of Librarians, Library Staff, Trustees, and library supporters whose purpose is to promote the profession of librarianship and to improve the visibility, accessibility, responsiveness and effectiveness of library and information services throughout Rhode Island.

South Carolina Library Association

http://www.scla.org/

The basic purpose of the South Carolina Library Association is to promote the development of quality library service freely available to all citizens of South Carolina and to provide for the needs and welfare of the members of the Association.

South Dakota Library Association

http://www.usd.edu/sdla/

The purposes of the Association shall be:

1. To promote library service of the highest quality for all present and potential users of libraries in the State of South Dakota;

2. To provide opportunities for professional involvement of all persons engaged in any phase of librarianship within the State; and

3. To further the professional development of librarians, trustees, and library employees in the State.

Tennessee Library Association

http://www.lib.uytk.edu/~tla/

The purpose of the Tennessee Library Association is to "promote the establishment, maintenance, and support of adequate library services for all people of the state; to cooperate with public and private agencies with related interests; and to support and further professional interests of the membership of the Association."

Texas Library Association

http://www.txla.org/

The Texas Library Association was established in 1902 to promote and improve library services in Texas. Specific objectives are:

1. To encourage the identification, development, and maintenance of library services which will meet the informational, cultural, educational, and recreational needs of the citizens of Texas.

2. To provide for and stimulate the professional and career development of personnel in academic, public, school, and special libraries of Texas;

3. To facilitate effective cooperation among library personnel in academic, public, school, and special libraries of Texas;

4. To increase the effectiveness of libraries;

5. To advance the standards and ideals of the profession;

6. To provide a vehicle whereby library personnel may be aware of and cooperate with other associations and organizations which have similar or allied interests;

7. To increase attention to intellectual freedom and social responsibility as an action-oriented association;

8. To provide appropriate services to members for the benefit of the profession;

9. To work cooperatively with other associations in developing joint activities which relate to the provision of library services, the selection, distribution and use of books and other materials, the support of intellectual freedom, and the enhancement of educational opportunities, provided that:

   a. The purpose of the joint activity is supportive of the emphases named above;

   b. The other association has a major role in those activities relating to libraries;

c. The financial commitment required does not place a major burden upon the regular financial responsibilities of the Association;

d. The activity has been approved by the Executive Board.

e. To operate exclusively for charitable, scientific, literary, and educational purposes.

Utah Library Association

http://www.ula.org/

The mission of the Utah Library Association is to serve the professional development and educational needs of its members and to provide leadership and direction in developing and improving library and information services in the state.

Vermont Library Association

http://www.vermontlibraries.org/

The Vermont Library Association is an educational organization working to develop, promote, and improve library and information services and librarianship in the state of Vermont.

Virginia Library Association

http://www.vla.org/

The Virginia Library Association is a statewide organization whose purpose is to develop, promote, and improve library and information services and the profession of librarianship in order to advance literacy and learning and to ensure access to information in the Commonwealth of Virginia.

Washington Library Association

http://www.wla.org/

The purpose of the Washington Library Association is to promote library services, continuing education and library advocacy on behalf of the people of Washington State.

West Virginia Library Association

http://www.wvla.org/

The association promotes library service and librarianship in West Virginia.

Wisconsin Library Association

http://www.wla.lib.wi.us/

WLA is committed to "improving and promoting library and information service within the Wisconsin library community."

Wyoming Library Association

http://www.wyla.org/

It is the mission of the Wyoming Library Association: To provide leadership and to serve as a collective voice and advocate for advancement of Wyoming libraries, to educate the library community and users about contemporary library services, issues and technology, to provide members with a network for interaction on professional and social levels, and to promote the profession of librarianship and participation of Wyoming libraries in regional, national and global library arenas.

NATIONAL ASSOCIATIONS

American Library Association

www.ala.org

The American Library Association is the oldest and largest library association in the world, with more than 64,000 members. Its mission is to promote the highest quality library and information services and public access to information. ALA offers professional services and publications to members and nonmembers, including online news stories from American Libraries and analysis of crucial issues from the Washington Office. The ALA Web page urges you to "Be a part of it—library worker or advocate—join today!"

Within ALA, the Association of College & Research Libraries (ACRL) enhances the effectiveness of academic and research librarians to advance learning, teaching, and research in higher education. CJCLS (the Community and Junior College Libraries Section) is a part of ACRL. Its purpose is "to contribute to library service and librarianship through those activities which relate to libraries and learning resources centers and services and which support the educational programs in community and junior colleges and equivalent institutions." http://www.ala.org/ala/acrl/aboutacrl/acrlsections/commjr/abouts/aboutcjcls.htm

League for Innovation

http://www.league.org/welcome.htm

The League for Innovation is an international organization dedicated to catalyzing the community college movement. It hosts conferences and institutes, develops Web resources, conducts research, produces publications, provides services, and leads projects and initiatives with its member colleges, corporate part-ners, and other agencies in its continuing efforts to make a positive difference for students and communities.

Since 1968, the League has been making a difference in community college education and in the lives of millions of educators and students. This thumbnail sketch captures highlights of the League's 32 years of accomplishments and con-tributions and offers a glimpse into why *Change* magazine calls the League the "most dynamic organization in the community college world."

The League is the only major international organization specifically commit-ted to improving community colleges through innovation, experimentation, and institutional transformation.

INTERNATIONAL ASSOCIATIONS

The International Federation of Library Associations and Institutions (IFLA)

http://www.ifla.org/

IFLA is the leading international body representing the interests of library and information services and their users. It is the global voice of the library and information profession.

Founded in Edinburgh, Scotland, in 1927 at an international conference, IFLA celebrated its 75th birthday at its conference in Glasgow, Scotland in Au-gust 2002. IFLA now has over 1,700 members in more than 150 countries around the world. IFLA was registered in the Netherlands in 1971. The Royal Library, the national library of the Netherlands, in The Hague, generously provides the facilities for its headquarters. IFLA's conferences take place in locations around the world, from Boston to Glasgow, from Rio to Seoul.

AFFILIATE ASSOCIATIONS

American Association of Law Libraries

http://www.aallnet.org/

The American Association of Law Libraries was founded in 1906 to promote and enhance the value of law libraries to the legal and public communities, to foster the profession of law librarianship, and to provide leadership in the field of legal information.

American Indian Library Association

http://www.nativeculture.com/lisamitten/aila.html

The American Indian Library Association is a membership action group that addresses the library-related needs of American Indians and Alaska Natives.

Members are individuals and institutions interested in the development of programs to improve Indian library, cultural, and informational services in school, public, and research libraries on reservations. AILA is also committed to disseminating information about Indian cultures, languages, values, and information needs to the library community.

American Society for Information Science and Technology

http://www.asis.org/

The American Society for Information Science and Technology, ASIST, is a nonprofit 501(c)3 professional association organized for scientific, literary, and educational purposes and dedicated to the creation, organization, dissemination and application of knowledge concerning information and its transfer. The Society provides education and conference programs, highly regarded publications and journals, and other professional services for information systems developers, online professionals, information resource managers, librarians, record managers, and others who bridge the gaps between research and application, and between developer and user.

American Theological Library Association

http://www.atla.com/

Established in 1946, the American Theological Library Association (ATLA) is a professional association of more than 800 individual, institutional, and affiliate members providing programs, products, and services in support of theological and religious studies libraries and librarians. ATLA's ecumenical membership represents many religious traditions and denominations.

Art Libraries Society of North America

http://www.arlisna.org/

Founded in 1972, the Art Libraries Society of North America represents a creative diversity of expertise and interests. Through its many works and activities—conferences, publications, awards, ARLIS-L the electronic discussion list, and Web site—ARLIS/NA plays a leadership role for the twenty-first century by providing resources and services for the worldwide arts information community.

Asian/Pacific American Librarians Association

http://www.apalaweb.org/

The purpose of APALA is:

- To provide a forum for discussing problems of APA librarians.
- To provide a forum for the exchange of ideas by APA librarians with other librarians.

178

- To support and encourage library services to APA communities.
- To recruit and mentor APA librarians in the library/information science professions.
- To seek funding for scholarships in library/information science masters programs for APAs.
- To provide a vehicle whereby APA librarians can cooperate with other associations and organizations having similar or allied interests.

Association for Library and Information Science Education

http://www.alise.org/

The mission of ALISE is to promote excellence in research, teaching, and service for library and information science education.

Association of Research Libraries

http://www.arl.org/

ARL is a not-for-profit membership organization comprising the leading research libraries in North America. Its mission is to shape and influence forces affecting the future of research libraries in the process of scholarly communication. ARL programs and services promote equitable access to and effective use of recorded knowledge in support of teaching, research, scholarship, and community service.

Beta Phi Mu

http://www.beta-phi-mu.org/

The purposes of Beta Phi Mu are to recognize distinguished achievement in and scholarly contributions to librarianship, information studies or library education, and to sponsor and support appropriate professional and scholarly projects related to these fields by:

1. Awarding scholarships, fellowships, and research grants to qualified students and scholars.
2. Publishing newsletters and scholarly works related to librarianship, information studies or library education.
3. Promoting, organizing and holding meetings, seminars, workshops, conferences and similar activities.

Canadian Library Association

http://www.cla.ca/

The Canadian Library Association (CLA) is the national English language association that represents those who work in or advocate for Canada's estimated 21,000 libraries. CLA members work in college, university, public, special (corporate, non-profit and government) and school libraries. Others sit on boards of public libraries, work for companies that provide goods and services to libraries, or are students in graduate level or community college programs.

The CLA mission is to promote, develop and support library and information services in Canada and to work in cooperation with all who share our values in order to present a unified voice on issues of mutual concern.

Within CLA is a section devoted to community and technical college issues, the Technical College Libraries Section (http://www.cla.ca/divisions/cacul/ctcl.htm). CTCL exists:

- to foster cooperation and exchange of information among the libraries of Community and Technical Colleges;
- to open channels of communication, via CACUL and CLA, to other members of the library community
- to promote professional development through workshops, meetings, etc.
- to provide current standards for the development of Community and Technical College libraries;
- to maintain liaison with other organizations with similar aims such as AUCC, AMTEC, etc.; and
- to act as an advocate for quality library service in community and technical colleges.

The CTCL Executive Council comprises three individuals including: the Chair; and Secretary.

Chinese-American Librarians Association

http://www.cala-web.org/

The objectives of the Chinese American Librarians Association (CALA) shall be:

1. To enhance communication among Chinese American librarians as well as between Chinese American librarians and other librarians;
2. To serve as a forum for discussion of mutual problems and professional concerns among Chinese American librarians;
3. To promote Sino-American librarianship and library services; and
4. To provide a vehicle whereby Chinese American librarians may cooperate with other Associations and organizations having similar or allied interests.

Council of Library/Media Technicians

http://colt.ucr.edu/

The Council on Library/Media Technicians (COLT) objectives:

- To function as a clearinghouse for information relating to library support staff personnel

- To advance the status of library support staff personnel
- To initiate, promote and support activities leading toward the appropriate placement, employment and certification of library support staff personnel
- To promote effective communication between and among library staff at all levels
- To initiate, promote and support research projects and publications for the advancement of knowledge and understanding among library support staff personnel
- To study and develop curricula for the education of library support staff and develop appropriate standards for that education
- To cooperate usefully with other organizations whose purposes and objectives are similar to and consistent with, those of COLT.

Friends of Libraries USA

http://www.folusa.org/

Friends of Libraries USA (FOLUSA) is a nationwide membership organization of local Friends groups, libraries, and individuals. Their Mission is to motivate and support local Friends groups across the country in their efforts to preserve and strengthen libraries, and to create awareness and appreciation of library services by:

- Assisting in developing Friends of the Library groups in order to generate local and state support
- Providing guidance, education, and counsel throughout the Friends network
- Promoting the development of strong library advocacy programs
- Serving as a clearinghouse of information and expertise.

Medical Library Association

http://www.mlanet.org/

The Medical Library Association (MLA) is organized exclusively for scientific and educational purposes, and is dedicated to the support of health sciences research, education, and patient care. MLA fosters excellence in the professional achievement and leadership of health sciences library and information professionals to enhance the quality of health care, education, and research.

Music Library Association

http://www.musiclibraryassoc.org/

The Music Library Association is the professional organization in the United States devoted to music librarianship and to all aspects of music materials in libraries. Founded in 1931, MLA provides a forum for study and action on issues that affect music libraries and their users. MLA and its members make significant contributions to librarianship, publishing, standards and scholarship, and the development of new information technologies. In the forefront of contemporary librarianship, MLA assures that users of music materials will be well served by their libraries.

National Storytelling Network

http://www.storynet.org/

Bringing together and nurturing individuals and organizations that use the power of storytelling in all its forms.

Oral History Association

http://omega.dickinson.edu/organizations/oha/

The Oral History Association, established in 1966, seeks to bring together all persons interested in oral history as a way of collecting human memories. With an international membership, the OHA serves a broad and diverse audience. Local historians, librarians and archivists, students, journalists, teachers, and academic scholars from many fields have found that the OHA provides both professional guidance and collegial environment for sharing information.

Patent and Trademark Depository Library Association

http://www.ptdla.org/

The objectives of the PTDLA are to discover the interests, needs, opinions, and goals of the Patent and Trademark Depository Libraries (PTDLs), and to advise the United States Patent and Trademark Office (PTO) in these matters for the benefit of PTDLs and their users, and to assist the PTO in planning and implementing appropriate services.

ProLiteracy Worldwide

http://www.proliteracy.org/

ProLiteracy Worldwide's mission is to sponsor educational programs and services designed to empower adults and their families by assisting them to acquire the literacy practices and skills they need to function more effectively in their daily lives and participate in the transformation of their societies.

REFORMA

http://www.reforma.org/

REFORMA is committed to the improvement of the full spectrum of library and information services for the approximately 56.2 million Spanish-speaking and Latino people in the United States. The goals of REFORMA include:

- Development of Spanish-language and Latino-oriented library collections
- Recruitment of bilingual, multicultural library personnel
- Promotion of public awareness of libraries and librarianship among Latinos
- Advocacy on behalf of the information needs of the Latino community
- Liaison to other professional organizations

Sociedad de Bibliotecarios de Puerto Rico

http://upracd.upr.clu.edu:9090/novedades/sociebib.htm

This association does not appear to be active.

Theatre Library Association

http://tla.library.unt.edu/

The purpose of the Association shall be to promote the acquisition, growth, preservation and use of performing arts materials in libraries, museums, archives and other collections; to support access to these materials; to further studies in performing arts bibliography and scholarship; to promote education in performing arts librarianship and curatorship and to foster excellence in these professions.

Urban Libraries Council

http://www.urbanlibraries.org/

The Urban Libraries Council is an association of public libraries in metropolitan areas and the corporations that serve them. Believing that thriving public libraries are a result of collaborative leadership, the trustees, library directors, and corporate officers of member institutions work together to address shared issues, grasp new opportunities, and conduct research that improves professional practice.

A CALL TO ACTION: SO MANY OPPORTUNITIES, SO LITTLE TIME, SO FEW TO DO SO MUCH

This chapter clarifies the alphabet soup of library associations and speaks to the myriad of opportunities that are available to those who wish to take advantage. It also speaks to the reasons why professional association work is necessary and gratifying.

What is unfortunate is that not enough community college librarians seem to understand that the opportunities to do association work are also imperatives if the profession and libraries themselves are to remain visible and viable. Think back to the Peggy Sullivan's concept of divine discontent and Max De Pree's (1990) servant-leadership. Library professionals must come together and work with passion, purpose, patience, persistence and perspective. No one but community college librarians can do the work of community college librarians. If we are not ready to accept the responsibility for furthering our work and our profession, who will?

If you are not now a member of a professional association, start by joining at least one. Offer to do something, anything that captures your interest and imagination. The alphabet soup spells commitment to our profession. Take a taste. Finish the whole bowl. You'll like it.

REFERENCES

American Association of Community Colleges. 2002. *Position Statement on Library and Learning Resource Center Programs*. Washington, DC: AACC.

American Library Association. 2005. "Number of Libraries in the United States," *ALA Library Fact Sheet 1*.

Change. 1998.

Cohen, Scott. 2003. Interview with Bill Nelson. http://faculty.jscc.edu/scohen/nelsoninterview.htm l. Accessed August 2004.

De Pree, Max. 1990. *Leadership Is an Art*. New York: Dell.

Fourie, Denise K. and David R. Dowell. 2002. *Libraries in the Information Age: An Introduction and Career Exploration*. Westport, CT: Libraries Unlimited.

Greenleaf, Robert K. 1970. *The Servant as Leader*. Indianapolis, IN: Robert K. Greenleaf Center for Servant Leadership.

V

KEEPING STEPS AHEAD THROUGH PLANNING, MANAGING, AND KEEPING THE COLLECTIONS PRODUCTIVE; IDEAS ABOUT BUILDINGS

13 LONG-RANGE PLANNING: A VIEWPOINT ON AN ESSENTIAL PROCESS

Patricia Vierthaler

"Once upon a time … "; "It was a dark and stormy night … "; or, as Shakespeare wrote in the play *Macbeth,* "Boil, boil, toil and trouble … " These were beginnings I thought about using for this chapter. I almost chose the latter because, for some people, planning ranks only slightly higher than witches' brew and comes in a distant last on their to-do lists. However, another well-known saying that serves as motivation for many actions also applies to planning: Benjamin Franklin's admonition that "a stitch in time saves nine. " In other words, proper planning can encourage future growth and save the planner many headaches.

The terms "long-range planning" or "strategic long-range planning" may infuse prospective planners with feelings of dread or apprehension. The terms, what they stand for, and the work involved in this process can also be intimidating. This dread, apprehension, or intimidation is reduced when people involved in the process can see planning as a tool that, when used appropriately, is a dynamic device for strengthening and revitalizing organizations. Because there is no one established method of long-range planning and no one way to plan for the future growth and development of the organization, in this chapter I discuss planning as I have developed, implemented, and experienced it with libraries that are part of academic institutions.

PURPOSE OF PLANNING

Planning, as a tool available to library leaders for assisting in the process of change and improvement, can be used to guide libraries in a forward and progressive direction. By choosing to develop and implement a planning process, leaders will be guiding the future of their libraries.

To plan, think process. To understand and establish a process, library leaders must work from a common understanding about planning. Some of the elements of this understanding are as follows:

Planning

- maintains that change is inevitable and that in order to be progressive and up-to-date, organizations must develop and implement strategies to enhance success of the plans and activities to stimulate future growth.
- supports the mission of the institution of which the library is a part and integrates the goals of the library with those of the institution.
- requires a strategic long-range plan to be implemented effectively in order to develop long-range results.
- employs a strategy for using human and nonhuman resources to effect change and improvement for the library.
- requires a systematic method for evaluating the planning process.
- is a continuous process involving input from all individuals in the library.
- aligns budget with activities so that, upon achieving these activities, budget allocation and expenditures will reflect achievement of the library.

To succeed, the planning process should be utilized institutionwide as a proactive (not reactive) tool. Administrators should devise strategies to solve any barriers to success before problems occur. Learning from past experiences and anticipating future trends allows planners to have strategies in place to prevent possible problems from becoming a certainty.

Planning is a process that must begin at the top. The idea for the development of a strategic long-range plan for an institution must emanate from and be supported by the president of the institution. In order for long-range planning in the academic library to be successful, the practice of planning must have the same meaning for the academic departments, the library, student services, and so on as it has for the admissions office, the registrar's office, plant facilities, information services, and so on. In addition, this planning process must have the same emphasis in the president's office as for the other areas of the institution (Parekh 1977, 13).

INSTITUTIONAL MISSION

The first step toward a successful planning process is developing a clear sense of institutional identity. This identity may be expressed by the aims and purposes of the institution and is often published in a catalog or other official document (Parekh 1977, 13) Another way of looking at institutional identity is by examining what the institution is actually doing. In this sense, mission is seen in terms of what is happening rather than in a statement of intent or purpose. Many institutions have a very clear definition of purpose or mission, whereas others may operate in an atmosphere where the purpose is generally assumed to be understood by those connected with the institution.

Tying planning to the mission of the institution is vital. Not only should the institution have a mission statement, but the academic library, an important component of the institution, should have a library mission statement, a well-defined vision and documented long-range planning that supports the mission of the institution. Leaders must see the link between planning and mission statement as essential because resources—federal funds, corporate grants, and private gifts—are more likely to be awarded to institutions that can demonstrate the clarity of their mission and their plan for future growth (Parekh 1977, 13) So, an institution's proposal for growth and evolution is demonstrated through a planning document, and an academic library's planning demonstrates support and continuity within the institution. Done properly, these processes evidence carefully considered procedures and well-developed methods of evaluation. They then support the institution, adding to the likelihood of gaining financial support from outside organizations.

NEEDS ASSESSMENT

Prior to beginning the planning process, the planning group should conduct a needs assessment to examine the environment of the organization for which the long-range planning document is being developed, whether it is the overall institution or the library. A needs assessment examines what is happening in and with an organization and also determines strategies that should be in place to eliminate possible barriers and enhance critical success factors.

The needs assessment should not be lengthy or overly complicated. Enough knowledge of a particular area exists within the personnel of that area to identify the needs without resorting to outside surveys. A good two-hour study session with a facilitator who knows how to use consensus techniques will usually produce an effective assessment.

In looking at the overall institution, all personnel should be involved in the assessment and planning process. Everyone is encouraged to discuss the strengths and weaknesses of the institution. From these discussions, results of the needs assessment process should enable leaders to look objectively at their institution and begin the planning process. From the mission of the institution, planners will be able to use the needs assessment process to develop written goals for the institution to provide guidance for leaders in directing the institution's future. By keeping the goals of the institution in mind, the staffs of the library, student services, instructional departments, the president's office, and so on can plan in such a way that activities and resources support the institution as a whole.

STRATEGIC LONG-RANGE PLANNING

Various methods of planning are discussed throughout the literature. Strategic long-range planning or long-range planning is discussed in this chapter. This method, when continuously implemented and developed by leaders, will enable them to plan successfully for the future of their organizations.

Strategic long-range planning differs from the usual long-range planning. Simply put, long-range planning means: (1) setting goals and developing objectives to meet the goals, (2) identifying activities that will achieve the objectives, (3) assigning responsibility for the activities, (4) establishing beginning and ending times, and (5) determining performance evaluation measures (PEMs).

The strategic part comes between developing objectives and actually creating the procedure for accomplishing the objectives. Strategic planning means preparing the environment for the detailed planning—identifying potential barriers and critical success factors and developing strategies to clear the way for planning by eliminating barriers and enhancing success factors.

When the planning team has determined the objectives, members should begin listing the barriers to achieving the objectives. For example, in many organizations a major barrier to success is a shortage of available funding or perhaps lethargy among the staff responsible for the necessary activities. Strategies must be devised to provide funding, whether seeking outside funding, reducing internal budget spending, or obtaining a commitment from affected departments to underwrite part of the cost. Strategies for involving the staff and developing enthusiasm must stimulate the process in order to eliminate the lethargy. If the planning team lists more than four serious barriers, they probably need to rethink the objective. In addition, if they cannot identify strategies to cope with any one of the serious barriers, they need to rethink the objective.

Critical success factors for a library might include eliciting support from the faculty and administration. The strategic part of the planning is finding ways to get those people to support the goals that will be in the plan, perhaps by involving possible critics in discussion early in the planning. Another critical success factor might be commitment of staff time to pursue the activities that will be listed. The strategy here might be to reduce other workload or to pay overtime.

In summary, this process does not occur overnight and may cover a time period of three or more years. Remember, the planning process will occur at a smoother pace with the involvement of those in the institution (i.e., faculty, staff, and students). Also, it is essential that it be understood by all involved that strategic long-range planning works with the mission of the institution. Next, and key to the process, is the needs assessment, that when performed by the institution, will produce results that will indicate the various needs of the institution to be addressed within the planning document. Remember, it is these needs that are used to develop and write the planning document. As mentioned previously, the needs of the institution will help determine the goals and objectives of the institution. Once these goals and objectives are determined for the institution, each area/department establishes its own set of goals and objectives needed to assist in accomplishing these institutional goals. In the planning process, the steps are to establish (1) goals, (2) objectives, (3) barriers and strategies to eliminate barriers, (4) critical success factors and strategies to enhance these factors, (5) activities, (6) evaluation of the process and determination if the activity is completed, ongoing, or needs to be deleted, and (7) revision of objective as needed.

Processes of Strategic Planning

1. *Goals* are detailed and measurable and should be accomplished in an established time period. A goal should be written so that the meaning is clear and the individual or group working to reach this goal is held accountable. A goal may cover three years or more. Goals begin with an action verb preceded by the word *To*. They should indicate current and desired or projected results and state a time span for accomplishing the goal.
2. *Objectives* are developed to guide effort toward achieving the long-range goal. The goal is divided into logical parts so the objectives become statements of results to be achieved by an individual or a group within a shorter time period of three months to one year. Objectives should be limited in number, say three, and a new one should not be added until one has been completed or discarded.
3. *Barriers* are obstacles that could make it difficult for an activity to occur, i.e., apathy, cost, not enough staff, and so on. *Strategies to eliminate barriers* are statements describing how the planning area (i.e., the library) intends to eliminate barriers (obstacles or situations that may hinder the achievement of the activities) and might involve providing rewards for efforts to overcome any barriers. Strategies prepare the environment for fewest problems and greatest effectiveness of the endeavor.
4. *Critical success factors* are attitudes, behaviors, and resources that are crucial to successfully achieving the objectives. *Strategies to enhance these critical success factors* stage will help correct weaknesses and improve the overall library. An example is provision of funding.
5. *Activities* are steps in achieving each objective, including a description of the activity, identification of the responsible party, a beginning and ending time line, PEMs, and resources needed. Activities are performed by an individual or group—that is, director, library staff, librarian, and so on. PEMs are observable changes, measurable results, or tangible objects (e.g., reports, memos, surveys) growing out of the activity as it pertains to the objective and establishing that the activities are completed satisfactorily. PEMs are a necessary aspect of documentation in order to maintain that the planning process is working and help ensure accountability.
6. *Evaluation* of the plan assists in determining whether the activity was (a) completed successfully, (b) partially completed (to be continued, revised, or discarded), or (c) postponed (to be continued, revised, or discarded), or (d) unattainable (eliminated from the plan). This follow-up also serves to hold the individual and/or group accountable for their responsibilities in the planning process.

7. *Revision* of the plan will occur naturally, following upon the evaluation as the team uses the categories, eliminating what did not work and adding new, more feasible objectives as needed.

THE PLAN

When developing its strategic plan, the library should develop its goals in line with achieving and supporting those of the goals of the institution. For example,

Institutional goal: To increase enrollment by 10 percent in 2007.

In response to this institutional goal, the goal of the distance education department might be as follows:

Distance Education goal 1: To develop 10 online course offerings by 2006.

The library will need to plan support services around this goal of the institution. So a goal for the library might be as follows:

Library goal 1: To increase the number of databases remotely accessible for off-campus users by 100 percent by 2007.

Following this goal the library would need to establish objectives to meet these goals.

Objective 1.1: Determine the most heavily used area that would benefit most by the use of online database (e.g., English, history, math, science).

Objective 1.2: Plan trials and demonstrations for use with instructors and classes.

Objective 1.3: License appropriate database(s).

The next stage in the strategic long-range planning process is determining what the possible barriers would be and choose strategies for removing or reducing those barriers as well as identifying what factors are critical to achieving each objective and enhancing those. Once this is done, the planners are ready to develop the activities, persons responsible, time frame, and PEMs.

Objective 1.1: Determine the most heavily used area that would benefit most by the use of online database (e.g., English, history, math, science).

Barrier 1.1a: Library staff apathy.
Strategy to eliminate barrier 1.1a: The library director/dean will work closely with staff to assist on the survey and keep the staff on a time line.
Critical success factor 1.1a: Library staff will not have sufficient time to work on survey instrument.
Strategy to enhance critical success factor 1.1a: The library director will provide library staff time away from library duties to work on survey instrument.

Activity 1.1a: The library staff will develop a survey by _____ of faculty to learn usage statistics of classes and students of the library as evidence by approval of the survey form by _____.
Evaluation 1.1.a: A copy of the survey form will be on file.

Barrier 1.1.b: Faculty will not complete and return survey instrument.
Strategy to eliminate barrier 1.1.b: The library director will send follow-up memos to faculty and work with department chairs to encourage faculty to return survey.
Critical success factor 1.1.b: Upon return of survey faculty will be given item(s) as token of appreciation for their participation in survey.
Strategy to enhance critical success factor 1.1.b: Appreciation items will be provided free to library by database vendors.
Activity 1.1.b: The library staff will administer the survey by _____ and tabulate the resulting statistics of the survey by _____.
Evaluation 1.1.b: The scheduled dates of administration, completed forms, and statistics summary results will be on file. Copies of results will also be submitted to department chairpersons.

Objective 1.2: Plan trials and demonstrations for use with instructors and classes.

Barrier 1.2.a: Instructors will be apathetic.
Strategy to eliminate barrier 1.2.a: Librarians will attempt to educate departments on databases.
Critical success factor 1.2.a: Instructors will not welcome library instruction.
Strategy to enhance critical success factor 1.2.a: Library staff will offer to educate instructors and classes on use of databases.
Activity 1.2.a: Library staff will contact instructors regarding their class usage times, determine best dates for instructors to have access to database trials and determine timeline for testing databases by _____.
Evaluation 1.2.a: Instructor schedules and timelines will be on file.

Barrier 1.2.b: Library staff apathy.
Strategy to eliminate barrier 1.2.b: The library director/dean will establish time for staff to view and investigate other sites, discuss findings, and follow up on progress of staff.
Critical success factor 1.2.b: Library staff will not have adequate time to work on viewing other sites for recommendation.
Strategy to enhance critical success factor 1.2.b: The library director will provide library staff time away from library duties to view other Web sites.
Activity 1.2.b: Library staff will search other institutional sites and observe their database choices and follow upon professional materials regarding databases by _____.

Evaluation 1.2.b: List of databases, their subject content, and institutions that use them will be on file.

Barrier 1.2.c: Library staff will not contact vendors in a timely manner.
Strategy to eliminate barrier 1.2.c: The library director/dean will establish time for staff to contact vendors, discuss findings, and follow up on progress of staff.
Critical success factor 1.2.c:
Strategy to enhance critical success factor 1.2.c:
Activity 1.2.c: Library staff will contact database vendors and establish trials of certain databases by _____.
Evaluation 1.2.c: Library will have access to database trials for a select time period.

Objective 1.3: License appropriate database(s).

Barrier 1.3.a: Library staff apathy to contacting vendors.
Strategy to eliminate barrier 1.3.a: Library director/dean will keep abreast with progress of library staff and work with them to contact vendors of selected databases.
Critical success factor 1.3.a: Library staff will not be able to contact vendors in a timely manner.
Strategy to enhance critical success factor 1.3.a: Library director will provide staff time to contact and deal with database vendors.
Activity 1.3.a: Contact vendors of appropriate databases by _____.
Evaluation 1.3.a: Records of telephone calls and correspondence will be on file.

Barrier 1.3.b: Library staff will not work in a timely manner to obtain quotes from vendors.
Strategy to eliminate barrier 1.3.b: Library director/dean will work with staff to contact vendors and negotiate fees.
Critical success factor 1.3.b: Library staff will not be able to contact vendors in a timely manner.
Strategy to enhance critical success factor 1.3.b:
Activity 1.3.b: Obtain reasonable fees and costs for databases by _____.
Evaluation 1.3.b: Fees/quotes for databases will be on file.

Barrier 1.3.c: Vendor is slow to send contract.
Strategy to eliminate barrier 1.3c: Director/dean will advise vendor of library timeline.
Critical success factor 1.3c:
Strategy to enhance critical success factor 1.3c:
Activity 1.3.c: Obtain contract(s) for reading and finalizing by _____.
Evaluation 1.3.c: Final contract between library and database vendors will be on file.

OUTCOMES OF STRATEGIC LONG-RANGE PLANNING

By using the planning process, all departments (e.g., library, admissions, student services, information services) develop similar goals and can move in the same direction to assist in the progress and growth of the institution. Achieving these goals encourages teamwork, leading to positive results, a stronger institution, and better morale. Furthermore, this planning process fosters effective decision making. When people within an institution know the direction they are going, decisions become easier to make. The planning process outlined here enables leaders and other personnel to evaluate their areas objectively and determine what resources are needed to achieve the desired results.

By utilizing the strategic long-range planning process, the institution, the library, and other departments develop a direction for their future. Unity among areas within the institution develops because all are working toward the successful achievement of the same institutional mission. Such unity creates a better working environment, which can lead to improved employee morale, and good employee morale spreads to affect the students at the institution and to affect the surrounding community. A positive experience by students and the community can only strengthen the institution and its parts.

Thus, when done properly, strategic long-range planning can inspire teamwork, foster effective decision making, and improve morale, which in turn is reflected to the students and the community.

FOLLOW-THROUGH ON THE PLAN

The purpose of strategic long-range planning is to improve upon and provide direction for the future of an organization. The planning process, which involves everyone, contains strategies that enable leaders charged with spearheading the plan to think the process through and take into account all who will be affected. Strategies are put in place to eliminate barriers and work with the resources the institution has available. Activities enable various employees to be involved, in the process, and the evaluation stage serves as a review or follow-up method for determining if the objective, with its strategies and activities, has been accomplished. By evaluating the achievement of each objective, planners can determine if it is complete or requires revision and continuation. Sometimes it can help eliminate excess activity that accomplishes nothing.

After developing the long-range plan for the organization, it should be published in a document and the results, whether negative or positive, "distributed to all areas of the institution" (Parekh 1977, 76). The results should be readily available to all employees, because feedback is a crucial element in the planning process and needs to be heard at all levels.

This planning document should become a way of life for the institution. Departments should develop their goals and objectives around those of the institution. The institutional goals should be included in campus meetings and their importance stated to all.

Finally, "a plan is only as good as the commitment of the people who implement it" (Parekh 1977, 77). This commitment must be nurtured and employees should realize that the plan is a beneficial tool and not a threat. Planning requires management to recognize the limitations of the plan rather than the people involved. Also, it is important to remember that strategic long-range planning is an ongoing process—"planning is permanent but a plan is not" (Parekh, 1977 77). If the plan is not generating the anticipated results, it should be modified or discarded so that one that works can emerge.

So remember, strategic long-range planning can assist in:

1. supporting the survival, advancement, and growth of the institution;
2. providing a common understanding "about the mission and goals of the institution and the strategies used to implement them" (Parekh 1977, 77);
3. encouraging a "better allocation of institutional resources" (Parekh 1977, 77);
4. directing "energies away from nonessential activities" (Parekh 1977, 77);
5. providing an objective method for evaluating processes and implementing them simultaneously; and
6. assisting in generating funds by strengthening the institutional case with granting agencies (Parekh, 1977, 77).

REFERENCE

Parekh, Satish B. 1977. *Long-Range Planning: An Institution-Wide Approach to Increasing Academic Vitality*. New York, Change Magazine Press.

14 AN ANALYSIS OF THE COLLECTIONS AT JFK LIBRARY: A CASE STUDY

Robert Kelly

Hutchinson Community College and Area Vocational School (HCC) is located in Hutchinson, Kansas, the seat of Reno County (pop. 63,700). With a city population of more than 40,700, Hutchinson is centrally located in the state and is classified as a "Large Town" by the National Center for Education Statistics. A regional agricultural, educational, and medical hub, Hutchinson annually hosts the Kansas State Fair and the National Junior College Athletic Association men's basketball championships, and is preparing to host the 2006 USGA Seniors Golf Championship. An organized initiative to grow the county population to 80,000 by 2020 is underway as a means to improve regional economic development. Reno, Harvey (pop. 32,800), McPherson (pop. 29,500), and Rice (pop. 10,700) counties yield a total primary service area of 136,700. Wichita, the state's largest city, is 59 miles to the southeast. Located in Sedgwick County (pop. 452,800), it is a secondary market for students attracted to HCC programs, particularly at HCC's Newton site, as a convenient and less expensive alternative to Wichita State University and numerous private colleges in the area. Hutchinson Community College maintains a main and south campus (15 miles south), and sites in Newton (35 miles to the east) and McPherson (35 miles to the northeast). Growth in distance education programs and courses are a significant factor in HCC achieving record head count enrollment of more than 5,000 students in 2003–2004. Distance education services are offered to students at the sites previously mentioned and to those enrolled via Internet (WebCT), telecourse, and interactive television (ITV) relationships with 10 area high schools. Programs at HCC are supported by John F. Kennedy Library (JFKL). Practical nursing (McPherson), Fire Science (South Campus), and Fine Arts (Main Campus) are supported by departmental libraries as well. JFKL is housed in the basement of Rimmer Learning Resource Center, a facility that reopened in April 2003 after a year-long renovation. Prior to the renovation, JFKL took up the bulk of the main floor and shared space with other campus offices and services in the basement. JFKL is nearly at full capacity for shelving space with approximately 43,500 monographs and 2,000 VHS/DVD/Audio resources.

PURPOSE

For some years there has been a trend in the academic library arena to institute qualitative methods of evaluating collections and services rather than relying exclusively upon quantitative figures. Susan Anderson briefly describes the changes in approach since her tenure as editor for the 1994 edition of the Association of College and Research Libraries' (ACRL) Community and Junior College Library Standards and notes the relationship these changes have to initiatives taken by higher education regional accreditation associations.[1] Hutchinson Community College participates in the Academic Quality Improvement Program (AQIP) alternative reaccreditation process. Established in 1999 by the Higher Learning Commission (HLC), an independent corporation that is a member of the North Central Association (NCA) and is charged with accrediting degree granting higher education institutions within NCA's region, AQIP is a self-assessment process that is "structured around quality improvement principles and practices" and involves the creation of action projects for institutional improvement.[2] JFKL supports institutional efforts to accomplish the projects and looks toward the ACRL Standards for Libraries in Higher Education for guidance in evaluating library abilities to meet institutional needs.[3]

Buckland states that library services are based in the roles of facilitating access to documents and supporting the mission of the institution or the interests of the population it serves.[4] Dowell and Scott assert that the "overarching goal of the community college is instruction."[5] To support this teaching mission and meet the needs of clientele, address accreditation concerns, and meet the quality standards established by ACRL, current practices and resources require evaluation to identify their effectiveness. Maloy finds that libraries operate in "both the print and electronic worlds, which compete for our time and resources."[6] Maintaining a balance between the worlds, collection developers face challenges that include keeping up with new technologies and user needs, updating of quality content and the various forms it takes, managing the infrastructure to host or access the content, and marketing to users. Collection development, Carrigan argues, is an important determinant of the nature and level of services libraries offer.[7] Furthermore, benefits that users reap from quality collections and services necessitate that collection developers and their methods be included in collection evaluation.

How well the library reflects the teaching nature of the community college, how well the library supports accreditation activities, and how well the library meets professional standards for libraries are the concluding questions evaluation processes must answer. The current study does not fully answer those questions, although it may add some insight. Rather, the current study seeks to identify (1) how well JFKL collections support curricula, (2) how well are JFKL collections meeting clientele needs, and (3) what the future costs may be to adequately meet curricular and overall clientele needs.

METHODOLOGY

Collection of data was accomplished through several means:

1. Discussion of institutional enrollment and graduation information with appropriate campus administration,
2. Evaluation of budget expenditures from previous years,
3. Evaluation of reports generated by library staff,
4. Collection of relevant data from published sources regarding purchasing/subscription costs of resources, and
5. Collection of course enrollment information from college course catalogs, campus intranet enrollment updates, and notices of additional offerings appearing in campus email.

Information gathered includes the following:

1. Cumulative e-book usage,
2. Fiscal year expenditures by Dewey number,
3. Circulation by Dewey number including in-house collection usage,
4. Collection age by Dewey number,
5. Article and reference database usage,
6. Number of volumes by Dewey number,
7. Identification of periodical titles by content area,
8. Applicable standards from professional and accreditation organizations sources,
9. Overall and full-time enrollment,
10. Numbers of graduates and 2001/02–2003–2004 degrees/certificates conferred,
11. Ethnic, gender, and age diversity of the student body,
12. Number of courses with three or more sections that are offered by departments during the school year,
13. Periodical subscription trends from *Library Journal*, April 15, 2003, and 2004,
14. Book prices trends from *The Bowker Annual: Library and Book Trade Almanac*, and
15. Interlibrary loan activity.

Table 14.1
Degrees (D) and Certificates (C) Earned by Major

Major	Award	2001/02	2002/03	2003/04
Liberal Arts	D	92	80	98
Biology	D	43	34	51
Business	D	41	46	40
Fire Science	D	28	29	35
Nursing	D	28	29	30
Health Information	D	26	16	17
Education	D	25	24	25
Practical Nursing	C	24	33	43
Office Technology	C, D	24	14	21
Applied Management	D	16	9	11
Radiology	D	15	16	15
Ag Science	D	13	15	17
Computer Support Specialist	C, D	13	20	21
Psychology	D	11	6	7
Paramedic (18 month program)	D	11	1	2
Farm & Ranch Management	D	11	3	6

DISCUSSION

Clientele

Defining the makeup of HCC's clientele is a first step to describing how well their needs are being met. Quite obviously, faculty, administrative staff, and students are the primary clientele. Patrons from the surrounding community are welcome to use JFKL collections and services, albeit with limited privileges. Unlike students, staff, or faculty, community members are limited in the number of items they may borrow, must pay for documents printed from library computers, and are ineligible for interlibrary loan services.

Faculty at all sites and campuses number approximately 310, of which 110 are full-time. Spring 2004 student enrollment was a record 5,066, approximately a 1 percent increase over the previous spring. On-campus housing averages 365 and is expected to increase to more than 400 with an additional dormitory wing opening for the 2005–2006 school year. Of the total enrollment, 2,544 students have declared majors, including 1,446 of 1,886 full-time students. Table 14.1 details the number of degrees and certificates awarded for recent time periods in popular major areas. A total of 546 students earned degrees (D) or certificates (C) during 2001–2002, 487 in 2002–2003, and 597 in 2003–2004.

Table 14.2 provides a demographic picture of HCC's student population. Enrollment in all listed ethnic groups has been growing, with minorities increasing nearly two percentage points in the three years covered. Age and gender distribution maintain steady figures, although an interesting phenomena has been the consistent disparity in median and mean age between the fall and spring semesters.

Growth in student population translates into additional courses being offered and increased numbers of course sections. Table 14.3 provides a visual of the growth. I examined the number of courses offering three or more sections, sensing that this measure would not only reflect enrollment increases but also show what content areas are seeing the growth. Spring 2004 saw an increase in numbers of courses (10) and total sections (13), especially those offered by distance education (67) over fall 2003. The figures illustrate that distance education methods (i.e., WebCT, ITV, and telecourse) have been the largest source of recent enrollment increases for HCC.

Table 14.2
Student Body Demographics

	2001-2002		2002-2003		2003-2004	
Ethic Diversity	Number	Percent	Number	Percent	Number	Percent
White	6,965	87.6	6,829	86.6	6,972	85.9
Black	241	3.0	282	3.6	335	4.1
Hispanic	305	3.8	329	4.2	331	4.1
American Indian	81	1.0	76	1.0	101	1.2
Asian	54	0.7	53	0.7	69	0.9
Other	302	3.8	319	4.0	308	3.8
Total	7,948		7,885		8,116	
Gender						
Female	4,602	57.9	4,607	58.4	4,634	57.1
Male	3,346	42.1	3,278	41.6	3,482	42.9
Age	Fall	Spring	Fall	Spring	Fall	Spring
Mean	28.5	31.0	28.5	29.9	27.6	29.1
Median	22	25	22	24	21	24

Table 14.3
Number of Classes with Three or More Sections

Fall 2003			Spring 2004		
Department	Classes	Sections*	Department	Classes	Sections*
Applied Mgmt	1	2	Art	1	7
Art	1	6	Biology	3	14 (4)
Biology	2	10	Bus. Admin.	5	26 (8)
Bus. Admin.	6	25 (6)	Chemistry	1	4 (1)
Chemistry	1	4	Comp. Info. Sys.	6	27 (9)
Comp. Info. Sys.	6	41 (5)	Drama	1	3 (1)
Economics	1	6 (1)	Economics	2	10 (3)
Education	3	21	Emer. Med. Serv.	1	3
Emer. Med. Serv.	1	3	English	7	68 (6)
English	5	71 (3)	Family & Con. Sci.	1	4 (2)
Family & Con. Sci.	1	3	Fire Science	7	30 (2)
Fire Science	5	21 (1)	Geography	1	5 (2)
Health Info. Tech	1	3	Health Info. Tech.	3	9 (7)
History	2	20	History	2	9 (2)
Mathematics	6	43 (3)	Mathematics	7	45 (2)
Music	2	8 (2)	Music	4	20 (2)
Nursing	1	3 (1)	Office Tech.	1	4 (2)
Office Tech.	1	3	Philosophy	2	10 (2)
Philosophy	2	9 (1)	Phys. Ed. & Rec.	3	26
Phys. Ed. & Rec.	3	31 (1)	Physics	1	3
Physics	1	3	Pol. Science	3	3 (1)
Pol. Science	1	3	Psychology	3	37 (5)
Psychology	3	35 (5)	Sociology	3	33 (2)
Sociology	3	17 (2)	Spanish	2	8 (2)
Spanish	2	8 (2)	Speech	1	17 (2)
Speech	1	13 (1)	Total	71	425 (67)
Total	61	412 (34)	Newton Site		
Newton Site			Comp. Info. Sys.	3	9
Comp. Info. Sys.	3	10	McPherson Site		
Office Tech.	1	3	Comp. Info. Sys.	1	3

*Parentheses denote number of included distance and off-campus sections.

Resources and Funding

A number of non- funding-related physical and technological influences have affected the nature of and methods of access to JFKL resources and services.

Until the early 1990s, when the first subscription to a CD-ROM article indexing database was purchased, resources were provided in print and microform. Library services also included media resources (e.g., videocassettes, 16 mm films, slides) and supporting services. Since that time the creation and expansion of an Instruction Technology and Distance Education (ITDE) department absorbed media staff and services. JFKL faced and continues to contend with the challenge of providing resources to students enrolled in classes at the growing McPherson, Newton, and South Campus locations and through distance education technologies. JFKL migrated to Web-based databases in the late 1990s and has enhanced accessibility as well as content since that time, adding proxy access to online databases in January 2004. As more electronic resources have been offered to our clientele, budgetary shifts away from more traditional information forms have been necessary.

The development of JFKL's online database offerings versus subscriptions to periodical and indexing resources is illustrated in Table 14.4. Of note is the impact of a 10 percent campuswide budget reduction that was implemented at the beginning of the 2003–2004 fiscal year. Commitments to changes in database subscriptions required expansion of a planned cut in periodical subscriptions. Extensive work with faculty yielded a reduction to 140 subscriptions from more than 200. *Biography Index* and *Reader's Guide to Periodical Literature* subscriptions were also retained, and some publication titles were replaced by others. The following were included among the criteria used to guide decisions:

- Supportiveness of department or curricular needs;
- Cost;
- Accreditation concerns (Nursing);
- Availability of full-text, illustrations, pictures, and so on in online resources;
- Duplication of print and microform subscriptions;
- Indexed in print or online resources;
- Student recreational interest.

Table 14.5 illustrates the impact online database commitments have had on funding for books. Supplementary funding, to support interlibrary loan and community borrowing of materials, has been provided by South Central Kansas Library System (SCKLS). The SCKLS expenditures shown in Table 14.5 are not indicative of the amount of funds received in past years. Rather, the figures reflect amounts spent from accumulated funds. Less than expected increases in database subscription costs have enabled funding for books to be increased for 2004–2005.

Table 14.4
Expenditures for Electronic Databases and Periodical Subscriptions by Fiscal Year

Year	Electronic Databases	Periodical Subscriptions
1999-00	$16,333.24	$19,194.27
2000-01	13,768.63	19,745.91
2001-02	31,588.48*	21,118.04
2002-03	28,835.00**	21,289.46
2003-04 Pre-Cut	27,877.00	16,936.00
2003-04 Post-cut	25,129.30	15,242.40
2004-05	26,001.00	15,853.47

*Includes a $2,710 purchase of a NetLibrary e-book collection Newsbank subscription.
**Includes a $2,535 purchase of a NetLibrary e-book collection.

Table 14.5
Detail of Book Expenditures by Fiscal Year

Year	Volumes added	Expenditures		
		Budget	SCKLS	Total
1999-00*	1,235	$12,773.01	$ 746.21	$13,519.22
2000-01	477	11,893.46	130.00	12,023.46
2001-02**	277	10,049.84	1,856.07	11,905.91
2002-03	315	10,474.74	1,983.37	12,458.11
2003-04***	404	8,806.50	6,150.80	14,957.30
2004-05		9,624.00		

*Numbers are artificially high due to an error in documenting purchased versus donated acquisitions when a large number of law books were acquired.
**Includes a $2,700 purchase of a NetLibrary e-book collection.
***Includes a $2,250 purchase of a NetLibrary e-book collection.

Facilities

Resource use has been affected by the dramatic changes that have occurred in recent years in terms of physical facilities and student computing services. This must be kept in mind when reviewing related statistical data. Prior to the 2002–2003 renovation, JFKL filled the main floor and two-thirds of the basement in what is now the Rimmer Learning Resource Center building. The building reopened in spring 2003 with Student Tutoring Services and a large computer lab (70 computers) on the main floor, with JFKL housed in the expanded basement.

JFKL now is approximately a third to a half of its original size in terms of floor space, offering seating for 52 in addition to a lab of 15 computers. From January 2002 to January 2003 significant portions of the book collections, along with the back file of the periodical collection, were placed in storage while library services were temporarily relocated to a portion of the student union. Low-circulating nonfiction (000s, 200s, 400s, and 500s) and the majority of the fiction, reference, and juvenile collections were placed into storage. Full access to library collections and resources did not become available until JFKL reopened in the remodeled facility in April 2003.

Usage

Partially documented earlier, technological change's impact on JFKL has led to making information available in new forms and through new methods at the expense of the more traditional or incumbent. Gathering and interpreting use statistics related to all of the resources JFKL provides access to is key to learning how well curricular and client needs are being met and for identifying what resources may be required to meet future needs.

Innovations in technology and communication enable distance education and commuting students similar access to information that resident students enjoy, including library-managed resources. Tables 14.4 and 14.5 illustrate expenditure swings associated with technological change. Expenditures on electronic databases and e-book collections have diverted funding away from periodical subscriptions and book purchases. Interlibrary loan activity has also been affected. Save for meeting the needs of a few faculty pursuing articles needed for doctoral study, borrowing requests are almost exclusively for monographs.

A focus of attention is the substantial decline in the use of the circulating nonfiction collection, illustrated in Tables 14.6 through 14.8. Although the remodeling project can shoulder some of the blame, analysis of use statistics for other resources may help provide a clearer explanation for the decline.

E-books, Circulating Nonfiction, and Interlibrary Loans

Use of e-books, circulating nonfiction, and interlibrary loan services can be examined together because each provides a different perspective on subject demand. Tables 14.6 through 14.10 provide usage data for each of the areas. The date ranges covered do vary between the areas in which data was gathered. E-books were only first offered during 2001–2002, so data is since inception. Data for the circulating nonfiction is provided for the most recent academic five years to illustrate trends in book usage both prior to and after JFKL's renovation in 2002 and 2003. Interlibrary loan data is provided for 2000 through 2003 primarily because the range was felt to be large enough to establish a feel for which subjects generate the most borrowing requests. Only the interlibrary loan borrowing activity in Table 14.10 visually provides a breakdown of specific areas of demand

Table 14.6
Circulation Statistics by Classification, 1999–2001

1990/00			2000/01		
Dewey No.	Circ	In-house	Dewey No.	Circ.	In-house
300s	1,514	703	300s	1,104	428
700s	1,078	230	600s	697	246
600s	955	380	700s	544	166
900s	488	226	900s	505	191
100s	379	102	100s	307	70
800s	356	175	800s	292	116
500s	165	98	500s	178	71
200s	112	35	200s	140	73
000s	85	26	000s	71	11
400s	48	9	400s	50	9
Total	5,180	1,984	Total	3,888	1,381

Table 14.7
Circulation Statistics by Classification, 2001–2003

2001/02			2002/03		
Dewey No.	Circ	In-house	Dewey No.	Circ	In-house
300s	678	95	300s	763	9
900s	495	131	600s	446	12
600s	457	73	900s	294	1
700s	339	97	100s	228	2
100s	263	21	700s	205	2
800s	261	77	800s	162	12
200s	89	8	500s	71	1
500s	62	6	200s	47	1
000s	25	1	000s	26	0
400s	20	0	400s	9	0
Total	2,689	509	Total	2,251	41

Table 14.8
Circulation Statistics by Classification, 2003–2004

2003/04		
Dewey No.	Circ	In-house
300s	1,028	152
600s	642	89
700s	367	62
900s	331	75
800s	295	80
100s	243	23
200s	89	8
500s	80	29
000s	69	11
400s	30	10
Total	3,174	539

Table 14.9
E-book Usage by Classification

2001/02		2002/03		2003/04	
Dewey No.	Accesses	Dewey No.	Accesses	Dewey No.	Accesses
300s	6	300s	89	300s	398
600s	6	600s	53	600s	280
000s	3	000s	40	000s	61
800s	2	100s	13	100s	34
900s	2	900s	13	500s	26
100s	1	500s	11	900s	24
700s	0	700s	8	800s	23
500s	0	800s	7	200s	22
200s	0	200s	1	700s	14
400s	0	400s	0	400s	0
Total Accesses	20	Total Accesses	235	Total Accesses	882
Total Records	18	Total Records	167	Total Records	522

Table 14.10
ILL Borrowing Activity by Dewey Classification, 2000–2003

Range	Requests Filled	Specific Areas of Demand In Order*
300 – 399	152	370, 300, 360, 320, 340, 390, 350, 380
900 – 999	58	970, 920, 910, 940, 950
800 – 899	57	820, 800, 810, 830
700 – 799	51	790, 740, 730, 780, 750, 720
100 – 100	41	150, 130, 170
600 – 699	39	610, 650, 620, 630
500 – 599	19	500, 570
200 – 299	13	220, 290
000 – 099	11	020
400 – 499	0	n/a

*Bolded areas represent noted high-demand areas.

within Dewey subject areas. E-book and nonfiction circulating book data has been included in discussions in summary only.

By a substantial margin and in all three statistical areas, Social Sciences (300s) receives the most activity. Except for interlibrary loan activity, Social Problems and Services (360s) generated as much as 75 percent more use than Generalities (300s), itself a high use area. Education (370s); Economics (330s); Law (340s); and Customs, Etiquette, and Folklore (390s) have also been areas of substantial use. Interest in Public Administration (350s) resources has dropped dramatically.

Technology-Applied Sciences (600s) is consistently one of the next strongest areas of activity. Medical Sciences (610s) receives very strong interest in all three areas and is the second highest area of use. Management and Auxiliary Services (650) is the only other area receiving substantial use in various forms. Agriculture and Related Technologies (630), Home Economics and Family Living (640s), and Chemical and Related Technologies (660s) receive moderate use in e-book and/or book form.

Geography and History (900s) is another consistently strong area of activity. Although not a top area of e-book interest, the area generates significant interlibrary loan traffic relative to other areas. North America (970s) and Europe (940s) dominate the use although moderate attention is received by Biography and Genealogy (920s), General Geography and Travel (910s), Ancient World (930s), Generalities (900s), and Asia (950s).

The Arts (700s) is an area that has seen wide fluctuations in use, dropping from a very high area of book use in 1999–2000 to the fifth highest in 2002–

2003 before rebounding a bit in 2003–2004. E-book usage is only slight, and interlibrary loan activity is moderate. Recreational and Performing Arts (790s) leads the category in attention. Drawing, Decorative and Minor Arts (740s) is a leading interlibrary loan area, although it received only light e-book and book attention. Generalities (700s), Painting (750s), Music (780s), Plastic Arts and Sculpture (730s), and Architecture (720s) also receive light to moderate attention.

A most steady area of interest is Philosophy and Related Disciplines (100s). Psychology (150s) leads the category in all forms of activity, including 70 percent of e-book usage. Ethics—Moral Logic (170s) and Paranormal Psychology (130s) receive moderate attention. Epistemology and so on (120s) and Logic (160s) also receive e-book activity.

Literature (800s) book collection use is dominated by American Literature in English (810s) and to a lesser degree English and Anglo Saxon Literature (820s) and Generalities (800s). The 820s also are a leading subject in e-book use and are also a leading area in interlibrary loan activity. Other areas receive only occasional attention.

Pure Sciences (500s) leads the lowest usage tier of subjects that includes Religion (200s), Generalities (000s), and Language (400s). The 500s are led in terms of e-book and book usage by Life Sciences (570s). Mathematics (510s) showed some noted e-book usage while receiving only occasional book use. Most other areas received light to occasional e-book and book use.

Other and Comparative Religion (290s) leads the 200s in overall use. Bible (220s) receives interlibrary loan and book attention, and almost all other subjects receive light e-book and/or book use.

Generalities (000s) physical collections have traditionally been the second lightest used area of activity, although the area has received the third most e-book usage. Computer science topics have led the specific General (000) to rank as the highest used subject area. Library and Information Science (020s), Bibliography (010s), and General Collections (070s) receive light attention, and Library and Information Science is the only noted area trafficking in interlibrary loan.

Languages (400s) have received neither interlibrary loan nor e-book usage. Spanish and Portuguese (460s) has been the highest subject of use in the book collections. Linguistics (410s) and English and Anglo Saxon (420s) get occasional attention.

Table 14.11 details expenditures on monographs and video recordings for 2002–2003 and 2003–2004. Figures 14.1 and 14.2 provide a visual of use relative to expenditures by general Dewey subject area. An accumulation of overall use data from 1999–2000 through 2002–2003 was contrasted to gain information on use versus funding. The confirmed suspicion was an imbalance of expenditures relative to use. Efforts were made to rudimentarily diversify spending in 2003–2004 pending a more complete examination of JFKL resources and client and curricular need. One noteworthy consideration is the impact the purchase of large and/or expensive reference book and video recording sets can have. An

Table 14.11
Expenditures by Classification 2002–2004

Expenditures by Classification 2002/03		Expenditures by Classification 2003/04	
Classification	Amount	Classification	Amount
300 – Social Sciences	$5,332.38	300 – Social Sciences	$4,610.21
330 – Economics	1,744.70	300 – General	2,046.93
360 – Soc. Problems	927.76	330 – Economics	805.14
370 – Education	802.26	360 – Soc. Problems	772.47
300 – General	463.79	340 – Law	347.81
320 – Political Science	462.85	370 – Education	223.22
350 – Public Admin.	233.59	320 – Political Science	163.56
390 – Customs, Folklore	206.07	310 – Statistics	132.00
340 – Law	190.36	350 – Public Admin.	63.48
380 – Commerce	177.00	380 – Commerce	30.95
		390 – Commerce	24.65
600 – Technology	$4,373.92	600 – Technology	$1,828.88
620 – Engineering	3,521.89	610 – Medical Science	960.70
610 – Medical Science	631.65	620 – Engineering	600.53
660 – Chemical Tech.	86.00	650 – Management	135.56
650 – Management	49.95	600 – General	97.66
640 – Home Economics	36.06	690 – Buildings	21.21
		640 – Home Economics	13.09
700 – The Arts	$1,747.91	700 – The Arts	$2,484.94
790 – Rec. & Performing	964.19	780 – Music	990.48
700 – General	339.64	790 – Rec. & Performing	615.04
780 – Music	214.58	750 – Painting	214.77
730 – Plastic & Sculpture	125.00	700 – General	189.75
720 – Architecture	64.52	730 – Plastic & Sculpture	184.71
750 – Painting	39.38	720 – Architecture	139.82
		770 – Photography	129.41
		710 – Civic & Landscape	20.96

Table 14.11
(continued)

Expenditures by Classification 2002/03		Expenditures by Classification 2003/04	
Classification	Amount	Classification	Amount
000 – Generalities	$1,247.25	000 – Generalities	$2,178.42
000 – General	719.85	030 – Gen. Encyclopedia	1,102.95
030 – Gen. Encyclopedia	239.95	010 – Bibliography	505.00
020 – Lib. & Info. Science	199.00	000 – General	483.69
010 – Bibliography	88.45	020 – Lib. & Info. Science	66.83
		070 – Journalism	19.95
900 – Geography & History	$995.59	900 – Geography & History	$853.60
970 – N. America	367.33	970 – N. America	294.26
940 – Europe	317.65	920 – Biography	130.00
920 – Biography	187.12	950 – Asia	127.55
900 – General	39.27	940 – Europe	118.52
930 – Ancient World	38.58	910 – Geography & Travel	108.41
950 – Asia	29.52	930 – Ancient World	43.42
910 – Geography & Travel	16.12	960 – Africa	15.72
		900 – General	15.72
500 – Pure Sciences	$395.50	500 – Pure Sciences	$357.59
570 – Life Science	218.91	570 – Life Science	143.52
540 – Chemistry & Related	139.95	500 – General	71.46
590 – Zoological Science	36.64	520 – Astronomy	56.97
		530 – Physics	39.90
		510 – Mathematics	29.62
		550 – Earth & Other	16.12
200 – Religion	$315.47	200 – Religion	$126.20
290 – Comparative	225.56	200 – General	57.97
240 – Christian Moral	73.80	290 – Comparative	37.16

Table 14.11
(continued)

Expenditures by Classification 2002/03		Expenditures by Classification 2003/04	
Classification	Amount	Classification	Amount
260 – Social, Ecclesias-tical	16.11	280 – Christian Denom.	16.71
		270 – History & Geography	14.36
800 – Literature	$270.97	800 – Literature	$1,273.40
810 – American in English	256.74	810 – American in English	469.84
820 – English, Anglo-Saxon	14.13	820 – English, Anglo-Saxo	463.02
		800 – General	194.42
		860 – Spanish	125.67
		840 – Romance	20.45
100 – Philosophy & Related	$119.17	100 – Philosophy & Related	$952.20
170 – Ethics	58.61	150 – Psychology	812.58
150 – Psychology	43.46	170 – Ethics	87.03
130 – Paranormal	19.96	130 – Paranormal	35.53
		190 – Modern Western	17.06
400 – Language	$109.56	400 – Language	$399.27
420 – English, Anglo-Saxon	96.00	460 – Spanish	251.25
410 – Linguistics	13.56	420 – English, Anglo-Saxon	67.32
		440 – Romance	52.25
		430 – Germanic	28.45
Fiction	$30.86	Fiction	$131.29
Juvenile Fiction	$18.86	Juvenile Fiction	$15.42
Total	$14,957.30	Total	$15,211.39

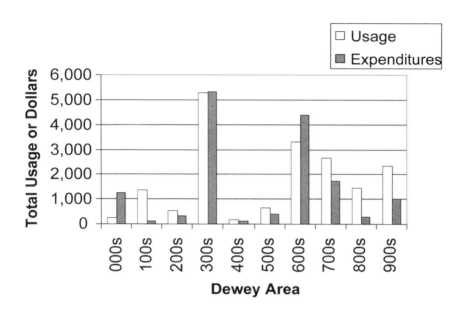

Figure 14.1   July 1999–June 2003 Usage versus February 2003 Expenditures

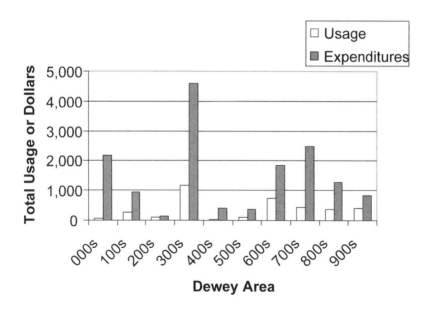

Figure 14.2   March 2004 Usage versus Expenditures

updated general encyclopedia set, cataloged in 030, acquired in 2003–2004 and a large set of fire science videos, cataloged in 620, acquired in 2002–2003 both caused a misrepresentative spike in expenditures in their general Dewey call number areas.

Article and Reference Databases

State-level initiatives in Kansas have broadened access to information by making several databases available to the general public and students enrolled in Kansas higher education institutions. The Kan-Ed Network, an organization formed by the Kansas State Board of Regents, sponsors Heritage Quest; Gale's Literature Resource Center; Custom Newspapers; ProQuest Nursing Journals; and Worldbook. Access began August 2003. The Kansas Library Network Board, the research and development division of the Kansas State Library, sponsors access to FirstSearch; Infotrac Web; SIRS Discoverer; !Informe! (Revistas en Español); and a collection of NetLibrary e-books.[8] SIRS Discoverer is the only resource not included in JFKL's database offerings due to the low level of its intended audience.

The state level offerings complement JFKL's subscriptions to LexisNexis Academic, JSTOR's Language & Literature and Arts & Sciences I, and Ebscohost's CINAHL and Academic Search Premier. The Ebscohost Academic Search databases have served as core, interdisciplinary resources offering full text articles of research oriented publications. Overall, JFKL database subscriptions meet curriculum-specific needs in the areas of business, legal, literature, and nursing information including outside nursing accreditation concerns. Other needs continue to include access to full text newspaper articles and off-campus database accessibility, particularly for distance education students. Recent changes, illustrated in Tables 14.12 and 14.13, which improved JFKL abilities to meet campus needs, have included upgrading to Ebscohost's Academic Search Premier, the addition of LexisNexis Academic and JSTOR Language & Literature and Arts & Sciences I, and the implementation of proxy software in January 2004 to improve remote database access. Academic Search Premier was upgraded from a combination of Academic Search Elite and PsychInfo because the value added was determined to be worth the increase in expense. LexisNexis Academic was added at the expense of Newsbank because it provided full text newspaper articles in addition to rich medical, legal, and business content. JSTOR's offerings were added, and ultimately retained at the expense of CQ Researcher, to provide a full text literature resource. Budget reductions combined with the addition of LexisNexis Academic necessitated cutting either the JSTOR databases or CQ Researcher in early 2003–2004. Faculty assistance from the Language and Literature Department and consideration of use statistics for both databases were key in the decision making process. Tables 14.4, 14.12, and 14.13 collectively portray the growth in database usage of and institutional reliance on database subscriptions and the related increases in spending on them.

Table 14.12
Article and Reference Database Usage

2002-2003		2003-2004	
Vendor/Database	**Searches**	**Vendor/Database**	**Searches**
Ebscohost – Total	20,766	Ebscohost – Total	27,459
Academic Search Elite	10,556	Academic Search Elite	2,142
CINAHL	1,296	Academic Search Premier	16,849
Clinical Pharmacology	45	CINAHL	2,154
		Pre-Cinahl	79
ERIC	1,548	ERIC	1,841
Health Source, Nursing Academic	2,390	Health Source, Nursing Academic	260
Image Collection	13	Image Collection	20
MAS Ultra	2,653	MAS Ultra	2,167
Military & Government	738	Military & Government	638
PsychInfo	1,523	American Humanities (Trial)	540
USP DI Vol. II, Advice...	29	Comm & Mass Media (Trial)	707
Newsbank	1,991	PsychInfo	69
CQ Researcher	321	CQ Researcher	209
JSTOR – Arts & Sciences 1	712	JSTOR – Arts & Sciences 1	870
LexisNexis Academic	5	LexisNexis Academic	3,352
InfoTrac	4,969	InfoTrac – Total*	11,896
		Business & Company ASAP	289
		Business & Company Resource Center	215
FirstSearch	3,602	Computer Database	165
		Custom Newspapers	4,529
		Expanded Academic ASAP	3,043
		Health Reference Center Academic	941
		Health and Wellness Resource Center	1,153
		Informe	26
		Literature Resource Center	1,153
		National Newspaper Index	382
		FirstSearch	3,887
		Grove Music Online (free/yr)	129
Total	32,366	Total	47,802

*July 2004 statistics not available.

Table 14.13
Database Subscription Costs

2002-2003		2003-2004	
Vendor/Database	**Cost**	**Vendor/Database**	**Searches**
Ebscohost – Total	$19,650	Ebscohost – Total	$20,663
Academic Search Elite		Academic Search Premier	
CINAHL		CINAHL	
ERIC		ERIC	
MAS Ultra		MAS Ultra	
PsychInfo		PsychInfo	
Other free or trial databases		Other free or trial databases	
Newsbank (pd Jan.02)	2,535	JSTOR	
CQ Researcher	660	Arts & Sciences 1	1,500
JSTOR		Language & Literature	490
Archive fee	1,000	LexisNexis Academic	2,506
Arts & Sciences 1	1,500		
Language & Literature	490		
Total	$25,835	Total	$25,159

2004-2005	
Vendor/Database	**Cost**
Ebscohost	$20,663
Academic Search Premier	
ERIC	
CINAHL	
MAS Ultra	
Other free or trial databases	
JSTOR (est.)	
Arts & Sciences 1	2,000
Language & Literature	490
LexisNexis Academic	2,848
Groves Online (1-year free)	
Total (est.)	$26,001

Curricular Support

Hutchinson Community College has experienced enrollment growth, especially at non-main campus sites and via distance education methods (i.e., telecourse, ITV, WebCT). Table 14.3 illustrates this by documenting 2003–2004 semester to semester increases in classes with at least three sections (10) and increases in course sections (32). Even with fall's Education students, who were enrolled in freshman-level general campus orientation courses, bolstering content courses in the spring, the dispersion does not account completely for the increase in content courses and the number of sections.

Strong enrollment is seen in Business Administration, Computer Information Systems, English, Fire Science, Mathematics, Physical Education, Psychology, Sociology, and Speech courses. Biology, Economics, Music, and Philosophy also have several sections of classes. Majors that have generated the largest number of graduates, listed in Table 14.1, include Liberal Arts; Office Technologies; fields of study in Biology; Nursing and other Allied Health; Agriculture; Business and Management; Education; and Computer Science. Other fields not listed in the table that graduated a number of students in Spring 2004 include Welding Technology (18), Visual and Performing Arts (17), Paralegal (9), and Communications (9). Some major areas see enrollment strength that does not show up in listings of high graduation areas or numbers of course and section offerings. Spring 2003 enrollment figures revealed Law Enforcement/Corrections (77), Engineering (32), Automotive Mechanics and Body Repair Technology (41), and Child Care (33) as popular areas.

Complete programs are offered away from the main campus location, presenting challenges as diverse as their programs of study. Welding Technology is offered on the main campus and at the McPherson site. Practical Nursing is offered only at the McPherson site. Automotive Mechanics and Body Repair Technology is offered in conjunction with and located at nearby Hutchinson High School. Fire Science, Paramedic, Law Enforcement, and Agriculture programs are located at South Campus. In addition, Health Information Technology offers a completely online program.

There has been an effort to describe individual course descriptions with Dewey content areas to assist in materials selection and evaluation.[9] In the spirit of that effort some general analysis can be done comparing programs with resource usage statistics and expenditures listed in Table 14.11 and graphically illustrated in Figures 11.1 and 11.2. A strong influence on the entirety of collections JFKL facilitates access to is introductory composition classes. These freshman-level, especially first-semester, courses enable students to explore a wide variety of subjects with a unifying "cause and effect" theme. Composition faculty members flavor this theme with their own emphases (e.g., causes of success for a famous individual, 1920s-era topics, causes of an issue being prominent in American culture). The sheer breadth of student interests affects all collection management decisions.

Business and Office Technology business specific courses are supported by a variety of databases. LexisNexis Academic is a primary source, but offerings provided by Ebscohost, FirstSearch, and Gale's Infotrac services provide additional support. These currently include Business & Company ASAP and Resource Center databases, ABI-Inform, and Business Source Premier. E-book use in the Management and Auxiliary Services (650) has revealed weaknesses in physical collections, stimulating a slight funding increase in 2003–2004. Economics (330) saw a substantial reduction in funding relative to overall use.

Fire Science and Paramedic programs rely primarily on resources housed at South Campus and on accessibility to article databases. Program supporting databases include CINAHL, LexisNexis Academic, Medline, and Academic Search Premier. Neither program contributes significantly to interlibrary loan, e-book, or book collection use in the Medical Science (610), Engineering (620), or Social Problems (360) areas. Life Sciences (570), which have led the Pure Sciences (500) in book and e-book usage, and Botanical Sciences (580) are also relevant Fire Science areas. Primarily videos are purchased for their programs and are often housed at South Campus. Although both programs are away from the main HCC campus, JFKL neglectfully supports them in terms of monographic materials.

Nursing, Practical Nursing, Health Information Technology, Radiology, and Pre-Medicine and Pre-Dentistry Biology majors are supported by databases that include CINAHL, Medline, ProQuest Nursing Journals, LexisNexis Academic, and Academic Search Premier. Medical Science (610) is arguably the most highly used area of e-book and monographic collections. Life Sciences (570) and Ethics—Moral Logic (170) may receive attention as students explore developmental issues. The Medical Science area is highly funded on an annual basis relative to other subject areas. Practical Nursing, located in McPherson, is supported by a departmental library in addition to JFKL-supplied materials. Nursing, Radiology, and Health Information programs are hosted in Davis Hall, located approximately 10 residential blocks from the main campus site, which is inconvenient for faculty and students to visit JFKL.

Liberal Arts students enroll in a breadth of classes encompassing social sciences, mathematics, science, language, and literature. Literature, as a significant component of the major, is specifically supported by the JSTOR offerings and Gale's Literature Resource Center. Primary demand is in General Literature (800), American Literature in English (810), and English and Anglo-Saxon Literature (820). Light to moderate use has been documented, but expenditures have been limited and with a narrow focus. Interlibrary loan traffic has been notable in the area, with a faculty doctoral candidate having an influence. Beginning in 2003–2004, work with a new faculty member in languages has assisted in efforts to develop appropriate Spanish and French collections in the 800s and 400s.

Agriculture and Farm and Ranch Management programs, located at South Campus, primarily are supported with interdisciplinary databases. Students may be dealing with veterinary, ecological, pesticide, machinery, and botanical concerns in addition to business issues, as they all constitute a knowledge base those working in faming and ranch management should be familiar with. Agriculture (630) is a primary area of interest, although industry information will surface in Economics (330). Specific to these majors, materials receive only light use overall, with Agriculture e-book materials receiving the majority. No materials specific to these majors have been purchased the past two school years.

Software emphasis Office Technology courses and various computer science majors are primarily supported by Generalities (000). A low area of in-house use, the subject receives significant e-book usage. Overall, the broader Generalities area is the second least used section of physical collections but is the third highest area of use in the e-book collections. Software issues that appear in Management and Auxiliary Services (650) also receive attention, although exclusively in e-book form. Although expenditures have been made in the two specific areas, few materials related to software have been purchased. Interdisciplinary and business-oriented databases that include technology and software publications support the majors. Infotrac's Computer Database is also a primary supporting database.

Psychology, although not graduating large numbers of students, is an area with large numbers of course sections offered. Psychology is a common major requirement. Psychology and related materials found in the Social Sciences (300s) receive substantial use. Academic Search Premier serves as the primary database serving the subject. Expanded Academic ASAP is also a useful resource. Ebsco-host currently provides the Psychology and Behavioral Sciences Collection database on a complementary basis. Psychological aspects of different subjects (e.g., marketing techniques, child development) can also be researched using more subject specific databases. Expenditures on physical materials was bolstered in 2003–2004 to better meet demand and respond to faculty requests for more pure Psychology resources.

Other high enrollment areas such as Child Care, Law Enforcement/Corrections, Engineering, and Automotive Care and Body Repair Technology vary widely in the amount of support they receive from JFKL resources.

Child Care touches upon issues including the psychological (150) and educational (370) aspects. Each of those content areas has received vastly different funding. Similarly, Law Enforcement/Criminology interests have been supported primarily in the avenues of Law (340) and Social Problems and Services (360). Various databases including Academic Search Premier, ERIC, CINAHL, Expanded Academic ASAP, and LexisNexis Academic support one or both subjects.

The Automotive and other various engineering topics are included primarily in Engineering and Allied Operations (620). Monetary support in the area has primarily gone to Fire Science resources. Combined, Expanded Academic ASAP and Ebscohost's MAS Ultra and Academic Search Premier databases are useful, although not exhaustive, sources of automotive articles. Academic Search Premier is the primary support for the spectrum of engineering topics.

As noted in Table 14.3, numerous other curricular areas have substantial enrollments, if not actual students majoring in the area. Art, Biology, Chemistry, Drama, English, Geography, History, Math, Music, Physical Education, Physics, Political Science, Sociology, Spanish, and Speech are the more visible general subjects. Many subjects, including those discussed previously, emphasize the biographical, remedial and skill development topics, specific time periods or cultural eras, field overviews, reference materials, and the vocationally relevant. These aspects influence the types of materials faculty and students desire.

FUTURE CONSIDERATIONS

Hutchinson Community College continues to experience increased enrollment. Programs such as Fire Science and Practical Nursing are among those enjoying the growth. Web- and telecommunications-based courses and programming at South Campus, Newton, and McPherson contribute significantly to the increases. Student populations continue to have a higher female to male ratio, exhibit consistent age characteristics, and draw primarily from the immediate four-county area plus Sedgwick County. However, the percentage of ethnic minority students is increasing. The population of students living in campus housing will also increase with the opening of the expanded residence hall by fall 2005. Located across the street from the JFKL, Gowans Stadium renovations continue on the coattails of the recent openings of the Rimmer Learning Resource Center, which houses JFKL, and Stringer Fine Arts Center. Campus reinvestments have improved the attractiveness and functionality of campus, and enabled programs to expand and the infrastructure to be placed to support them. Institutional growth and change challenge JFKL's abilities to effectively support academic programs.

Efforts to improve the content of and remote access to JFKL managed resources has been documented in Tables 14.4 and 14.5. Although we cannot count numbers of remote users accessing e-book resources, some data has become available regarding access to databases; namely, 2,346 accesses to a Web site providing remote user access to databases were recorded from November 2003 through October 2004. Students are able to log in to the site by using HCC's WebCT or Campus Connect software, faculty are able to reach the site through a separate faculty access process. Clearly, databases are a heavily used resource, e-book use is rising, and users are taking advantage of remote access to databases. Substantial time is committed during JFKL staff's general and course-integrated instructional sessions to teaching electronic resource accessibility and use.

After a considerable decline in use from 1999–2000 through 2002–2003 monographic collections saw a rebound in 2003–2004. Investments in e-book collections have yielded information use/need data that confirms the popularity of some subject matter as well as revealed areas of weakness in monographic collections. Interlibrary Loan statistics have also served as an indicator of collection needs. Expenditure information has painted a picture of declining funding for books, as more financial resources have been needed for e-book collection purchases and database subscriptions, and a need to distribute funding across broader subject stratification. It is too preliminary to make judgments regarding how much funding is needed to meet curricular needs for all programs, a great deal more legwork will be required to describe those needs in detail.

Many program areas have received little or no funding. Selection practices may have been a contributing factor. Communication with faculty regarding resource needs has been reactive in nature; contact primarily occurred when faculty, particularly freshman English Composition course instructors, visited or phoned JFKL when instruction or general tour sessions were scheduled or if a faculty member had a specific request. Resources often have been chosen based upon faculty emphases in those courses or otherwise reactive to current student research interests. Primary review sources that staff members use are *Library Journal*, *Choice*, and *New York Times Book Review*. They have also relied heavily on catalogs. Reviews appearing in most other professional, trade, and scholarly publications have not been routinely scanned. Segments of collections are more difficult to develop when relying on traditional review sources because some subjects are inconsistently or under represented, or not covered at all.

An inhibitor to increasing the quantity of resources, and the overall quality of resources, managed by JFKL is price increases. Actual budgetary changes can be seen in Tables 14.4, 14.5, and 14.13. Table 14.13 documents past and expected database costs for 2002–2003 through 2004–2005, and Table 4 compares electronic database versus periodical subscription expenditures since 1999–2000. Note the declining budgeting for books since 1999–2000 in Table 14.5, although an effort is being made to reverse that trend for 2004–2005.

Before any forward-looking statements can be made regarding anticipated costs of curricular support, we must examine recent and anticipated pricing trends.

Recent volumes of *The Bowker Annual: Library and Book Trade Almanac* reveal mixed pricing trends, detailed in Table 14.14, relevant to JFKL purchasing practices.[10] U.S. College Books, North American Academic Books, and U.S. Paperbacks especially paint a picture of per-volume costs consistent with JFKL selection practices. U.S. College Books are a set of titles, reviewed in *Choice*, of interest to college librarians regardless of format. North American Academic Books are a set of titles treated for approval plan customers by Baker and Taylor/ BP and Blackwell North America. U.S. Paperbacks is compiled from Bowker's *Books in Print* database and excludes mass market paperbacks. Typically JFKL has purchased trade paperback editions. Hardbacks have been considered based on cost and anticipated use, physical shelf life, and timelessness. It has been somewhat atypical for mass market paperback editions of title selections to be available. The mixed trend has been somewhat of a benefit to JFKL. Although budget allocations have been declining, the increased cost of some formats has been offset by declines in others. As an industry, the net effect has been relative price stabilization. Moderate inflation, 2–5 percent, is the expectation for future costs.

Table 14.14
Average Book Prices by Market

Year	Mass Market Pbs	U. S. PBs	HBs Under $81	U. S. College Books	HB Books	No. Am. Acad. Books
1997	$5.36	$38.45				
1999	5.64	32.93	$35.96	$52.04	$62.32	$56.30
2000	5.77	31.07	36.20	53.22	60.84	57.42
2001	6.31	38.20	36.48	54.24	70.05	57.65
2002	6.39	31.33	35.74		62.84	
2003	6.34	30.02	35.24		62.94	

To stretch budgets and improve access to monographic materials to non-residential and distance education, students investments have been made in NetLibrary shared e-book collections. Primarily purchased through Bibliographic Center for Research (BCR), an Aurora, Colorado–based nonprofit library services cooperative, four collections are now accessible. More than 11,000 titles are accessible to campus clientele, including the BCR's Ready Reference, Community College, and Shared Collections. Integrated into JFKL's online catalog as well as available to search separately, use of e-book collections is developing into a viable resource. However, as older titles and title editions within the collections are superseded by the new, more active management of e-book collections must also occur than simply purchasing access to a new collection.

Although periodical subscriptions have not been included within the scope of the study, their overall impact on materials budgeting warrants inclusion. As described previously, subscriptions were reduced from more than 200 to 140 in fall 2003. And although minor adjustments were made in fall 2004, the number of titles has remained the same. Table 14.4 documents past and anticipated expenditures for periodicals, including the impact of an institutionwide budget cut at the beginning of 2003–2004. In its April 15 issue, *Library Journal* typically analyzes trends in periodical costs for titles included in Academic Search Elite, for the benefit of small academic libraries, and MAS Ultra, for school and small public libraries. Both are representative of JFKL's roster of periodical subscriptions. Anticipated 6–13 percent price increases, projected in the 2004 issue, for 2004–2005 were confirmed upon the arrival of renewal notices.[11] These increases built on 9–13 percent increases that were projected for 2003–2004 in the 2003 issue.[12] As *Library Journal* has used a standard database to identify pools of periodicals for study, pricing trends identified within those pools invariably extend to the database.

Databases and electronic book collections have commanded an increasing amount of financial resources. Anticipated database costs for 2004–2005 show only a slight increase from 2003–2004, primarily because Ebscohost froze prices as a result of the recessionary American economy. This one-time benefit is expected to yield to future price increases. Full-time equivalent–based subscription services such as LexisNexis have also increased in cost as HCC's enrollment has grown. Expectations are for upper-single to low-double digit percentage price increases similar to those *Library Journal* anticipated for periodical subscriptions in databases comparable to those to which JFKL subscribes.

Without surveying clientele on an informal and formal basis, preliminary indications are that there are instances in which particular program and student interests are receiving adequate support, most notably Nursing and related allied health areas. Communication with faculty assists in selection of resources to support freshman level English Composition courses and has led to improvements in materials selection in subjects such as Mathematics, arts categories, Spanish and French language materials, and Fire Science. However, numerous content areas, particularly the natural and physical sciences, are inadequately supported. Efforts are needed to gain a thorough grasp of the nature of all HCC programs, including the personalities driving and teaching within each program. As knowledge is gained, processes to identify and manage program supportive resources, and to meet client—especially student —needs, can then be improved. Regardless of current material format a 5–20 percent overall increase in annual resource costs is the near-term expectation to maintain current acquisition levels. However, as information technology continues to evolve and new formats and standards spread, additional costs and budget adjustments will be incurred to take advantage of the known formats currently included at JFKL (e.g., MP3, electronic periodical subscriptions, open access publications) and those that may be developed in the future.

REFERENCES

ACRL College and Research Libraries Task Force. 2004. "Standards for Libraries in Higher Education: the Final, Approved Standard," *College & Research Libraries News*. 65 (October): 534–43.

Anderson, Susan. 2003. "Standards," *Community & Junior College Libraries*. 11 (3): 63–64.

Bogart, Dave, ed. 2002. *The Bowker Annual: Library and Book Trade Almanac 2002*. 47th Ed. Medford, NJ: Information Today.

———, ed. 2003. *The Bowker Annual: Library and Book Trade Almanac 2003*. 48th Ed. Medford, NJ: Information Today.

———, ed. 2004. *The Bowker Annual: Library and Book Trade Almanac 2004*. 49th Ed. Medford, NJ: Information Today.

Buckland, Michael. 1992. *Redesigning Library Services: A Manifesto*. Chicago: American Library Association.

Carrigan, Dennis. 1996. "Collection Development—Evaluation," *Journal of Academic Librarianship*. 22 (4): 273–78.

Dowell, David R., and Jack S. Scott. 1995. "What Community Colleges Need from Their Libraries." In *Academic Libraries: Their Rationale and Role in American Higher Education*, Gerard B McCabe and Ruth Person, eds. (Contributions in Librarianship and Information Science; no. 84) Westport, CT: Greenwood Press.

The Higher Learning Commission. 2003. *Overview of Accreditation*. Available from: <http://www.ncahigherlearningcommission.org/overview/index.html#Programs>. Accessed 22 September 2004.

Kansas State Library. *Kansas Library Card: Databases Available*. Available from <http://www.kslc.org/databases.jsp>. Accessed 2 November 2004.

Maloy, Frances. 2004. "Creativity as a Leadership Strategy in Times of Change: The 2004–05 ACRL President's Theme," *College and Research Libraries News*. 65 (8): 444–46, 469.

Orsdel, Lee Van, and Kathleen Born. 2003. "Periodicals Price Survey 2003: Big Chill or the Big Deal?" *Library Journal*. 128 (April): 51–56.

———. 2004. "Periodicals Price Survey 2004: Closing in on Open Access," *Library Journal*. 129 (April): 45–50.

Shook, Gary. 2003. "New Frontiers in Collection Development: Preparing a Plan to Meet New Standards." Presentation at Sirsi Midwest User's Group Meeting, 24–25 May, at College of St. Mary's, Omaha, Nebraska.

NOTES

All URLs cited in the text were retrieved 12/2004.

1. Susan Anderson, "Standards," *Community & Junior College Libraries* 11, no. 3 (2003): 63.

2. The Higher Learning Commission, "Overview of Accreditation," 2003. 22 September, 2004 <http://www.ncahigherlearningcommission.org/overview/index.html#Programs>

3. ACRL College and Research Libraries Task Force, "Standards for Libraries in Higher Education: the Final, Approved Standard," *College and Research Libraries News*. 65, no. 9 (October, 2004): 534–543.

4. Michael Buckland, *Redesigning Library Services: A Manifesto* (Chicago: American Library Association, 1992), p. 3.

5. David R. Dowell and Jack A. Scott, "What Community Colleges Need from Their Libraries," in *Academic Libraries: Their Rationale and Role in American Higher Education*, eds. Gerard B. McCabe and Ruth Person (Westport, CT: Greenwood Press, 1995), p. 17.

6. Frances Maloy, "Creativity as a Leadership Strategy in Times of Change: The 2004–05 ACRL President's Theme," *College & Research Libraries News* 65, no. 8 (2004): 445.

7. Dennis Carrigan, "Collection Development—Evaluation," *The Journal of Academic Librarianship* 22, no. 4 (1996): 273.

8. Kansas State Library, "The Kansas Library Card: Databases Available," 2 November, 2004 <http://www.kslc.org/databases.jsp>

9. Gary Shook, "New Frontiers in Collection Development : Preparing a Plan to Meet New Standards" (Presentation at Sirsi Midwest Users Group Meeting, Omaha, Nebraska, July 24–25, 2003).

10. Data was drawn from the 2002–2004 editions. Updated U.S. College Book and North American Academic Book information updating 2001 information was not in the 2004 annual.

11. Lee Van Orsdel and Kathleen Born, "Periodicals Price Survey 2004: Closing in on Open Access," *Library Journal* 129 no. 7 (15 April, 2004): 49–50.

12. Lee Van Orsdel and Kathleen Born, "Periodicals Price Survey 2003: Big Chill or the Big Deal?" *Library Journal* 128, no. 7 (15 April, 2003): 55–56.

15 LEADERSHIP IN ENERGY AND ENVIRONMENTAL DESIGN: NEW TECHNOLOGIES THAT SIMPLIFY BUILDING MANAGEMENT

Gerard B. McCabe

The Leadership in Energy and Environmental Design Green Building Rating System, established in 2000, is a voluntary, consensus-based national standard for developing high-performance, sustainable buildings developed and administered by the U.S. Green Building Council....LEED standards are currently available for new construction and major renovation projects, existing building operations, commercial interiors projects, and core and shell projects. 'Environmentally responsible' seems to be the consensus when it comes to defining a green building....the basic LEED standard considers site sustainability, water efficiency, content of materials and resources, indoor environmental quality and innovative design.

(http://texas.construction.com/common/print.asp? accessed 3/19/04)

THE DIRECTOR'S ROLE

The natural inclination for library directors is concern for adequate space for readers, services, and staff. For readers the concern is for suitable surroundings, group studies, accessible collections, quiet study areas, and comfortable chairs and workplaces. For staff, well-designed space with ample room for equipment is ever the issue. Rightfully, these matters do require and deserve the major portion of the director's attention. Employing a qualified library consultant is advantageous to a planning project. If this isn't possible, the burden falls almost entirely on the director. The director should encourage staff contribution to the process to avoid overlooking important matters and provide for staff morale. If an architect with library building experience is employed, there is some advantage. This person will understand infrastructure requirements, but the director should bring some knowledge of special requirements to the planning process.

The director must be aware of current developments in technologies that will help operate the library effectively and minimize loss of time on the part of readers, staff, and the director. An informed library leader is an effective member of the planning team, fulfilling the role of a cooperative colleague with other members of the team. This chapter begins with a statement on Leadership in Energy and Environmental Design (LEED) because the LEED precepts must be clearly in the forefront of the planning process. I then discuss some new technological developments that will help in the planning process, help improve understanding, and provide relief from minor but disruptive annoyances in the future when the library building is operational.

DEMOGRAPHICS

In planning for renovation/expansion or for a new building, enrollment projections are important, but it's even more important to know the possible makeup or characteristics of the forthcoming student population. U.S. Census data is helpful in determining these factors and should be used. Consideration for students with physical disabilities must be part of the planning process. It is naïve to think that planning need only follow guidelines accompanying the Americans with Disabilities Act (ADA). More thoughtfulness is necessary than would first appear. It's better to have an understanding of what to expect in the enrollment mix then to just plan accommodations and think that's enough.

Several of the suggestions in this chapter will appear to go beyond ADA requirements. To determine what the enrollment mix could very well be, search the U.S. Census 2000 first for your state and then the county or counties your library serves. Find Quick Tables DP-2. Profile of Selected Social Characteristics: 2000. A few lines above the bottom of the first page is a row titled "Disability Status of the Civilian Noninstitutionalized." Succeeding lines give the population with a disability by age ranges. Elsewhere in the Census reports information explains that this is long-term disabilities.

Much of this data is of importance to public libraries, but it's safe to assume that the future enrollment will include students with digital, hearing, mobility, and vision impairments, possibly in larger numbers than past enrollment experience would indicate. Media reports also show that persons with disabilities are more proactive than has been the prior case and so mere conformity to ADA requirements will not do. Better to be alert to these issues in the planning process than to be surprised by negative reactions when the building becomes operational. For more awareness, see the *Seattle Times* entry in the Selected Bibliography.

Awareness of LEED qualifications and needs of persons with disabilities is of initial importance, and that is why this chapter begins with these two topics.

TRICKLE-DOWN TECHNOLOGY

Most if not all the technologies described in this chapter originated to meet demands from business and industry. Some relate to construction or operation of buildings, and others, designed for application in the internal working environment, are adaptations or modifications for use in libraries. Much of the recent new technologies seen at library association conference exhibits are the latter: adaptations or modifications of industrial technologies. The original manufacturers are not dependent solely on the library market. Two simple examples are described.

Delivery and Inventory Control

The cutting-edge advancements unveiled recently at United Parcel Service Inc. start with what appears to be a simple white sticker.

But the stickers are very high-tech labels. All are encoded with information that helps guide 13 million boxes and envelopes across the nation and to 20 countries to the correct conveyor belt, the correct delivery van, even to the exact shelf in the van. (Cohn 2004, D1)

For libraries employing UPS for interlibrary loan service, this is how the shipments are handled. There are many other technological advances adapted specifically for libraries. They offer many advantages and have been tested under often more severe working demands than libraries provide. This leaves very little concern for librarians who need only assess the capability of these technologies to meet their libraries particular conditions.

Radio frequency identification technology is sweeping through industry. Vendors are offering adaptations for libraries. For more information, see Boss (2004).

Technology for Buildings

From the early 1960s through the early 1970s many new academic institutions, including community, technical colleges, and institutes came into existence. Some venerable institutions tracing their origins to the early twentieth century or even before that took on new missions or redefined their roles in the educational sphere of our country. With a new campus came a new library building. Now an aging 30 or more years old, these once sparkling buildings must be renovated, expanded, or, in some cases, replaced with an entirely new facility. In some locales population growth is forcing the development of whole new campuses, or to facilitate library service in a practical way for both students and community residents, public and community college libraries are uniting into single large buildings to better serve both groups. In some areas, cultural demands are bringing museums and libraries together (see Dilevko and Gottlieb 2004). A very large number of building projects are either underway, being planned, or receiving attention that will result in a project in the near future. In short, many readers of this book are involved or will be involved in planning new buildings or major renovations.

Whether your project is for a freestanding building or a shared building, for the greater benefit of service to the academic community, the building must be modern, economical to operate, and energy efficient.

Nationwide the concern of both government and the construction industry is for energy efficiency and sustainability. Architects and contractors are responding to the challenge. Media coverage is extensive because significant changes are occurring in construction technology; states are granting tax relief for such projects, and all levels of construction from large high-rise buildings to residences of varying sizes are affected. Publications are appearing on- and offline. Newspapers report on so-called green building projects that are planned with innovative energy saving and sustainable features. Fairley writes about the increasing use of solar power through use of photovoltaic glass (PV) in *Architectural Record:* "The use of solar power is growing rapidly. PV installations in the U.S. jumped 53 percent in 2002 and rose another 30 to 40 percent last year, according to the Solar Energy Industries Association" (Fairley 2004, 161).

Activity Increases

Will new accommodations cause significant growth in use of library services? Shill and Tonner, in a landmark study, believe the results will be positive:

> The investigators found that 80 percent of the libraries completing a major space improvement project between 1995 and 2002 experienced greater facility usage in 2001–2002 than they did in a preproject baseline year, whereas 20 percent of the responding libraries reported lesser usage. The median change in post-occupancy usage was a 37.4 percent increase. (Shill and Tonner 2004, 148)

The authors' study revealed that certain improvements directly influenced growth in activity, most involving computer services for both tabletop and laptop computers, better seating and physical comfort. This article and its predecessor are worth reading. You will be better prepared with ideas for improvements that students appreciate.

Affordability

Before describing some of the sustainability issues that can affect library construction, it is clear that construction costs will be higher, but operational cost savings over a period of time, dependent upon the scope of the project, will recover the additional costs. There is disagreement on the extent of extra costs. One source in California suggests about 2 percent more whereas sources in

Maryland suggest 10 percent but foresee falling prices (Hopkins 2003, D4). There is no disagreement on the lowering of operational costs. This is the important consideration for college librarians—keeping the library open daily as long as necessary is critical to the success of its mission. Again, Fairley (2004, 161) writes "When combined with high energy prices, the payback period for investment in PV can be as little as four years." The question for libraries is not "Can we afford this?" but rather "Can we afford to bypass new technologies that will reduce daily operating costs?" In some of this country's geographic areas some other technology may provide similar results.

When beginning planning, never rule out any technological advance as being "too expensive," not "affordable for our budget." This process takes time, sometimes extending several years; costs might and probably will decrease. Sometimes funds will suddenly become available and the order is given to proceed with the project as it exists without an opportunity to review and change the included technologies for more advanced items. The results of the bid procedure could well produce acceptable costs.

BUSINESS AND INDUSTRY: BUILDING FEATURES IN COMMON WITH LIBRARIES/LEARNING RESOURCE CENTERS

There are library areas that are not dissimilar from areas in business or industrial buildings. One area common to all is office space. In November 2003 *Architectural Record* published *Architectural Record Review Office Buildings*, a very useful supplement for library office planners. One of the more important and useful features is the trend toward under-floor air distribution and under-floor power/communications supply. Merkel (2003a, 10–11) quotes architect Bruce Fowle: "the move to under floor air distribution for environmental reasons, along with task and indirect lighting [and mobile communications], really frees up office space," allowing maximal flexibility and higher more interesting ceilings". In another article in the same supplement Merkel reviews a postoccupancy evaluation of an office building (Merkel 2003b, 31). Here are some pointers:

- Bringing employees into the design process helps them to accept change.
- Open office space can encourage teamwork.
- Consider office space a business tool.
- Under-floor air and cabling improves heating and cooling functions and makes moving people easy.

Following the trend to under-floor air distribution, *Baltimore Sun* staff writer Jamie Smith Hopkins, supports a column one Business section article with sidebars featuring Maryland green building projects. With an illustrating photograph, one reports "RTKL Associates Inc. Its year-old Baltimore office is a pilot project for green interiors, with bamboo floors, a built-in shower for people bicycling to work and air distribution through the floor instead of the ceiling to save on energy" (Hopkins 2003, D1).

In this well-researched article, Hopkins goes on to discuss other green, or, as some now prefer, high-performance buildings (Hopkins 2003, D4). This quotation makes the case for green very compelling and presents strong talking points for planning library projects.

"A study conducted for California's Sustainable Building Task Force, released last month, found that an average so-called green building uses 30 percent less energy than a conventional counterpart. A strategy as simple as more windows means facilities are less reliant on artificial lighting, which in turn keeps the indoor air cooler—which means less money spent on air conditioning. Builders can buy windows made of high-tech glass that keeps heat from seeping in or out" (Hopkins 2003, D4).

A fine example of what is described here is Santa Monica College Library's new addition. This now modernized California community college library is the subject of a feature article in the December 2004 issue of *Architectural Record*.

This brings up the next topic. Again, there is a common interest with business and industry.

Lighting

I can't write about lighting without including windows/window glass, sensors, atria, and skylights. These all affect the quality of lighting, and achieving a balance requires understanding of how each relates to the objective(good quality lighting to meet the needs of all persons in any area of the library). Most librarians are aware now of the benefits of natural light and that to obtain the objective of as much natural light as possible in work and reader spaces means having windows of a good size. Librarians aren't alone in this concern. It's an issue for business and industry. For the business/industrial interests, the concern is for workspace, whereas librarians' broader interests include reader space. The solutions are the same because readers are workers too.

Glass

Window glass is available that blocks ultraviolet rays and reduces glare. Sensors near windows will adjust artificial light levels as natural light brightens or fades. Acoustical glass for interior use aids in noise containment. Atria and skylights can admit natural light into the interior. I encourage their use; the benefits are substantial.

In fall 2005, Vista Community College, Berkeley, opens a new 165,000 gross square feet campus building. A major building is a six-story atrium with a skylight. Centrally located, the atrium will bring natural light into the building. For the exterior consider a glass canopy over the main entry. Options for this canopy are the use of photovoltaic glass or solar panels. Either will generate some power for lighting the exterior. If in locations where vandalism is a factor, request impact-resistant safety glass for windows on lower floors.

There are many options for using glass to help make the library attractive. Among these are stained glass and overlay and tinted or colored glass. If glass will enhance the attractiveness of an area, don't hesitate to request it.

For open areas where computers are in use and in computer laboratories, if these are used, ambient lighting is preferable for no or minimal glare on monitor screens.

The photographs that follow show Cuesta College Library's entry way and Circulation counter. The skylight illuminates the counter and traffic area attractively.

Shatford Library, Pasadena City College, California, uses sensors to regulate and adjust natural and artificial lighting intensity during daylight hours. A fine example of the use of mirror glass for exterior windows is that of MiraCosta College's new library at its Oceanside, California, campus opened in December 2002. This attractive building has a large wheel-like skylight over an area described as "The Hub." This library, as well as the Cuesta Library and the Shatford Library have excellent interior lighting.

The need for and the actual craving for natural light by students and staff is so critical that every means for gaining natural light should be utilized. Exterior win-

Cuesta College Library—Circulation counter entry traffic area, skylight above, and windows behind the counter. To the right sunlight from a Palladian window falls on the floor. Used with permission of Cuesta College. Photo by Stephen Gunsaulus.

Cuesta College Library, view of well-lighted Circulation workspace. Square windows on far wall are balanced by square campus photographs.

dows should be large, and clerestory windows should be used when walls might block natural light. The Natural Resources Defense Council advocates use of clerestory windows and other means for extending natural light into buildings (NRDC).

Clerestory windows on interior workrooms and study rooms allowing the extension of artificial lighting will reduce lighting costs, even if remote from natural light sources. In extreme cases, the use of roof mounted tubing extending into these areas with light diffusers will bring the benefits of natural light to people working in those areas.

Carpet

The benefits of using electrostatic carpet appear obvious, but errors can occur. The specifications and bid documents should state this requirement, clearly and a replacement clause should be in the purchase contract if the carpet proves defective or inferior to the specifications. In a recent year-old public library carpeted in all areas where carpet is appropriate, the carpet was neither electrostatic nor commercial grade. Wear in several traffic areas was very noticeable. Students will complain if static electricity interferes with their computer work. Replacing shabby badly worn carpet in only a few years is costly and time consuming for heavily used academic libraries.

The means of keeping carpet clean begins at the main entry. Some methods for removing dirt, rain, snow, or ice melting chemicals from footgear should be provided both on the exterior and interior of the main entry doors. These simple provisions will help preserve carpeting and reduce fading from harmful chemicals. Hotels and restaurants provide excellent examples at their entries.

Doors

For the main entry to the building, sliding glass doors are preferable and are appearing on renovated and new buildings with high public traffic. Sliding doors are used for retail stores, supermarkets, restaurants, hotels, and public libraries. They provide the easiest and safest access for all persons and are especially appreciated by those with mobility impairments.

The interior use of sliding and pocket doors may not occur to either you or your architect. These should be used for entries to interior classrooms and laboratories. When visiting older buildings, it's not unusual to see the swinging doors to rooms of these types propped open. Recessing these doors during service hours provides even easier access for the mobility-impaired.

Keys and the Key Plan

The choice of and planning for a key system is often very difficult. There are new technologies for metal key systems, and then there are card systems. It has been several years since I last registered at a hotel and was given a metal key. I favor a card system for a library building. The advantages are several, including reuse of plastic cards, lightness, easy replacement, and better security when a card is lost. Yet persuading other campus planners to convert isn't easy. In some buildings, compromise is possible in that both card and metal key systems can be used. Facilities maintenance staff might prefer metal keys for accessing utility rooms. This issue of key access is worth serious discussion.

Regardless of the final outcome some decisions should be made early in the planning process. Think carefully about which rooms or service spaces should have controlled access or might require control later if experience indicates a need. Retrofitting for key control or ease of access/entry can be expensive if something was overlooked. One good example is that of a staff entrance to the building. Plan to use a keypad. Incoming staff can quickly punch a code into a keypad to open this door. This feature provides for security and will be much appreciated during bad weather when fumbling through pockets or purse for a key or card can be annoying. Regardless of whether you are planning for metal keys or plastic cards, keep the plan simple so the number of either is minimal.

Restrooms

Nationally, the trend is to "hands-free" restrooms. Modern restrooms have automatic faucets, automatic flushing, electronic soap dispensers, and paper towel dispensers. Sometimes electronic hand dryers are used, though health experts consider them less efficient then paper towels for removing bacteria from hands and power usage is high. Electronic paper towel dispensers in my view are superior. "Hands-free" is something to insist on; should an outbreak of some contagion occur, complaints about the restrooms should be minimal. The industry is competitive and choices are available for all of these advanced devices.

Wireless Computer Service—"Wi-Fi"

Whether or not plans for your new library include computer laboratories or classrooms, it would be wise to plan for wireless service throughout the building. In so doing provide for exterior access to the system from surrounding patios. Boston Public Library provides wireless service in its main building and all other locations. In San Diego, the strikingly beautiful Point Loma branch public library has an exterior patio above street level with wireless accessibility for laptop computers. During pleasant weather students can sit outside their college library and continue their academic work. Indications are that costs for installing wireless are very affordable.

During spring 2004, media reported on wireless security issues, including concerns for security of laptops. At this writing, most if not all of these issues should be resolved. This is a matter to discuss with the vendors, but is not cause for declining to move ahead with wireless technology.

If your campus is in a remote area and online service seems unattainable, consider the experience of the city of Cerritos, California. Unable to obtain either cable or DSL service, city officials signed an agreement with a wireless service company "to install a citywide Wi-Fi network" ("Cerritos Goes Wi-Fi" 2003). If in similar circumstances advise your college administration to consider this possibility.

Planning Thoroughly

Quite often the planning sequences will seem repetitious, but repetition is a means of avoiding oversights. Never decline to bring up a question even though the answer might be obvious because it may lead to a chain of interrelated actions that have a direct bearing on success. Don't leave planning to others in a misplaced fit of confidence; sometimes people forget common solutions; why be embarrassed later when suddenly something seemingly routine is noticed as missing, as in the case of the new public library's nonelectrostatic and noticeably worn carpet? Engage the staff in the planning effort. They will work in the building for a long time; their morale will be positive when they know they contributed to a successful project. An academic library is important and will serve for many years; everyone working together can ensure the best of outcomes.

REFERENCES

Boss, Richard W. 2004. *RFID Technology for Libraries*. Chicago: American Library Association.

Boston Public Library. *Wireless Access at the Boston Public Library*. http://www.bpl.org/general/wireless.htm. Accessed 23 August 2005.

"Cerritos Goes Wi-Fi." 2003. *Information Week Wireless* (December 12), n.p.

Cohn, Meredith. 2004. "UPS Is Scurrying to Stay out Ahead," *Baltimore Sun* (May 23), D1, D2.

Dilevko, Juris, and Lisa Gottlieb. 2004. *The Evolution of Library and Museum Partnerships: Historical Antecedents, Contemporary Manifestations, and Future Directions*. Westport, CT: Libraries Unlimited, The Libraries Unlimited Library Management Collection.

Fairley, Peter. 2004. "In the U.S., Architects Are Ramping up the Design Power of Photovoltaics," *Architectural Record* (March), 161–64.

Hopkins, Jamie Smith. 2003. "Buildings Save when Friendly to Environment," *Baltimore Sun*. (November 30) Business, D1, D4.

Merkel, Jayne. 2003a. "The Fluid Office," *Architectural Record Review* (November), 7–14.

———. 2003b. "Post-Occupancy 2003 Owens Corning Toledo, Ohio," *Architectural Record Review* (November), 31.

Natural Resources Defense Council. http://www.nrdc.org. Accessed November 2004.

Shill, Harold B., and Shawn Tonner. 2004. "Does the Building Still Matter? Usage Patterns in New, Expanded and Renovated Libraries, 1995–2002," *College & Research Libraries* 65 (2), 123–50.

Vista Community College. http://vista.peralta.edu/new_building/default.htm. Accessed 23 August 2005.

SELECTED BIBLIOGRAPHY

"Accessibility in Libraries Tutorial." 2004. An Educational Service of the American Library Association's Office for Information Technology Policy. http://www.ala.org/ala/washoff/oitp/emailtutorials/accessibilitya/01.htm. Accessed November 30, 2004.

"Acclaimed Library Disappoints Disabled, but Corrections Promised." 2004. *Seattle Times* (June 20) http://seattletimes.nwsource.com/html/localnews/2001960578_library20m.html. Accessed August 6, 2004.

ALA Tech Notes. http://www.ala.org/ala/pla/plapubs/technotes/rfidtechnology.htm. Accessed May 31, 2004.

"The Business Case for Sustainable Design in Federal Facilities." 2003. U.S. Department of Energy. Federal Energy Management Program. www.eere.energy.gov/femp. Accessed November 29, 2004.

California Energy Commission. 2003. "Windows and Offices: A Study of Office Worker Performance and the Indoor Environment." technical report, California Energy Commission. Prepared by Heschong Mahone Group. http://www.newbuildings.org/pier/downloadsFinal.htm. Accessed November 29, 2004.

Newman, Morris. 2004. "Santa Monica College Library, Santa Monica, California," *Architectural Record* (December), 204–10.

Shill, Harold B., and Shawn Tonner. 2003. "Creating a Better Place: Physical Improvements in Academic Libraries, 1995–2002." *College & Research Libraries* 64 (6), 431–66.

VI

CONTROLLING THE FISCAL REALITY: POLICIES CAN SOLVE PROBLEMS

16 BUDGETING: MOVING FROM PLANNING TO ACTION

David R. Dowell

One of the realities of managing a college library is that the available financial resources are never enough to support all the collections and services that would facilitate student learning. This is so obvious that it hardly needs to be said. However, that statement frames the discussion of this chapter and links it to the earlier chapter on planning. It is not the intent of this chapter to provide a detailed, step-by-step, and encyclopedic guide to successful fiscal management of college libraries. Many texts already exist on budget management. The knowledge, skills, and techniques needed to manage library budgets are similar to those required in many other settings. Therefore, this chapter only covers the broad outlines and adds an eclectic pattern of observations about subtle differences that occur within the college library venue.

BUDGETING: BEGINNING THE PLANNING PROCESS

Once objectives have been established as part of the planning process, it is time to develop the map that will guide the implementation of these objectives. As Vierthaler indicates in Chapter 13, "supporting the survival, advancement, and growth of the institution" is a goal of most organizations. In actuality, just supporting the status quo is the goal of some. It is easy for the budget to become a silent instigator for maintaining the status quo. In most organizations, the institutional processes create subtle pressure toward inertia by rolling the previous year's budget into the current year. Active intervention is required to initiate any movement in the goals of advancement and growth to better meet the needs of student learning.

Such a process also ignores the sage advice of Peter Drucker and other strategic thinkers who suggest that the first step in any rational budget planning process is to identify what current activities have outlived their usefulness and can be given up. This process, if used effectively, will have the potential to free up resources for activities that have a higher potential to help students learn. Such assessments cannot be effective unless all the sacred cows of the library staff come under scrutiny. If such rigorous reviews are used systematically, they are time intensive and can be emotionally draining. This should not be undertaken lightly or so frequently that it becomes merely an exercise.

On the other hand, such techniques as zero-based budgeting do have their place. One good time is during the first budget planning cycle after new directors are selected. To be successful, it will mean that this cycle will have to begin much earlier than normal. The process of examining every activity in the library can be a great learning opportunity for both the new director and the staff. At that point the director's ego is not as firmly attached to the status quo as it may become later. Therefore staff can be encouraged to make suggestions without fearing that they will seem to be criticizing the library leader. The goal should be that each activity of the library is either validated or resources are redirected to higher priorities.

Managing fiscal resources in college libraries is all about setting and carrying out priorities. It involves a number of distinctly different components. Stueart and Moran (2002, 440–41) list the following three:

1. "Preparation of the budget;
2. Presentation to funding authorities, with full justification linking inputs with outputs (results); and
3. Implementation of the actual beginning of the phase for which the budget has been allocated."

These important phases seem to downplay the importance of monitoring incremental progress toward following the plan outlined in the budget and making midcourse corrections if necessary. Each of these activities are discussed in subsequent sections.

Budget Preparation and Long-Range Planning

Developing the annual budget in a college library is primarily about outlining the spending plan for the coming year. This should flow from a longer-range planning process. For those skeptical of the effectiveness of long-range planning, it may be useful to look at planning as making today's operational decisions, taking into account what the long-term ramifications will be. As the old Chinese proverb says, "A trip of 1,000 miles begins with one step." Sometimes managers fail to realize that deciding to preserve the status quo, or even refusing to make a decision today, will often have long-range consequences as significant as making a decision to implement radical change.

242

BUDGET PLANNING AND ENHANCING REVENUE

Managing finances, or putting planning into action, involves more than just dealing with the annual operating budget. It involves deciding whether to invest time and effort to try to enhance revenue flow by such activities as the following:

- Applying for grants;
- Organizing a Friends of the Library auxiliary organization; or
- Initiating other fundraising activities.

These activities, if undertaken, need to be coordinated with the fundraising arm of the college and/or with the upper levels of the administration. It is not in the interest of the college for the library to go out and secure a $1,000 gift from a local individual or company when there was the potential for a $50,000 or a $100,000 or even a larger gift from that same source. Directors of the libraries, acting alone, are usually not in a position to secure such large gifts. Gifts of that size and larger usually require the effort of a team that includes the college president and a director of development. Grants and other increments to the general operating funds of the college can be very useful—particularly for special projects. Friends of the Library organizations need a strong partnership between the college and its community to succeed. Strong leadership from volunteers is also a real plus. Such organizations are much more likely to be found in university and other large libraries that have the critical mass needed to launch and sustain such efforts; but they exist in smaller colleges as well (Gamewell and Dowell 1999). Any fund-raising effort can consume an immense amount of energy and should not be relied upon for support of ongoing operations. Unless used with skill and care, securing such fund-raising activities can drain more resources from the library than they return. Used adroitly, they can add new dimensions to the learning opportunities libraries can make available to students.

Infrastructure and Financial Base

Various components of the library need to be balanced in order to optimize service. Dowell and Scott (1995, 22–24) used the metaphor of a table to describe the components of library infrastructure necessary to convert financial resources into services that facilitate student learning:

> Library infrastructure is the vehicle that coverts resources into library services for the benefit of constituencies. To better communicate an understanding of this infrastructure, it will be described as a table with four legs. Experience with four-legged tables tells us how important it is that all four legs are the same length and that the floor that supports them is strong and stable. In this analogy, resources (primarily financial) serve as a floor, or the base, for supporting the library table. It

is important to the library that the funding base is strong and stable.

This library infrastructure is a little different than the four-legged table you have been imagining. It really does not look like a folding card table or even a study table in the library. Actually from the outside it looks like a one-legged pedestal table. [See Figure 16.1.] Only when one examines a cross section of this infrastructure is it possible to see the four distinct legs. Each overlaps with each of the other three legs. Therefore, it is even more important that all of them are the same length.

The four legs of this table represent the staff, collections, technology, and facilities. [See Figure 16.2.] The "staff" leg of the table includes recruiting, and developing, and retaining a first-rate library faculty and supporting staff. [See Chapters 1,2, and 3.] The "collections" leg includes all information recorded on paper, plastic, electronic disk, or other media. The "technology" leg includes bibliographic tools such as library catalogs, indexes, finding aids and holdings lists (whether on paper, mechanic or electronic form). Actually, the card catalog was one of the most durable technologies of the twentieth century, and its life almost exactly spanned that time period. The final component of the library table is the "facilities" leg. Its purpose is to house the staff, collections and technology.

Functioning, useful, and productive tables exist not to have legs but to support something. This library table exists to support library services. Excellent library services can be provided to the various clientele of the library when adequate resources have been made available to the library and when those resources have been managed wisely to build four strong legs, each in the proportion that properly supplements the other three legs. (Dowell and Scott 1995, 22–24)

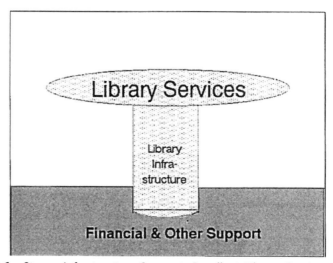

Figure 16.1 Strong Infrastructure Supports Excellent Library Services

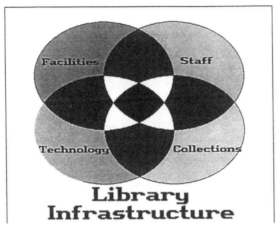

Figure 16.2 A Cross-Section of Library Infrastructure

The Budget within the College Plan

Several college staff members have separate and distinct but sometimes overlapping roles in the funding of library services that support student learning. Although the library director has the primary responsibility for securing and expending the budget, it is important that other supporting players also play their roles effectively. Other librarians and other library staff members share the responsibility for identifying and advocating for maximum library services. Other instructional managers also have a role in identifying and advocating as well. The college foundation, if one exists, has a role in bringing in additional dollars. Fiscal managers and staff have a role in making sure that the college as a whole remains financially stable and viable to continue into the foreseeable future. However, they should not have final authority for setting spending priorities. The chief instructional officer must help the library director understand collegewide priorities and also must lobby for the resources needed to achieve these objectives once they have been agreed on.

There are many techniques for developing systematic budget proposals. The quantitative skill level of the library manager and the upper management who review and approve budget requests will determine which of these may be effective. Stueart and Moran (2002, 443-469) describe a number of techniques generally popular in management literature, such as the following:

- Line item budgets,
- Formula budgets,
- Program budgeting,
- Performance budgeting,
- Planning programming budgeting system, and
- Zero-based budgeting.

Any manager wishing to learn more or wishing to try any of these techniques should consult the "Budgeting Techniques" section of Steuart and Moran (2002, 443–59).

BUDGET DEVELOPMENT AND REAL COSTS

No matter which techniques are employed to develop the budget, it is important for budget managers to be honest with themselves about the total cost of what is being proposed. There is a concept emerging in some colleges to consider the "total cost of ownership" of any increments to the budget. For example, it may be possible to add 50 computer workstations for $50,000. However, the true cost may add two or three times that amount if they overload the network or electrical capacity of the facilities. Technicians to maintain them in good working order are also an issue. Students cannot be expected to learn unless the resources can be counted on to operate reliably.

The total cost of ownership of a staff position is also often underestimated. A new technician may start at $15 an hour. The annual salary cost for such a person would be approximately $30,000 dollars. Fringe benefits alone will likely boost this cost at least 20–30 percent. Then there may be the additional equipment and facilities costs for providing a workstation for the staff member. Training and supervision costs can be substantial and should be considered.

In situations in which true costs of activities are required, another level of complexity should be considered in understanding the true cost of an employee. As we get further into outcomes measurement, it may be important to figure the true staff cost for activities. If we need to know what it really costs to catalog a book or maintain 50 data projectors or extend library hours during the weekend, there are hidden costs that are generally disregarded. Often, we can safely ignore them. However, we should understand them. For a full-time staff member to produce one hour of service, there are vacation, sick leave, holidays, training, and meeting time costs that must be paid for as well. Even the ubiquitous coffee break reduces an 8-hour day to 7.5 hours. The list is endless. The bottom line is that it costs the institution at least 40 percent to 50 percent more for a productive hour of service than the hourly wage of the employee would suggest.

The Budget: Fitting into the College Plan

In reality, the options available to individual budget managers largely will be determined by the budget preparation process of the college of which they are a part. However, in order to participate effectively within these processes, the managers must understand clearly how the college process works. For example, some colleges have a unit planning process that feeds into the overall institutional budgeting process. A copy of the template that outlines one such process is included as Appendix 10.

In the institution in which this document is used, the budget for the library for the next year is assumed to be a rollover of the current budget, plus any increments that result from the justifications and priority setting start with the library's unit plan. All units are instructed to review college goals and specific priorities adopted by the governing board for the coming year as they begin to put together their plan. Detailed information is requested for any item requested. These items are first listed in categories of permanent personnel, operations, equipment, and facilities. The operations category includes student and hourly personnel as well as supplies, software, and so on. It must be specified for each requested item whether it is needed immediately (i.e., in the next year), in the intermediate future (i.e., the second or third year out) or in the longer-range future (i.e., the fourth or fifth year out). All items listed as immediate needs must be prioritized within the category of expenditure. This reflects that at the college level different categories may have different sources of funding and different processes for approval of expenditure. Finally, all items must be listed in an overall priority list.

The library unit plan that emerges is combined with those similar academic support units into a cluster plan. Again, priorities must be set within each category and also for the overall cluster. A great deal of "horse trading" takes place among unit managers at this stage. The resulting cluster plans are then submitted to the college planning and budget committee.

In such situations it is often critical to include in the unit plan any item that may be included in the subsequent budget request or otherwise need to be purchased in the following year. Often the first response to any significant request for expenditure is this: "Is that in your unit plan?" Astute budget managers will be able to at answer in the affirmative. Even if the college does not have a formalized planning process, it will add credibility to a funding request if one is able to say and back up with documentation, "This item is part of our plan." It is even better to be able to say, "The Library is supporting this fiscal year's College Priority 5B by...."

The Budget and the Accounting Process

It is not the purpose of this section to provide an accounting or even a bookkeeping manual. Rather, the intent is to highlight some of the ways in which not-for-profit and/or governmental accounting generally differs from that practiced in the private sector and the form of fiscal control most commonly taught on our campuses. Fund accounting, not double-entry accounting is the vehicle of control employed here. Generally, such issues as cash flow and tax advantage are not involved in the equation.

Accountants and catalog librarians have a lot in common. Both need to be able to think linearly and to be able to follow through long, complex processes. Both need to be good at creating long and involved classification systems. Those of you who understand the intricacies of Dewey Decimal classification schemes should

Table 16.1
Decomposing a Fund Account Number

Category	Fund	Level	Department	Object	Source	Sub-activity
Code	10	03	0710	6130	00	0102
Meaning	General	Academic Vice President	Library	Multi-media	General	A specific satellite campus

have no trouble deciphering the account codes that get set up to record transactions in a fund accounting system. First one must get a copy of the chart of accounts for your college. This is the functional equivalent of our classification tables. The chart of accounts document for your institution may not be as thick as the class tables used in bibliographic categorization, but it can easily run to 30 pages.

The chart of accounts discussed next is partly real and partly fabricated to illustrate the complex but rational way in which fund account numbers are created. The chart of accounts of a college is an organic and ever-changing document. Fund account numbers may be composed of any or all of the following components:

- funds,
- administrative level,
- division/department,
- object,
- source, and
- subactivity.

Not all charts of accounts will have all these categories and some may have additional ones. The list is offered for illustration only. The account code 10–03–0710–6130–00–0102, which is decomposed in Table 16.1, might be assigned to a purchase order to track a transaction in which some digital video disks were purchased for a satellite campus library collection using general funds.

Most of the codes in the various classifications contain many subcategories. It is significant that some of them have two digits and that others have four. In the preceding example, the department, object, and subactivity codes each can be subdivided into as many as 9,999 subcategories. Although most library transactions will be completed by the repetitive use of a few codes, at times other codes will be used.

Budget Funds: Their Differences and Limitations

The most significant fund to college libraries is the general fund. They might also have capital outlay funds; income from endowments, gifts, and grants; and others. Although these may all have different origins and must be treated very differently by accountants, there are two distinctions that are very important to library budget managers. These are the difference between restricted funds and unrestricted funds and the difference between recurring funds and one-time or limited-time funds.

The difference between restricted funds and unrestricted is very simple to an experienced budget manager. However, to their staff, customers, and the general public these differences are not well understood. Restricted funds, whether they come from a gift, endowment earnings, grants, or categorical state funding, most often come with strings attached and can only be used for the purpose specified by the donor or funding authority. Unrestricted funds can be used for any purpose approved by the college. As simple as this is seems to be, library managers will find that they need to repeatedly remind their many constituencies of this fact of life. Money donated for art books cannot be used to patch the roof, no matter how much it needs it. Part of the bond money to construct a new facility cannot be used to create new staff positions even if the operation of that new facility requires more staff to operate it than did the old building. A small part of those millions of dollars of construction money for that gorgeous new building cannot be used to avoid layoffs and service hour reduction brought on by the latest college or state budget crisis. To those we lead and those who rely on us for services, these distinctions may not seem rational. There are, however, ethical and often legal limitations of our latitude to manage our resources to meet both immediate and long-term needs. The most successful library budget managers are the ones who orchestrate all the restricted and unrestricted components available to provide a balanced infrastructure that best assists student learning.

Budget Expenditures: Using Funds Correctly

One of the easiest traps into which a library director can fall is to use nonrecurring funds to pay for recurring expenses. This tactic can solve immediate problems but, in so doing, generally creates a ticking time bomb that will have to be dealt with at a later date. For this reason staff positions and periodical subscriptions generally should not be funded from temporary sources of funding. Limited-time appropriations, one-time gifts, and grants can greatly enhance library services. Many projects would be unthinkable without them. However, they should be used to fund activities that have a defined life cycle such as digitizing a specific collection, buying books for a new satellite campus, or purchasing expensive equipment that has little or no ongoing maintenance costs. Even in these examples there are at least modest ongoing costs that will need to be absorbed by future operational budgets. These continuing costs should not be minimized and should be included in the initial funding plan if at all possible. Funding new positions or initiating an increment to the number of periodicals subscribed to which the college may not have the resources to maintain is a disservice to staff and does not improve long-term student learning.

Budget Control and Rate of Expenditure

In managing expenditures it is good to understand the rate at which expenditures are made over the course of the budget year. The simplest way to do this is to determine if 1/12 of the allocated amount of any given budget line is expended each month. However, this is not the savviest way to manage the budget, even though some college accounting offices may try to enforce this kind of regimen on various departments. This approach to forcing fiscal discipline from a central authority is most likely to occur when budgets are tight and/or when specific departments have a history of overspending their budgets in previous years.

On the surface this seems to be a logical guideline to use to measure whether individual budget managers are exercising due diligence. Since a very high percentage of the budgets of most college departments—often as high as 80 percent to 90 percent—are personnel costs, these costs are relatively evenly dispersed through out the year. Depending on whether staff members are 12-month employees or academic year only; June, July, and August may be different than the rest of the year. Nevertheless, by the end of December, most personnel expenditures for the year should be about 50 percent of what will be the case for the entire year.

Within the library, however, there are a number of expenditures besides personnel, and these often must be paid out in proportions that are nowhere near the 1/12 per month rate. A prime example of this is the costs of periodical subscriptions. Generally, almost all of these must be renewed in the fall in order to continue receiving them for the following calendar year. If such subscriptions are a substantial percentage of the overall budget, this can have a significant effect on the bottom line as far as the percentage of budget that should be expended in the first half of the school (and budget) year. Often other parts of the acquisitions budget are also front-loaded in the first half of the fiscal year.

Central accounting offices and upper administrators on the campus may not understand this phenomenon. They may require mentoring from library budget managers in order to make sure libraries are allowed to manage their budgets in a prudent manner. In order to carry out this function and also to give library managers a more effective yardstick than the 1/12 per month rule, analysis of expenditure patterns of previous years will be quite instructive. This may show that whereas 50 percent of salary and benefits allocations are usually expended by December 31, more than 90 percent of the periodicals budget and 70 percent of the book budget is usually expended by that date.

In order to establish your own historic baseline, you may need to compile a trend line of the month-to-month expenditures by category for the past three to five years. It would be helpful to have a budget database that will allow you to request a report that will allow you to measure the current year expenditures to date against the average of previous years. If this does not exist, you may need to use a spreadsheet like Excel to build such a tool.

Two small practices that can be valuable are the use of blanket purchase orders and the use of credit cards. Each of these, if used well, can make operating within the budget easier. However, both have their pitfalls.

Blanket purchase orders can cut down on a lot of paperwork when there is a historic pattern on making multiple orders from the same vendor over the course of the budget year. If a predictable amount is spent with a specific vendor—whether a book vendor, a supply vendor, or an equipment vendor, a single purchase order can be processed in that amount. Then any orders, up to that amount, do not require a separate purchase order to be processed by the business office of the college—thus saving work for both the library and the business office. This would appear to be a win-win situation.

In practice, however, blanket purchase orders must be carefully monitored. Some business offices tend to encumber additional funds when invoices show up for payment. In other words, an initial amount, say $10,000 is encumbered for purchases to be made over the year from vendor A. When an invoice for a purchase of $495 comes in from Vendor A for payment, instead of charging this against the $10,000 already encumbered for this purpose, the transaction is charged against the library's account outside that blanket purchase order. As a result, a total of $10,495 is now encumbered or expended against the fund, but the library only considers $10,000 to be committed. After a few more transactions of this magnitude, the business office may decide that the library has overspent the amount budgeted for this kind of expenditure and try to rein in the overspending. In actual fact the library may have several thousand dollars still to spend.

Credit cards must be used wisely by libraries as well as by individuals. In some colleges it may be difficult to get a credit card, but the effort can be well worth it. There are now many sources for books and supplies that can only be used or are much easier to use with a credit card than they are through the traditional method of creating a requisition and having the business office send out a purchase order. Although such opportunities probably have long existed, the Internet has made them much more available. Often the advantage of having a credit card will be most obvious when speed is of the essence. If a book urgently needed for course reserve is found on the Internet, the deal can be closed almost instantly. The same is true when there is an emergency need for a relatively small item from a local merchant with whom the college does not regularly do business. A staff member can be dispatched to pick up the item, and the emergency is resolved. This should not become the way in which the majority of library purchases are made. Used with discretion, however, this can be a valuable tool.

Libraries will never have money to hire all the staff and buy all the collections and licenses and equipment that would be needed to create the absolutely ideal environment for student learning. However, by planning, setting priorities, justifying needs, and carefully managing fiscal resources, library managers can maximize the opportunities for students to reach their educational goals.

REFERENCES

Dowell, David R. and Jack A. Scott. 1995. "What Community Colleges Need from their Libraries." In McCabe, Gerard B. and Ruth J. Person, eds. *Academic Libraries: Their Rationale and Role in American Higher Education*. Westport, CT: Greenwood Press, 15–27.

Gamewell, Mary and David R. Dowell. 1999. "Spinning Straw into Gold: How Cuesta's Friends of the Library organization has been successful in raising almost $600,000," *College and Research Libraries News*, 60 (September): 649-51.

Stueart, Robert D. and Barbara B. Moran. 2002. *Library and Information Center Management*. 6th Ed. Greenwood Village, CO: Libraries Unlimited, 439–64.

17 IF IT ISN'T WRITTEN, IT DOESN'T EXIST: CREATING A LIBRARY POLICY MANUAL

Shelley Wood Burgett

INTRODUCTION

A wise administrator once said, "If it isn't written it doesn't exist." An even wiser administrator might say, "If it is written but neither accurate nor accessible it doesn't exist." Unfortunately, in many libraries policies are not written but rather exist in the form of oral traditions carried forward from one generation of worker to the next, often degrading each time they are repeated in much the same way messages are distorted in the children's telephone game. In those libraries that do have written policies, the policies may represent a hastily compiled document prepared the day before an accreditation visit, a pristine compilation of how a perfect library should operate that bears no resemblance to actual operation, or be so scattered and buried as to be virtually nonexistent. So, what is a library director to do? One solution is to develop a Library Policy Manual that reflects the actual policies in place that govern the operation of the library. Rather than a project with a specific beginning and ending, the development of a Library Policy Manual is best viewed as never-ending as the process of developing a library collection. This chapter is a systematic guide to help libraries begin that never-ending process.

STEP ONE: IDENTIFY WHY

There are a number of reasons to have a library policy manual, and probably the most important is that written, accessible, current polices provide for consistent library service. There is nothing more frustrating to a patron or embarrassing to a director than a debate at the circulation desk about who can check out library materials. Consistent policies provide for consistent service.

If library policy is known and related to job responsibilities, it can be used to train personnel. It can also be used as a method for evaluating a staff member's job performance. If employees do not adhere to the stated policies in performing their job responsibilities, a written policy can be used to document that. Conversely, a written policy can be used to document exceptional service.

Policies can be used to resolve conflicts between patrons and between staff members. If, for example, a patron insists having been told the library keeps all textbooks, a copy of the Collection Development policy that states "the library does not add textbooks to the library collection" is often effective is dissuading a patron from that incorrect stance. This can also be true if staff members disagree on the appropriate action for a given situation. What often happens is that a library starts with a policy and over the years, it is adapted and changed in practice but not in writing, and instances of unequal or different service result. Polices can be invaluable when there is trouble. A staff member knowing what to do if there is a fire, an incidence of violence, or an abusive patron is key to a well-functioning library. Predicting such problems is impossible; being prepared is not. Written policies can also demonstrate and define service.

Even if a library has written policies, they often do not have them in a convenient format. Often, a scheduled visit from an accrediting body is motivation for the assemblage of a policy manual. Having a pristine manual for review is a little suspicious. An accrediting team will be more impressed by a manual that shows wear, is comprehensive, and is evaluated and reviewed in a systematic manner, and by a staff that is implementing service according to the policies included.

STEP TWO: IDENTIFY WHAT

So, what is a policy? A policy is a guideline or statement that outlines how a library implements service. Ideally, a library's policies should relate directly to its mission. They differ from procedures in that a procedure is a systematic guide explaining how to complete a task. For example, a library's circulation policy should list eligible borrowers based on the library's mission. The procedures should detail how to issue a library card to each category of borrower. All libraries have policies. They may not be written, they may not be consistent, they may not be in the best interest of the library patrons, and they may not relate to the library's mission, but all libraries have policies.

To be effective, a policy needs to be comprehensive enough to address the implementation of the service offered but simple enough to be understood and remembered by library staff members. Having policies that make sense is a very good idea. Although this really is more of a procedure, the old standard for processing library materials was to stamp the top, side, and bottom; stamp the front inside cover, back inside cover, and title page, and finally to stamp page 22. The purpose of doing this was to be able to identify the book if someone should try to steal it. The insanity in this procedure was never addressed; that is, if someone steals the book, it will not matter if the ownership is stamped on every single page because the book will be gone—stamps and all. So, keep policies simple and keep them sane.

To identify what policies are needed, review existing library services. Yes, that is right, existing library services. Do not create a manual that contains policies for services the library no longer offers or services the library plans to offer but does not. To be useful, a Library Policy Manual must be current as well as comprehensive. In the area of public services an academic library would probably have policies governing circulation, confidentiality and privacy of records, library instruction, public use of computers, scheduling of library facilities, scheduling of library equipment, interlibrary loan, unattended children, telephone use, and copier use at a minimum.

Each policy should be constructed as much as possible in the order the service being defined is administered. This is beneficial in that it supports the procedures that support the policy. For example, a Circulation policy might contain the following sections:

1.1. CIRCULATION POLICY

Eligible Patrons
Collections (Location) – Circulation status
Loan Period by Type of Patron
Renewal
Holds
Recalls
Fines and Fees

In contrast, a collection development policy might include the following:

Introduction
Responsibility
Selection Guidelines
Selection Guides
Criteria for specific types of material
Maintenance of Collection
Challenged Materials

STEP THREE: IDENTIFY HOW

If the goal is to have a comprehensive library policy manual, then an easy method for completing this goal is to draft a table of contents. Determine the sections of the manual based on broad categories of library service: public services, technical services, audiovisual services, and administrative services, whatever is appropriate for the library organizational chart. Number the sections: one, two, three, and four. Then divide each section by individual services. Number these: 1.1, 1.2, and 1.3. Finally, assign a decimal for further subdivisions. Formatting a library policy manual in this way allows for short documents or word files for each policy. Making revising and replacing individual policies easy, allowing for expansion with new policies as services change, is good practice. Following is an example of a table of contents that can serve as an outline for the compilation of a library policy manual:

Library Mission

1. PUBLIC SERVICES

1.1	Circulation
1.1.1	Lost and Missing
1.1.5	Confidentiality and Privacy
1.2	Library Instruction
1.2.5	Library Instruction – Evaluation
1.2.6	Library Instruction—Assessment
1.3	Audiovisual Equipment
1.4	Interlibrary Loan
1.4.5	Intercampus Loan
1.5	Room Use
1.6	Reserves
1.7	Reciprocal Borrowing Agreements
1.8	Fax
1.9	Telephone
1.10	Photocopier
1.10.5	Microfiche Reader Printer
1.10.6	Change
1.11	Library Computers
1.11.5	Computer Cleanup
1.11.6	Internet Policy
1.12	Student Workers
1.13	Opening/Closing
1.14	Stack Maintenance
1.15	Periodical Maintenance
1.16	Collection Evaluation and Inventory
1.17	Courier Service
1.18	Local Newspaper
1.19	Unattended Children
1.20	Lost and Found
1.21	Tax Forms

2. TECHNICAL SERVICES

3. ADMINISTRATION

For ease in revision, add a last updated, last saved, or last printed footer. That way there is no question as to which is the current policy if individuals have different versions. For print copies, always use a three-ringed binder for ease in updating. Before the first policy is printed, determine the number of copies of the manual that are going to be maintained. Do you want each staff member to have a policy manual, do you want one complete manual with each staff member having copies of those policies that pertain to their job, or do you want the policies posted online for the entire college community to see? At this point, it is important to remember that every copy that exists requires maintenance. So think carefully before you print or post. If you post the policies online then every update will require updating the online postings. If every employee has a complete manual, every updated policy will require printing enough copies to update all staff copies. Limiting the number of copies in circulation limits the number of opportunities for confusion, but it also limits access thus increasing the opportunity for ignorance. A sample of how a simple policy statement can be formatted follows:

2.2 Acquisition Policy

It is the policy of the Somerset Community College to acquire materials selected according to the Collection Development Policy, q.v. through the most expedient and cost-effective measures available following all guidelines for purchasing documented in the Kentucky Community and Technical College System *Business Procedure Manual*, q.v.

Last printed 10/31/03

STEP FOUR: WHERE

Even a library that proclaims no written policies probably has some, although they may not be easily identified as library policies. Circulation policies are a good example of the written policy not easily viewed as a policy. It is not unusual for a library to note on bookmarks or book pockets the length of time an item circulates, the charges for an item not returned on its due date, the number of items a patron can have out at any given time, and how to renew items. This is a bare-bones written circulation policy. Therefore, with an outline and format established a library could gather all of the written policies number them according to the table of contents and file them in a three-ring binder. The library now has a rudimentary policy manual ready for review, revision, and expansion.

However, local internal library policies are only the beginning for a library that is part of a larger institution. By default, the library has policies dictated by the governing institution, and in general, the parent institution's policies trump internal library policy. These local but external policies may include employment, promotion and tenure, and student conduct—policies that stand on their own but may also apply to some area of library service. It is best to include a reference to the parent institution's policy even when an additional policy statement is necessary. For example, if a library's vacation policy is exactly the same as the college's vacation policy, a statement in the administration section of the policy manual might look like this:

3.8.5 Personnel Vacation Policy

Please see Do It Right Community College Vacation Policy at www.vacation.take offtime

3.8.5 Personal Vacation Policy Last printed 10/31/03

If, on the other hand, the library vacation policy is different, that difference should be noted in the library policy manual, like this:

3.8.5 Personnel Vacation Policy.

The Library follows the Do It Right Community College Vacation Policy, q.v. at www.vacation.takofftime with the following exceptions:

Library personnel must work through the Christmas break.
No two staff members can schedule vacation at the same time.

3.8.5 Personal Vacation Policy Last printed 10/31/03

The most important aspect of researching the parent institution's policies and referring to them is to avoid either duplicating existing policies or contradicting institutional policies. Last year we puzzled over what to do about unattended children in the library, only to discover that the system with which our college is affiliated has a policy dealing with unattended children on campus in the student code of conduct. Rather than agonizing over what to do, we just added a reference in the library policy manual and posted notices at all library locations.

If a library belongs to any network, consortium, or system, the policies of those groups must be considered in developing policies for a library as well. Again, either a reference to the existing policy or a copy of the policy should be included in the library's policy manual. It is important to remember these both when gathering policies to include in a library policy manual and when developing local policies.

After gathering the existing policies, fitting them into the table of contents, putting them into the standard format, and filing them in the newly established library policy manual, it is time to begin the process of developing policies for those areas of library services for which no written policies do exist. No library stands alone when it comes to library policies. There are wonderful sources where policies that can be adapted for local use can be located. A quick Google search for "Library Policies" resulted in more than 61,000 hits. The American Library Association and the Association of College and Research Libraries are excellent sources. If you belong to any list of librarians or library managers (e.g., the community college library list) an inquiry about any type of policy statement is likely to result in numerous offers of policies for review. Adopting a policy from another library without review, of course, is not recommended. Policies for similar libraries will have many of the same elements but local practice must prevail. Finally, there are books out there with sample policies (e.g., Larson and Totten 1998).

STEP FIVE: KEEPING IT CURRENT

Naturally, since any policy manual will be in a constant state of revision, print versions should be loose-leaf. Electronic copies can be updated by replacing the files. A word of caution here: Nothing, but nothing, is more annoying that having the entire policy manual on the library's home page, especially if that information is not current. Therefore, the library should not post in electronic form for the entire world to see policies if they are not committed to keeping them updated.

Changes in a policy manual will include expanding it to provide for new programs and services, revising it to reflect changes, and removing entire policies if the corresponding services no longer are offered. Review the entire manual each year. Depending on the size of the library, individuals responsible for services could be responsible for verifying the completeness and currency of the policies in their area. However it is done, it is important to involve the entire staff in the review. One approach is to have an individual responsible for the manual who makes notations in the master file during the year. During the time the manual is being reviewed, policies can be sent as attachments to emails for review and then at meeting revised, if needed and approved. Email update can provide for any revisions, and everyone who maintains copies of those policies can update their files.

INITIATING ACTION

If a library does not have a library policy manual, the steps mentioned here should help them get started developing one. If a library does have a library policy manual, these steps might offer assistance in how best to review the existing manual and improve it. A suitable approach when creating a comprehensive manual is to take a year, gather, review, revise, and slot the policies into a binder and then review them one by one with the library personnel. It may seem an overwhelming task when viewed in total, but if taken one step at a time, it is a manageable and rewarding project for any library manager.

REFERENCES

Larson, Jeanette and Herman L. Totten. 1998. *Model Policies for Small and Medium Public Libraries.* New York, Neal-Schuman, 1998.

Web Sites

The American Library Association. http://www.ala.org/. Accessed November 2004.
Association of College and Research Libraries. http://www.acrl.org. Accessed November 2004.

VII

TOWN AND GOWN TOGETHER:
A BIBLIOGRAPHIC ESSAY

18 LEADERSHIP ISSUES FOR COMMUNITY COLLEGE LIBRARIANS

Rashelle Karp

INTRODUCTION

The literature of community college libraries and regional campuses[1] presents an array of challenges and opportunities for library leaders. The challenges for community college library leaders are different from those in four-year institutions, in part because "the community college library is, in a sense, a peculiar hybrid. While officially academic in its classification and overall composition," it also closely resembles a public library because of its location in an institution of higher learning with an open admissions policy (Tolle 2001, 28). Community colleges are dynamic and diverse (MacAdam 2001); they not only serve the academic community, but also the larger communities within which they are located (Yang, Hashert, and Evans 2001). "Making library service available on and beyond its own campus is key to the mission of the community college library. While most academic libraries hold basic services to faculty, staff, and students at the center of their missions, the community college library rarely forgets to include its local community in its mission statement" (Fradkin 2003, 721).

The similarities between public libraries and community college libraries can also be seen in terms of needs to embrace diversity. The literature includes articles about needs to:

- speak in a student's native language at the reference desk rather than forcing the student to speak English (Marcus 2003)
- increase the library's collections in areas of diversity represented by the community/student population (Bryan 2001)

- increase foreign language materials collections (Perez 2000)
- help ameliorate the technology divide between the haves and have nots by loaning laptop computers to students for an entire semester (Duncan 2003).

Adding to the special challenges of community college librarians are challenges facing all academic librarians. At a recent ACRL national meeting, top issues facing academic librarianship were identified: (1) recruitment, education, and retention of librarians; (2) maintaining the role of the library in the academic enterprise by demonstrating to the campus community that the library remains central to academic effort; (3) the impact of information technology on library services; (4) creation, control, and preservation of digital resources; (5) advocating for continuing availability of scholarly research and communication through commercial publishers; (6) support of new users who come to library through distance education; and (7) higher education funding (Hisle 2002).

It is interesting that unlike the literature of academic libraries in general, the literature of community college libraries does not focus on declining budgets. One of the few articles that discussed the impact of budgets on community college libraries focused on the "haves" and "have-nots" in the world of newspaper access, pointing out that smaller academic libraries such as community college libraries could not afford to provide access to a broad range of full text newspapers through common, but expensive full text databases (Wiggins 2002). The lack of community college literature decrying small budgets may be because community college librarians have always dealt with inadequate budgets. Unlike other academic libraries, where declining budgets can often be balanced by endowments or "end-of-the-year" funding, community college libraries do not have this luxury. Rather than lamenting lack of money or declining budgets, the community college library literature presents a picture of innovative librarians and library administrators working with innovative community members to combine resources in ways that will meet a clear vision for service to students and the community. "Community college libraries deliver the best service possible given the available funding levels. Librarians and learning resources staffs ... innovate and redirect precious resources in order to be as relevant as possible to the students they serve, to support the curriculum in the best ways possible, and to use the best delivery methods. Service, after all, is what ... librarians and staffs do, no matter the budget or conditions" (Carr 2003, 5).

This review includes library literature since 1998 that focuses specifically on community colleges. Throughout the literature, it is clear that community college librarians are "leading the way in this new millennium with creative activities related to instructional support, active learning, resource cooperation, delivery of distance education, and integration of emerging technologies" (Poole 2000). Discussion of some of these topics and some of the challenges noted above are explicit in the literature of community college libraries; some discussions are implicit within the nuances of a community college library. For purposes of this essay, the literature of community college libraries has been divided into categories suggested by the special nature of the community college.

"JOINING"

Although the specter of privatizing community college libraries by outsourcing an entire library services program to a private company (Margolis 2000) does appear in the literature, it is not prevalent. Much more common in the literature is the concept of "joining" through joint-use facilities and programs. The literature of joint-use community college libraries includes many possibilities. Examples include descriptions of common collaborations such as joining the community college libraries with the public colleges and universities in the state through a shared online catalog system (Tope 1998; Liu 2000), electronic resource sharing (Mahoney 2000; Laun 1999), or electronic patron-initiated interlibrary loan requests (Montgomery and Cook 1999). The literature also includes descriptions of more ambitious collaborations such as combining a public, community college, and college library (Roshaven and Widman 2001), or combining a private college library and a public library (Lubans 2002). Particularly innovative collaborations have included collaborations among private, public and community colleges to provide 24/7 reference service, collaborations among community colleges, public libraries, and local community groups to encourage an entire city to read and discuss the same book (Bahr and Bolton 2002), and collaborations among community college libraries and K–12 councils to bring young people into the college environment (McKinstry and Garrison 2001). One article discusses the joining of libraries and museums in one unit (Bell 2003).

Budget pressures are often the catalyst for joint-use initiatives. The most common examples of budget-induced community college library/university library collaborations include sharing common management systems (Poole 2002) and networking through consortia with university libraries (Singley 1998). These types of collaborations force libraries to relinquish some local control of operations such as cataloging and classification, fund management, and after-hours reference services. However, they also have benefits such as cost savings over time, abilities to negotiate shared contracts for online information resources and add-on management modules, and more accountability through streamlined procedures at individual campuses.

Joining the community college library with a local public library (Connole 1999; Heezen 2000; "Building of Opportunities" 2000), a technical college library (Pennevaria 2002), or a university library (Fugate 2001a) as a joint-use library has its hazards and its benefits (Reno 1999; Sullivan and Taylor 1999). Benefits include shared online catalogs and circulation systems, shared library cards, and funding and operations budget increases. However, it is important to pay attention to the politics of partnering (Saferite 1999) and to carefully define the limits of partnering so that each entity preserves its autonomy, especially in areas such as mission, collection development policy (Mesling 2003), ownership of bibliographic records, and provision of reference and support services for specific groups of patrons (Dornseif and Willis 1999). Other issues related to joint libraries, especially joint community college-public libraries include hours of operation and working hours for librarians and staff, responsibilities for library instruction, balancing quiet study with the needs of children's programming, and parking for various constituencies (Anderson 1999; Brown 2002). Joining a community college and public library can also cause unique problems when the public library opts to install Internet blocking software, but the community college library does not want to do this. In some cases, the community college library is forced to install the software because it is a joint library (Kertesz 2000).

Some joint-use ventures have focused on joint-use buildings rather than joint-use libraries, where the cost and use of one building is shared among the local residents and the community college, but the services and many of the operations remain separated. For example, the shared facility that was built by the Front Range Community College and the Westminster Public Library (Westminster, Colorado) includes a shared online catalog but different classification schemes for materials. The public library uses Dewey and the college library uses Library of Congress. The concept for the library is that *two libraries* share the same building with open access to all patrons, rather than a concept of *one library* with two classification schemes. Similarly, rather than trying to force both libraries to configure their local area networks the same way and with the same firewalls and filters, each library developed its own local area network to meet the needs of its constituencies (Sisler and Smith 2000). The decision not to force a fit where the goals of two libraries in a joint facility sometimes don't match can also be found in public–community college joint-use facilities in which each library may have its own governing board, separate staff and work areas, and separate shelving areas. However, commonly shared facilities include shared computer labs and shared staffing in order to expand the library hours by using staffing from the college library and staffing from the public library ("Unique College, Unique Public Library" 1999).

Joining can also take the form of valuable joint research efforts, especially in the area of collections development. For example, an attempt in Florida to analyze the situation of community college libraries across the state focused on a statewide evaluation of all the community college collections, rather than individual collection evaluation efforts (Perrault, DePew, and Madaus 1999). The assessment showed that the collections followed a traditional bell curve in terms of the publication dates of held resources. These results led to statewide program review efforts to increase resources to the community college libraries for updated library collections (Perrault, Madaus, and Armbrister 1999) and to assess the results of increased collections budgets (Perrault, Adams, and Smith 2002; Perrault, DePew, Madaus, Arbrister, and Dixon 1999).

Other types of joining focus on placing disparate units within the library—for example, joining the library and the college's academic and/or student support services unit (Kriewall 2000; Dykshoorn 2001), or integrating library and learning resources in one library location (Rotenberg 2002).

Regardless of the type of joining, the literature is clear that a memorandum of understanding that includes an operational agreement and policies must be written and appropriately authorized (Gilmer 1998, 2001; Fugate 2001b; Woods 2001). The literature also clearly demonstrates that each agreement will be different because each must reflect the unique institutional culture, mission and circumstances of the library partners and their communities (Dornseif 2001).

ACCESS VERSUS OWNERSHIP

Like all academic libraries, community college librarians are constantly balancing needs to provide on-demand (often electronic) access to a wide range of library resources that the library does not own with the needs to provide ongoing stable access to a smaller range of physical resources that the library does own. Ownership of critical resources across time is important to the integrity of academic programming but it is often difficulty to justify. Duplicating resources in hard copy that are available online can seem like a waste of money to administrators in times of severe fiscal constraints. In some libraries that have become completely online, the librarians are concerned that there are few requests for hard copy items (Freedman 1999; Karr 2000), in spite of the fact that not all of the online references are linked to full text. Other librarians point out the need to develop guidelines for preservation of rare book materials in community college libraries which do not usually have rare book collections (Visser 2003), as well as needs to develop clear weeding criteria for materials that are not rare (Fohl 2001). A question that must be asked is whether the provision of totally online library services causes people to rely on what is convenient (i.e., what is available in full text online) rather than taking the extra time to find information that is only available through interlibrary loan or in hard copy. One justification for online resources that is, unfortunately, reflective of the difficult times in which we live:, Provision of electronic remote access to library materials allows a library to remain open, even during times of terrorism such as the destruction of the twin towers in New York on September 11, 2001 (Eng 2002).

INFORMATION LITERACY

Information literacy is recognized as an essential component of library services by accrediting agencies, the American Library Association, and by the American Association of Community Colleges (AACC). The AACC defines *information literacy* as the "ability to:

- Determine the nature and extent of information needed
- Access and use needed information effectively and efficiently
- Evaluate information and its sources critically, and incorporate selected information into one's knowledge base and value system

- Use information effectively to accomplish a specific purpose
- Understand many of the economic, legal, and social issues surrounding the use of information" (American Association of Community Colleges 2002).

Community college librarians, like other librarians, must expand concepts of library instruction beyond the more narrow focus on library instruction to a broader focus on information literacy, or as it is referred to in some states, "information competency" (Brose 2002). For some, "the new literacy for the 21st century and beyond is clearly the ability to utilize appropriate technological tools in an information society" (Evans 1999, 102). For most, however, information literacy is much more expansive, flowing across a college curriculum, and causing tremendous increases in workload as librarians try to provide instruction in the use of e-books (Doan 2001), the electronic and physical library (Bontenbal 2000a), discipline-based instruction, electronic and virtual reference services (Ryer and Nebeker 1999; Kelly, Siddons, and Jenkins 2002; Ashe 2003), desktop Internet videoconferencing (Jia 2003), and real-time online chat with reference librarians (Shamel 2001). "This is the best of times [for libraries] in that the information world, the heart of all libraries, is booming; information is the buzzword.... The public wants information and expects that all libraries can produce, with cyber-speed, the answers to a world wide web of questions and needs. And it is because of these increased expectations that, in some ways, these are the worst of times; because these infinite expectations are often beyond the real world of finite budgets for materials, equipment, and staff" (Martinez 1999, 10). At some community colleges, the lack of an adequate number of librarians has resulted in the librarians teaching discipline-based faculty to provide library/information literacy classes (Walsh 2002). Staffing issues are exacerbated in community college libraries because of unique needs to help adult and older patrons who are not only unfamiliar with libraries but also unfamiliar with computers (Bontenbal 2000b) and new definitions of plagiarism in a digital age (Liddell 2003). In a typical one-hour library instruction class, there is not enough time to instruct users on all topics. However, true to their innovative nature, community college librarians have developed creative solutions. For example, some library instruction classes place the students in groups so that the more proficient students can help the less proficient students as they master computer skills. This allows the librarian to concentrate on the library skills (Leeseberg 1998). Other librarians intersperse humor into their library instruction units in order to reduce boredom on the part of students and in order to reduce anxiety on the part of adult patrons who may feel overwhelmed by the amount of information and the electronic library (Arnsan 2000).

Library instruction in community college libraries includes models such as the following:

- A course-integrated or infusion model, where library research is addressed within the context of specific classroom assignments (Dodgen et al. 2003; Johnson, Burke, and Evans 2001);
- An elective for-credit model, where an information literacy class taught by library faculty is part of the university's elective curriculum;
- A required discipline-specific for-credit course model, where library instruction is addressed within the context of a specific discipline;
- Required core curriculum for-credit models, in which a certain level of competency is required for all students regardless of their major (Donnelly 1998; Hiss and Boatright 2003); and
- Self-guided library instruction that supports active learning theories (Marcus and Beck 2003).

In some libraries, credit-bearing classes include traditional and online classes on accessing electronic resources, followed by more extensive coverage of specific electronic resources (McCarthy 2003). These include classes such as the following:

- *Electronic Access to Information.* This one-credit, 15-hour class shows students how and when to use electronic resources available through the library's electronic databases, as well as research strategies using Boolean logic, and
- *Introduction to Internet Research.* This Web-based, one-credit, 15-hour class teaches methods of accessing information resources available through the Internet, how to design effective search strategies, and how to retrieve, evaluate, and cite Internet resources (Evans 2001).

Regardless of the instructional model, the literature seems to agree that it is critical that library instruction allow both the student and faculty member to use the computer while the instruction is being conducted in order to provide instant reinforcement of the concepts (Staines and Craig 1999). In some libraries, instruction is provided in mobile, wireless computer labs (Mathias and Heser 2002; Tolson 2001; Patton 2001). Other libraries use traditional computer lab facilities that are hardwired. Most recently, librarians have begun to use personal digital assistants to enhance library instruction (Matesic 2003), and virtual self-paced library orientation modules (Dent 2003). It is also commonly accepted is that the instruction should be linked to instruction in a content class and should be collaboratively designed by librarians and teaching faculty (Spanfelner 2000; MacNaughton 2000; Bower 2000; Weintraub and Cater 1999), especially if the library skills instruction is linked to developmental instruction (Thomas 2000). Another area of agreement in the literature on community college library instruction is the recognition that "college faculty are the key to whether or not students develop information literacy skills, because they control the class content, assignments and learning objectives, while also serving as role models and mentors for the students" (Moore and Ivory 2000, 4). However, faculty members in the disciplines are not necessarily the best faculty members to provide information literacy instruction for students because they often do not have the time to update information assignments regularly, nor do they have the time to consult with librarians on a regular basis to ensure the relevancy and accuracy of the information literacy units that they present (Davis 2002).

STUDENT LEARNING OUTCOMES ASSESSMENT

Information literacy has begun to replace "library services" as the standard used by regional accrediting agencies and other accrediting agencies (Middle States Commission 2002), causing increased pressures on librarians and discipline faculty to provide assessment data relative to student learning as a result of intentional information literacy instruction and experiences. The literature provides numerous examples of library instruction units that are virtual, online using streaming video and PowerPoint, on-demand, "just-in-time," or embedded within discipline-specific classes (Erazo 2003; Lee, Hime, and Domincis 2003). However, there exists very little literature that provides evidence of the impact of library instruction on universitywide student learning. The majority of the literature speaks to the results of user satisfaction data (Bahde 1999; Barbier 2003) as a means for evaluating library services. Indeed, most of the literature on assessment of Web sites focuses on a definition of *usability* as ease of use, rather than a more appropriate definition that focuses on usefulness (Vaughn and Callicott 2003). User satisfaction data does not provide the kind of granular detail that is needed to evaluate the impact of the library on student learning and performance. Assessment is difficult to conceive and difficult to implement, since it requires some statistical ability, commitment of faculty and staff time beyond the day-to-day provision of direct services, time to write up the results in ways that can be presented to the university, and a great deal of time working with individual teaching faculty and discipline-based programs. One example of a successful student learning assessment program can be found at the Glendale Community College (California). At Glendale, library faculty worked with English and Nursing faculty to develop infused library instruction that was geared toward student learning outcomes within the English and Nursing programs. Statistically significant quantitative data demonstrated that students who completed the library units as part of their English or English as a Second Language (ESL) classes had up to a 35 percent higher pass rate in their English and ESL composition classes than students who did not complete the workshops (Moore, Brewster, and Dorroh 2002). Another example in the literature is the infusion of information competency components into Allied Health classes at Gavilan College. The librarians, in collaboration with the teaching faculty, were able to show that students who had completed the information competency lessons demonstrated better health and medical research skills, and improved basic research, report writing, and computer skills (Hausrath et al. 2003).

At another community college library, transaction log analysis allowed librarians to examine searches performed by library patrons in the online catalog. Over a set period of time, the librarians found that 83 percent of the searches were executed as subject searches, 35 percent of all searches resulted in zero hits, and over 60 percent of the zero-hit searches were caused by problems with controlled vocabulary. The librarians used this data to develop interactive help algorithms to guide patrons through successful searches (Holloman 1999).

OUTREACH

Community college libraries must engage in community outreach because of their dependency on private boards, local and state governments, and other public agencies that provide funding. Community outreach provides confirmation to funding sources that the library, and indeed the college, is providing valuable services to the community—services that are worth funding. An innovative project that uses the talents of librarians and library systems personnel is the series of Web exhibits called *Through Our Parents' Eyes: Tucson's Diverse Community*, developed and maintained through the Pima Community College Library in Tucson, Arizona. The goal of the project is to acknowledge the community's multicultural heritage through digital histories that combine historical images and text with stories of Tucson told by some of Tucson's founding members. Many community organizations, as well as other colleges in the area, contribute content to the project. The librarians plan, set goals, meet with prospective participants, work with scholars and contributing authors, mark up the text in HTML, develop and revise the exhibit's appearance, configure the Web server, and write authoritative text to accompany the exhibits (Glogoff and Glogoff 1998). Another innovative example in the literature is the University of Illinois Fire Service Institute Library's workshops across the state for community college librarians and Illinois fire service personnel to teach them how and where to access up-to-date fire safety information over the Web (Ruan 2001).

At some community colleges, outreach involves offering university classes at community college sites. These classes generate revenues for both the university and the community college, and they are a good recruitment tool for institutions. However, unless an agreement on provision of library services is written, lack of resources at community college libraries to support university classes can cause great difficulty (Farrell and Manasco 2002). Along the same lines, some community colleges provide library resources for local vocational teaching programs (Garbart 1998), as well as classes and library services via assistive and adaptive technologies to individuals with disabilities and individuals who are homebound (Bowen 1999; Kumar 1999; Smith 2002; Williams and Corpus 2002).

Another form of outreach that benefits the community college library involves Friends of the Libraries. Friends of the Libraries groups can be helpful sources of funding and awareness-raising for community college libraries. Examples of activities that support these dual goals include ongoing book and magazine sales of withdrawn resources, donated resources, and new resources; literary and artistic social functions; literary and cultural bus tours to popular destinations; book clubs; and sales of t-shirts and other promotional materials (Gamewell and Dowell 1999).

Of course, librarians cannot forget the need to reach out to faculty and student affairs professionals (Poole 2003). A survey of six community colleges in the City University of New York (CUNY) found that without support from the teaching faculty, library services will be underutilized or not utilized effectively (Feldman and Sciammerella 2000). The survey also revealed serious mismatches among the perceptions of faculty and librarians. For example, although 94 percent of the librarian respondents felt that teaching faculty members were unfamiliar with the use of current research tools available to students in the library, 90 percent of the responding teaching faculty felt they were familiar with these resources. All efforts to reach out to teaching faculty, including activities that go beyond the usual traditional liaison structures, are helpful. One innovative strategy in the literature discusses using retail book-buying trips to local bookstores in which library faculty and teaching faculty visit the bookstore and purchase books off the shelf. Although the books that are purchased are not as scholarly as those that are purchased through normal academic library vendors, the librarians have found that the experience of purchasing books together from the bookstore has brought a new sense of partnership to the faculty–librarian relationship, and it has in some cases brought in donations from departments to support the book-buying trips (Brantz 2002). Another innovative approach to reaching faculty was used at the University of Washington's Bothell/Cascadia Community College Campus Library. A one-hour orientation was designed for faculty and administrators to introduce them to service points in the library, searching the library's online catalog and databases, ordering materials from other libraries, and the ways in which library staff might help them (Hurst 2003).

PARAPROFESSIONALS

In times when the use of the computer to access information is ubiquitous, it is important to be sure that library assistants are being paid at a level that will ensure quality services (Orenstein 2003). It is also necessary to carefully define the skills necessary for library paraprofessionals to work with patrons in ways not considered before the use of computers by end users (Slusar 1998). It is equally important to carefully differentiate those tasks that are appropriate and not appropriate for paraprofessionals to perform. For example, when does a general question appropriate for a paraprofessional become a reference question that should be answered by a librarian? What criteria does the library use to distinguish between computer hardware and software questions (which could might be answered by paraprofessionals), and electronic database questions (which should be answered by librarians)? The changing role of librarians puts them in the forefront of helping patrons with hardware and software problems (Donohue 2001), and makes these types of distinctions critical. Librarians in community colleges are increasingly revising skills standards for civil service and paraprofessional library employees, as indicated in conversations and information sharing about paraprofessional work, most often found in the journal, *Library Mosaics* ("Library Technician Skill Standards" 2000; Baker 1998). "Today every job description at every level requires some degree of computer expertise. Many libraries have developed new computer-related positions, while other libraries have incorporated these responsibilities into existing staff positions" (Born, Clayton, and Balash 2000, 1).

The experience in community college libraries has been that increased numbers of electronic resources and electronic delivery systems for patrons necessitates increased needs for librarians and staff to help users interpret and use the technology (Jackson and Parton 1999). Because increased staffing is usually difficult, continuing education for paraprofessionals is a focus in many community college libraries (Burke 2000), especially if the education can be provided through electronic delivery mechanisms that eliminate the need to travel (Dickey 2002). For example, the College of Dupage (Glen Ellyn, Illinois) maintains a Web site for Library Technical Assistants to help them participate in continuing education, including an award-winning teleconference series, "Soaring to Excellence," which provides satellite-delivered sessions on technical and workplace issues, covering topics as varied as skills for advancement, technology, and conducting effective meetings (Slusar 2000).

STUDENT ASSISTANTS

It has long been assumed that student assistants are important to the effective operations of all academic libraries. The recent literature, however, has begun to question this assumption. Although student assistants do provide a steady source of labor, they bring unique problems to the library work environment. For example, student assistants who are freshmen often come to the library without any training on how to behave in a work environment and how to relate with adults in a work relationship. Students in general come to the library without knowledge of basic library elements such as "classification and organization of materials, conservation of materials, issues of confidentiality and intellectual freedom, and ... thoughts of service" (Baird 2003, 23). This makes development of training programs and well-written job descriptions for student assistants a critical component of library operations (Kathman and Kathman 2000). Training programs should begin with a careful interview that is comprehensive in order to increase the likelihood of a good match between the student assistant and the job (Constantinou 1998). After a student is hired, the library training program should make sure that student assistants understand how important their work is to the library (Petty 1997), how to recognize situations where a judgment call is required by a library professional (Constantinou 1998), and details about library operations such as copyright checklists that specify what can and cannot be copied by library employees for patrons (Hershey 2003). Training programs should also include mechanisms for recognizing students who provide meritorious service. At some libraries, recognition includes plaques, cash awards, written performance appraisals, student employee scholarships, and university bookstore certificates (Hasty 2000; Cleaver 2001). Finally, the types of jobs performed by student assistants should be selected carefully. Traditional jobs such as shelving and preparing materials for circulation are helpful to the library's operations. Less traditional jobs such as using library peer tutors to provide basic library instruction, and using student assistants to perform more advanced duties (e.g., journal check-in and claims) can also be helpful, but training and job responsibilities must be well defined (Deese-Roberts 2000; Palmer 2000; Manasco, Gillespie, and Purks 1998). As well, training for disabled student assistants must also be well defined (Dick 1999). To cut down on the amount of time that must be spent training library student assistants, some libraries utilize online training modules (Epstein 2003). But, no matter how well a student is trained, and no matter how efficiently the training occurs, student assistants can be a drain on a library's financial and human resources. And, because they are temporary, or "contingent" employees, they often do not have the same commitment to the library as regular employees have. Library employers point to poor productivity, minimal return on training investment (the student workers leave before the library can reap the benefits of a trained employee), security and safety risks, and the fact that the presence of many student workers adversely affects the spirit of teamwork that should exist among library employees. Recent literature has discussed the cost-effectiveness of hiring a small number of regular employees using the same money that would have been spent to hire a large number of student employees (Gerlich 2002).

Conversely, however, librarians point to the benefits of hiring student employees, and especially the benefits of hiring diverse student employees, whose presence makes the library an inviting place for minority students, and whose perspectives on library operations can make the library more inclusive in the types of services offered for diverse students and how they are offered (Kathman and Kathman 1998). Another benefit of hiring student assistants for the library is the opportunity, and for some the perceived obligation, to recruit students into the profession of librarianship (Berry 1999, 2002; Echavarria 2001). Studies of factors that influence a person's decision to enter the profession of librarianship have found that factors such as information provided by role models, positions held as student library assistants, appreciation for the work of librarianship, and enjoyment of the library environment are important (Winston 1998; Jenkins 2001; Gresko 2003). A most comprehensive guide to using student assistants in academic libraries is Baldwin, Wilkinson, and Barkley's *Effective Management of Student Employment* (2000), in which librarians will find job descriptions for specific student assistant positions; guides to hiring, orienting, supervising, and disciplining student assistants; and helpful chapters on financial aid for student assistants and performance appraisals for student assistants.

DISTANCE EDUCATION AND ADULT LEARNERS

Because so many community college students are adult learners, the community college library must provide services and resources for users who may not be able to physically use the library when the library is open. The Western Cooperative for Educational Telecommunications defines distance education as "instruction that occurs when the instructor and student are separated by distance or time, or both. A wide array of technologies are currently used to link the instructor and student. Courses are offered via videotape, broadcast television, ITFS (instructional television fixed service), microwave, satellite, interactive video, audio tapes, audioconferencing, CD-ROM, and, increasingly, computer networking—including e-mail, the Internet, and its World Wide Web" (*Distance Education* 1997). Regional accrediting agencies accept distance learning or distributed learning as a "formal educational process in which some or all of the instruction occurs when the learner and the instructor are not in the same place at the same time; information or distributed learning technology is often the connector between the learner and the instructor or the site of origin" (Middle States Commission 2002, 45). Increasingly, accrediting agencies are revising their standards for accreditation by eliminating standards for physical libraries and replacing these with standards for information literacy.

The use of distance education delivery for degrees offered by a community college adds another level complexity to the provision of library services. For example, should library professionals provide instruction on how to use Yahoo, email attachments, discussion boards, blackboard, and other aspects of a course's electronic delivery system? Or should library professionals restrict their instruction to the use of electronic library resources? Should library professionals partner with the instructional technology staff on campus so that delivery and information services are provided seamlessly from several cooperating units on the campus? Should the instructional technology staff be a part of the library or part of the computing services unit? Should Web-based and online library instruction tutorials and classes replace or be provided in addition to classes where students come to the library and participate in face-to-face lectures (Levesque 2003; Birchfield 1998; Gray 1999; Davis 2000)? Questions such as these are important to answer in order to recruit and then retain distance learning students who need constant communication and feedback in order to avoid feeling isolated and helpless as they work from cyberspace (Yorke-Smith 2001).

Other issues related to distance education and distant learners include the proliferation of Web sites with valuable information. This has caused librarians, especially librarians at community colleges where budgets are very constrained, to identify free Web resources that provide authoritative information. Webliographies maintained by librarians have costs associated with them in terms of the personnel time to develop them and keep them updated, but when they are developed for a specific class or discipline, they can be manageable and helpful (Mathias 1998). Adding another layer to the Webliography concept, librarians also are responsible for developing toolkits and online library instruction programs to guide students through the steps in electronic research, selecting a research topic, using Internet search engines, using online reference sources and indexes, searching library catalogs, and evaluating and documenting sources (Cain 2001; Hayworth and Brantz 2002). Finally, librarians must use appropriate promotional strategies for their Web sites (e.g., submitting sites directly to search engines, sending announcements to current awareness services) so that patrons will be able to find sites that are critical to their research (Smith 2001).

Development of the library's Web site involves many decisions that previously did not have to be made. For example, will the library's Web site be an information tool, a reference tool, a research tool, an instructional tool, or all of the above? How often will the Web site be updated? How sophisticated will the search capabilities on the Web site be (Cohen and Still 1999). How can the Web site be developed so that it meets the needs of traditional library patrons, as well as distance education students (Buckstead 2001)? How will the Web site use jargon but also ensure that patrons unfamiliar with library jargon will understand the links? What type of information architecture will be used to structure the Web site (Swanson 2001)?

CHANGING ADMINISTRATIVE STRUCTURES AND RESPONSIBILITIES

New delivery mechanisms for classes and entire academic programs have necessitated creative thinking about administrative structures in order to eliminate "silos." The understanding of synergies among academic administrative structures dating back to the 1980s and 1990s no longer works in the twenty-first century, where technology and changing student demographics have blurred the distinctions that once differentiated these units. For example, learning and technology centers, once located within computing services divisions because they dealt primarily with technology implementation issues, are now dealing with broader issues of faculty professional development, instructional development, and collaboration. This has led to new administrative structures that place "disparate units that share the common purpose of supporting teaching and learning campus-wide" into the same division (Mundell, Celene-Martel, and Braziunas 2003). An example might be the North Seattle (Washington) Community College's Instructional and Information Support Services Division, which brings together the college's Library, Media Services, Distance Learning, and Teaching and Learning

Center under a dean with a required MLS (Mundell, Celene-Martel, and Brazi-unas 2003). It is also recommended in the literature that "more attention needs to be directed toward revising and updating library job descriptions to adequately reflect new technologies" (Poole and Denny 2001, 512) and the ethnic demo-graphics of students (Ayala et al. 2000), as well as to develop peer review pro-cesses for librarians that mirror the peer review processes used for teaching faculty (Petersohn 2000). Finally, the ubiquitous use of computers in libraries has also led to new administrative structures that provide for manual operations when the library's computers are not working (Morris 2001).

CONCLUSION

Community college librarians and all academic librarians must continue to change in anticipation of, and in response to, changing patterns of the world. The literature provides examples of what might be termed "best practices," or practices that have been "proven to be valuable or effective within one orga-nization and may have applicability and may be transferred to other organiza-tions" (Todaro 2002, 28). The most current literature seems to focus on areas such as collaboration, information literacy, and electronic library services. The key for community college librarians is to engage in a process referred to by To-daro (2002, 28) as "best practice benchmarking," or the process of "looking for, identifying, [and] studying the best practices that produce superior performance in specific areas and then applying or transferring the best practice to the orga-nization in need of change." One author has made an important distinction that perhaps describes the most pressing challenge for community college librarians in the coming years. Librarians must distinguish between "ease of use" and "use-fulness" as they develop services to meet the needs of the twenty-first century (Vaughn and Callicott 2003).

REFERENCES

American Association of Community Colleges. November 2002. *AACC Position Statement on Library and Learning Resource Center Programs*. www.aacc.nche.edu. Accessed on February 28, 2004.

Anderson, S.M. 1999. "Planning for the Future: Combining a Community and College Library," *Library Administration and Management*, 13 (2) 81–86.

Arnsan, D. 2000. "Libraries, Laughter and Learning: the Rubber Chicken School of Bibliographic Instruction," *Community and Junior College Libraries*, 9,(4): 53–58.

Ashe, J.C. 2003. Information Habits of Community College Students: A Litera-ture Survey," *Community and Junior College Libraries* 11 (4): 17–26.

Ayala, J., L. Chaparro, A. M. Cobos, and R. Rodriguez. 2000. "Serving the His-panic Student in the Community College Library." In *Library Services to*

Latinos. Salvador Guerena, Ed. Jefferson, NC: McFarland and Company: 111–20.

Bahde, W.J. 1999. "User Satisfaction: How We Measured It," *Community and Junior College Libraries,* 9, (1): 57–66.

Bahr, A. H., and N. Bolton. 2002. "Share the Experience: Academic Library, Public Library, and Community Partnerships," *The Southeastern Librarian,* 50 (2): 26–32.

Baird, L. N. 2003. "Student Employees in Academic Libraries: Training for Work, Educating for Life," *PNLA Quarterly,* 67 (2, Winter): 13, 23.

Baker, C. 1998. "Life of a Media Service Worker," *Library Mosaics,* 9 (4, July/August): 16.

Baldwin, D., F. C . Wilkinson, and D. C. Barkley. 2000. *Effective Management of Student Employment: Organizing for Student Employment in Academic Libraries.* Englewood, CO: Libraries Unlimited.

Barbier, P. 2003. "Evaluating Patron Satisfaction at the M.M. Bennett Library," *Community and Junior College Libraries,* 11 (2): 65–72.

Bell, C.J. 2003. "Library-Museum Connections in Community Colleges: Innovations for Lifelong Learning," *Community and Junior College Libraries,* 11 (4): 45–68.

Berry, J. 1999. "Recruiting: Whose Job Is It? *Library Journal,* 124 (20): 6.

———. 2002. "Addressing the Recruitment and Diversity Crisis," *American Libraries,* 33 (2): 7.

Birchfield, M. 1998. "Wide Load on the Information Highway; An Undergraduate Library Science Course via the Internet at Lexington Community College," *Kentucky Libraries,* 62,(4): 8–11.

Bontenbal, K. F. 2000a. "Challenges Faced by Reference Librarians in Familiarizing Adult Students with the Computerized Library of Today: The Cuesta College Experience," *The Reference Librarian,* 69/70: 69–76.

———. 2000b. "Introducing Older Students to the Library of the New Millenium: Same Library, New Technologies. *Community and Junior College Libraries,* 9 (4): 41–52.

Born, J., S. Clayton, and A. Balash. 2000. *Community College Library Job Descriptions and Organizational Charts.* Chicago: American Library Association.

Bowen, J.E. 1999. Assistive Technology at Cabrillo College Library," *Community and Junior College Libraries,* 9 (1): 47–56.

Bower, R.J. 2000. "The Development of an Online Library Instruction Tutorial at Pellissippi State Technical Community College," *Community and Junior College Libraries,* 9 (2): 15–24.

Brantz, M.H. 2002. "Library-Sponsored Faculty Book-Buying Trips," *College and Research Libraries News,* 63 (4): 264–66, 292.

Brose, F.K. 2002. "Information Competency and Community College Libraries: California Moves Toward a Graduation Requirement." *Community and Junior College Libraries,* 11 (2): 37–44.

Brown, M. M. 2002. "Story Hour Program at Texas Tech University Library." *School Library Journal*, 48 (4, April): 45.

Bryan, G. Winter 2001. "An Assessment of Library Services for a Culturally Diverse Population." *Louisiana Libraries*, 63 (3, Winter): 14–17.

Buckstead, J.R. 2001. "Developing an Effective Off-Campus Library Services Web Page: Don't Worry, Be Happy!" *Journal of Library Administration*, 31 (3–4): 93–107.

"A Building of Opportunities: Metro Sarpy Center and La Vista Public Library." 2000. *Nebraska Library Association Quarterly*, 31 (2, Summer): 8–10.

Burke, J. J. 2000. "Library Technical Assistant Programs: Library Education for Support Staff." *Community and Junior College Libraries*, 9 (3): 23–32.

Cain, K. 2001. "Of Blizzards, Bytes, and Virtual Beginnings: Front Range Community College's Boulder County Campus Libraries." *Colorado Libraries*, 27 (3, Fall): 4–6.

Carr, M. M. 2003. "Avoiding the Dire Hole, Community College Style." *Alki*, 9 (3, December): 5–6.

Cleaver, S. 2001. "Investing in Our Student Employees' Futures: One Page at a Time." *Indiana Libraries*, 20 (2): 29–30.

Cohen, L. B. and J. M. Still. 1999. "A Comparison of Research University and Two-Year College Library Web Sites: Content, Functionality, and Form." *College and Research Libraries*, 60 (3, May): 275–89.

Connole, T. 1999. "The Aurora Public Library-Community College of Aurora Relationship." *Colorado Libraries*, 25: 2, Summer): 33–36.

Constantinou, C. 1998. "Hiring Students with Disabilities in the Academic Library." *Catholic Library World*, 69 (2, December): 20–23.

Davis, H. M. 2000. "Distance Learning Students and Library Services: Issues, Solutions and the Rio Salado College Model." *Community and Junior College Libraries*, 9 (2): 3–14.

———. 2002. "Information Literacy Modules as an Integral Component of a K-12 Teacher Preparation Program: A Librarian/Faculty Partnership." *Journal of Library Administration*, 37 (1–2): 207–16.

Deese-Roberts, S. 2000. "Integrating a Library Strategies Peer Tutoring Program." *Research Strategies*, 17 (2/3): 223–29.

Dent, V. F. 2003. "Innovation on a Shoestring: An All-Virtual Model for Self-Paced Library Orientation on an Urban Campus." *College and Undergraduate Libraries*, 10 (2): 29–44.

Dick, M. A. 1999. "Hiring Students with Disabilities in the Academic Library." *Illinois Libraries*, 81 (2): 83–87.

Dickey, E. 2002. "Library and Information Technology." *Library Mosaics*, 13 (4, July/August): 12.

Distance Education: A Consumer's Guide. 1997). Boulder, CO: Western Cooperative for Educational Telecommunications. http://www.wcet.info/resources/publications/conguide/conguida.htm. Accessed on February 28, 2004

Doan, S. 2001. "NetLibrary: eBooks for the Academic Community." *Community and Junior College Libraries*, 10 (1): 41–46.

Dodgen, L., S. Naper, O. Palmer, and A. Rapp. 2003. "Not so SILI: Sociology Information Literacy Infusion as the Focus of Faculty and Librarian Collaboration." *Community and Junior College Libraries*, 11 (4): 27–34.

Donnelly, K. M. 1998. "Learning from the Teaching Libraries." *American Libraries*, 29 (11): 47.

Donohue, M. K. 2001. "The Autobiography of a Modern Community College Librarian." *Computers in Libraries*, 21 (10): 44–46.

Dornseif, K. A. 2001. "Joint-Use Libraries: Balancing Autonomy and Cooperation." *Resource Sharing and Information Networks*, 15 (1–2): 103–15.

Dornseif, K. and E. Willis. 1999. "Making the Joint-Use Library Work: Harmony Library, Fort Collins, Colorado." *Colorado Libraries*, 25 (2): 15–17.

Duncan, L. E. 2003. "The World in Their Laps." *Community and Junior College Libraries*, 11 (3): 11–16.

Dyckshoorn, S. 2001. "Learning Achievement Center: Budget Crunches." *Community and Junior College Libraries*, 10 (3): 55–60.

Echavarria, T. 2001. "Reach Out to Recruit New Librarians." *Alki*, 17 (1): 18–20.

Eng, S. 2002. "How Technology and Planning Saved my Library at Ground Zero." *Computers in Libraries*, 22 (4): 28–35.

Epstein, C. 2003. "Using Blackboard for Training and Communicating with Student Employees." *College and Undergraduate Libraries*, 10 (1): 21–25.

Erazo, E. 2003. "Using Technology to Promote Information Literacy in Florida's Community Colleges." *Florida Libraries*, 46 (2): 20–22.

Evans, R. 1999. "Serving Modern Students in a Modern Society at the Community College: Incorporating Basic Technological Literacy." *THE Journal*, 27 (3): 102–8.

———. 2001. "Faculty and Reference Librarians: A Virtual Dynamic Duo." *THE Journal*, 28 (6): 46–51.

Farrell, S. L. and J. E. Manasco. 2002. "Cooperative Support for the UK Engineering Program Paducah Campus—Based on a Report delivered at the 2001 Fall KLA Conference." *Kentucky Libraries*, 66 (3): 4–5.

Feldman, D. and S. Sciammerella. 2000. "Both Sides of the Looking Glass: Librarian and Teaching Faculty Perceptions of Librarianship at Six Community Colleges." *College and Research Libraries*, 61 (6): 291–498.

Fohl, C. 2001. "Weeding: An Experience at Columbus State Community College." *Community and Junior College Libraries*, 10 (3): 47–50.

Fradkin, B. 2003. "The Community College Library Perspective in an Age of Opportunity: Meeting Expectations in Times of Uncertainty." *College & Research Library News*, 64 (11): 721–23.

Freedman, J. 1999. "The St. Petersburg Junior College, Seminole Campus CyberLibrary—or When Is a Library not a Library?" *Florida Libraries*, 42 (3): 52–53.

Fugate, C. 2001a. "Common Ground: Making Library Services Work at a Collocated Campus." *Resource Sharing and Information Networks*, 15 (1–2): 55–64.

———— 2001b. "'Only Connected': The Collocation of the University of Washington, Bothel and Cascadia Community College." *College and Research Libraries News*, 62 (1): 9–10.

Gamewell, M. and D. R. Dowell. 1999. "Spinning Straw into Gold: A Look at Cuesta College's Friends of the Library." *College and Research Libraries News*, 60 (8): 649–51.

Garbart, K. A. 1998. "Career and Technical Education Resource Center." *Colorado Libraries*, 24 (4): 42–43.

Gerlich, B. K. 2002. "Rethinking the Contributions of Student Employees to Library Services." *Library Administration and Management*, 16 (3): 146–50.

Gilmer, L. C. 1998. "Writing Formal Documents for Program Planning and Development." In *The Eighth Off-Campus Library Services Conference Proceedings*. Steven P. Thomas and Marhelen Jones, compilers. Mount Pleasant, MI: Central Michigan University, 159–63.

————. 2001. "Straddling Multiple Administrative Relationships." *Journal of Library Administration*, 31 (3–4): 219–24.

Glogoff, L. G. and S. Glogoff. 1998. "Using the World Wide Web for Community Outreach: Enriching Library Service to the Community." *Internet Reference Services Quarterly*, 3 (1): 15–26.

Gray, D. 1999. "Online at Your Own Pace: Web-Based Tutorials in Community College Libraries." *Virginia Libraries*, 45 (1): 9–10.

Gresko, A. B. 2003. *Recruitment to the Profession: Student Workers in Academic Libraries as Potential Future Librarians*. Chapel Hill, NC: University of North Carolina.

Hasty, D. F. 2000. "Student Assistants as Library Ambassadors: An Academic Library's Public Relations Initiative." *Reference Services Review*, 31 (2): 141–53.

Hausrath, D., S. Auyeung, J. A. Howell, and K. Bedell. 2003. "Integrating Information Competencies into the Allied Health Curriculum at Gavilan College." *Community and Junior College Libraries*, 11 (2): 13–50.

Hayworth, G. and M. Brantz. 2002. "Developing an Online Library Instruction Program: ACCS Online Library Tutorial." *Colorado Libraries*, 28 (4): 39–42.

Heezen, R. 2000. "A History of Cooperation: Omaha Public Library and Metropolitan Community College as a Case Study." *Nebraska Library Association Quarterly*, 31 (2): 15–16.

Hershey, K. 2003. "Metropolitan Community College Copyright Checklist." *Nebraska Library Association Quarterly*, 34 (4): 32–34.

Hisle, W. L. 2002. "Top Issues Facing Libraries: A Report of the Focus on the Future Task Force." *College and Research Libraries News* (November): 715–16.

Hiss, S. and K. Boatright. 2003. "Keeping the Library Relevant to Community College Students: Library Skills as a Required Course." *Community and Junior College Libraries*, 11 (4): 9–16.

Holloman, M. 1999. *Scaling Down Transaction Log Analysis: A Study of OPAC Usage at a Small Academic Library*. Master's Thesis. Chapel Hill, NC: University of North Carolina.

Hurst, L. 2003. "The Special Library on Campus: A Model for Library Orientation Aimed at Academic Administration, Faculty, and Support Staff." *Community and Junior College Libraries*, 11 (2): 51–64.

Jackson, J. and B. Parton. 1999. "Virtual Reference Desk for Regional Education Center Libraries." *Illinois Libraries*, 81 (1): 39–41.

Jenkins, S. 2001. "Undergraduate Perceptions of the Reference Collection and the Reference Librarian in an Academic Library." *Reference Librarian*, 73, 229–41.

Jia, P. 2003. "Distance Referencing: Real-Time Conference Tools." *Community and Junior College Libraries*, 11 (3): 35–42.

Johnson, W. G., A. Burke, and B. Evans. 2001. "Bibliographic Instructional Design: A Case Study." *Community and Junior College Libraries*, 10 (3): 17–38.

Karr, J. 2000. "A Trial Virtual Library: Renovation and Innovation at Great Basin College." *Community and Junior College Libraries*, 9 (3): 47–50.

Kathman, J. M. and M. D. Kathman. May 2000. "Training Student Employees for Quality Service." *The Journal of Academic Librarianship*, 26 (3): 176–82.

———. 1998. "What Difference Does Diversity Make in Managing Student Employees?" *College and Research Libraries*, 59 (4): 378–89.

Kelly, M. S., J. Siddons, and L. Jenkins. 2002. "The Great Reference Debate." *Community and Junior College Libraries*, 11 (1): 5–16.

Kertesz, C. J. 2000. "County in Texas Orders Filters at All Its Libraries." *American Libraries*, 31 (5): 22.

Kniffel, L. 2001. "Community Colleges Fight Budget Cuts." *American Libraries*, 32 (8): 19–20.

Kriewall, G. 2000. "Integration of Academic Support Services into one Facility through a Construction Project." *Community and Junior College Libraries*, 9 (2): 37–46.

Kumar, S. 1999. "Assistive Technology for a Community College Library." *Illinois Libraries*, 81 (2): 88–93.

Laun, M. A. 1999. "On-Ramps to Electronic Highways: Database Trends, Practices, and Expenditures in California's Community College Libraries." *Community and Junior College Libraries*, 9 (1): 35–46.

Lee, L., L. Hime, and E. Domincis. 2003. "Just-in-Time Course Guides." *Florida Libraries*, 46 (2): 8–10.

Leeseberg, K. 1998. "Teaching the Electronic Way." *LLA Bulletin*, 60 (3): 109-13.

Levesque, C. 2003. "Taking Information Literacy Online." *Community and Junior College Libraries*, 11 (2): 7–12.

Library Technician Skill Standards. 2000. *Library Mosaics*, 11 (1, January/February): 8–12. For a word document copy of *Library Technician Skill Standards*, 38 pages, go to: www.highline.ctc.edu. Click on *"Library,"* and click on Library

Technical Program then click the "*Skill* Standards" document. Last accessed May 13, 2004.

Liddell, J. 2003. "A Comprehensive Definition of Plagiarism." *Community and Junior College Libraries*, 11 (3): 43–52.

Liu, V. 2000. Cooperative Online Resource Catalog (CORC): A Community College's Experience." *Community and Junior College Libraries*, 9 (3): 5–22.

Lubans, J. 2002. "A portrait of Collaborative Leadership: Donald E. Riggs and Nova Southeastern University's Joint-Use Library." *Library Administration and Management*, 16 (4), 176–78.

MacAdam, C.L. 2001. "JSTOR for Community College Libraries." *Community and Junior College Libraries*, 10 (3): 39–46.

MacNaughton, D. 2000. "Librarian and Instructor Collaboration: Development of a Customized Website at Lane Community College." *Community and Junior College Libraries*, 9 (3): 33–38.

Mahoney, B. D. 2000. "Electronic Resource Sharing in Community Colleges: A Snapshot of Florida, Wisconsin, Texas and Louisiana." *Community and Junior College Libraries*, 9 (2): 31–36.

Manasco, J. E., B. Gillespie, and J. Purks. 1998. "Duties of Student Employees in Carnegie I institution Branch Libraries." *Kentucky Libraries*, 62 (4): 14–18.

Marcus, S. 2003. "Multilingualism at the Reference Desk: Keeping Students Connected." *College and Research Libraries News*, 64 (5): 322–23, 336.

Marcus, S. and S. Beck. 2003. "A Library Adventure: Comparing a Treasure Hunt with a Traditional Freshman Orientation Tour." *College and Research Libraries*, 64 (1): 23–44.

Margolis, R. 2000. "Sparks Fly North of the Border." *School Library Journal*, 46 (1): 22.

Martinez, E. B. 1999. "A Tale of Two Libraries." *Library Mosaics*, 10 (4): 10–12.

Matesic, M. 2003. "CONSIDER THIS: Education, PDAs, and Wireless Networks: A New Convergence." *College and Undergraduate Libraries*, 10 (2): 19–28.

Mathias, J.H. 1998. "Creation of a Web List for Clinical Disciplines: A Step-by-Step Account of the 'Webliography' Process." *College and Research Libraries News*, 59 (10): 768–70.

Mathias, M.S. and S. Heser. 2002. "Mobilize Your Instruction Program with Wireless Technology." *Computers in Libraries*, 22 (3): 24–30.

McCarthy, S.C. 2003. "Online research 111." *Community and Junior College Libraries*, 11 (3): 17–28.

McKinstry, J. and A. Garrison. 2001. "Building Communities @ Your Library." *College and Research Libraries News*, 62 (2): 165–67, 186.

Mesling, C.F. 2003. "Collection Development Policies in Community College Libraries." *Community and Junior College Libraries*, 11 (2): 73–88.

Middle States Commission on Higher Education. 2002. *Characteristics of Excellence in Higher Education*. Philadelphia: Middle States Commission on Higher Education.

Montgomery, T. and D. Cook. 1999. "Southern Oregon University and Rogue College Libraries: Partners in Access." *OLA Quarterly*, 5 (1): 19.

Moore, A. C. and G. Ivory. 2000. *Investigating and Improving the Information Literacy of College Faculty.* East Lansing, MI: National Center for Research on Teacher Learning (ERIC Document ED449783).

Moore, D., S. Brewster, and C. Dorroh. 2002. "Information Competency Instruction in a Two-Year College: One Size Does Not Fit All." *Reference Services Review*, 30 (4): 300–306.

Morris, S. E. 2001. "When the Lights Go Out: How to Deal when the Catalog Is Down." *Community and Junior College Libraries*, 10 (4): 7–12.

Mundell, J., C. Celene-Martel, and T. Braziunas. 2003. "An Organizational Model for Instructional Support at a Community College." *Information Technology and Libraries*, 22 (2): 61–67.

Orenstein, D. 2003. "Fair Pay Is an Issue for Managers, Too." *Library Journal*, 128 (6): 45.

Palmer, C. S. 2000. "Integrating the Learning Library into the Undergraduate Curriculum: Extending Staff Resources for Library Instruction." *Research Strategies*, 17 (2/3): 167–75.

Patton, J. K. 2001. "Wireless Computing in the Library: A Successful Model at St. Louis Community College." *Community and Junior College Libraries*, 10 (3): 11–16.

Pennevaria, K. 2002. "Glasgow's New Regional Center: The First of Five." *Kentucky Libraries*, 66 (3): 14–15.

Perez, D. R. 2000. "The Support Role of Community Colleges Library/Learning Resources Programs in Academic Success." In *Library Services to Youth of Hispanic Heritage*, Barbara Immroth and Kathleen de la Peña McCook, eds. Jefferson, NC: McFarland and Company, 59–66.

Perrault, A. H., T. M. Adams, and R. M. Smith. 2002. "The Florida Community College Statewide Collection Assessment Project: Outcomes and Impact." *College and Research Libraries*, 63 (3): 240–49.

Perrault, A. H., J. N. DePew, and J. Madaus. 1999. "An Assessment of the Collective Resources Base of Florida Community College Library Collections: A Profile with Interpretative Analysis." *Resource Sharing and Information Networks*, 14 (1): 3–20.

Perrault, A. H., J. Madaus, and A. Ambrister. 1999. "The Effects of High Median Age on Currency of Resources in Community College Library Collections." *College and Research Libraries*, 60 (4): 316–39.

Petersohn, B. S. 2000. "Reinventing Peer Review for Librarians in a Two-Year College." *Community and Junior College Libraries*, 9 (4): 29–40.

Petty, J. B. 1997. "Management Perspectives: Administrative/Management Dilemmas Dealing with Work-Study Students in Academic Libraries." *Arkansas Libraries*, 54 (6): 15–17.

Poole, C. E. 2000. "Importance of Research and Publication by Community College Librarians." *College and Research Libraries*, 61 (6): 486–89.

———. 2002. "Libraries LINCC Lifelong Learners to Community Colleges." *Florida Libraries*, 45 (1): 10–13.

———. 2003. "A Missing Link: Counselor and Librarians Collaboration." *Community and Junior College Libraries*, 11 (4): 35–44.

Poole, C.E. and E. Denny. 2001. "Technological Change in the Workplace: A Statewide Survey of Community College Library and Learning Resources Personnel." *College and Research Libraries*, 62 (6): 513–16.

Reno, E.E. 1999. "Joint-Use Libraries: A College President's Perspective." *Colorado Libraries*, 25 (2): 10–11.

Roshaven, P. and R. Widman. 2001. "A Joint University, College and Public Library." *Resource Sharing and Information Networks*, 15 (1–2): 65–87.

Rotenberg, S. 2002. "The Information Commons at Solano Community College." *Community and Junior College Libraries*, 11 (2): 17–26.

Ruan, Lian. 2001. "Final Narrative Report—Internet Outreach to and Training Illinois Fire Service Personnel, Public and Community College Librarians for Electronic Access to Fire Safety Information." *Illinois Libraries*, 83 (1): 18–33.

Ryer, M. A. and B. Nebeker. 1999. "Implementing an "Ask a Librarian" Electronic Reference Service." *Community and Junior College Libraries*, 9, 1, 21–34.

Saferite, L. 1999. "Libraries Recap What They Sow." *Colorado Libraries*, 25 (2, Summer): 18–20.

Schneider, T. M. 2001. "The Regional Campus Library and Service to the Public." *The Journal of Academic Librarianship*, 27 (2, March): 122–27.

Shamel, C.L. 2001. "Centralized Library and Learning Resources: A Remote Access Demonstration Project." *Community and Junior College Libraries*, 10 (4): 13–28.

Singley, Y. 1998. "Status Report on Library Automation and Networking in Community Colleges." *Illinois Libraries*, 80 (1, Winter): 29–31.

Sisler, Eric and Veronica Smith. 2000. "Building a Library Network from Scratch: Eric and Veronica's Excellent Adventure." *Computers in Libraries*, 20 (9, October): 44–48.

Slusar, L. 1998. "A New Season of Excellence." *Library Mosaics*, 9 (6, November/December): 7.

———. 2000. "Soaring to Excellence "Has the Power!" *Library Mosaics*, 11 (1, January/February), 13.

Smith, K.J. 2001. "Publicizing Your Web Resources for Maximum Exposure." *Community and Junior College Libraries*, 10 (1): 35–40.

Smith, V. 2002. "The Future of Adaptive Technology in Libraries." *Colorado Libraries*, 28 (4): 35–38.

Spanfelner, D. L. 2000. "WebQuests, an Interactive Approach to the Web." *Community and Junior College Libraries*, 9 (4): 23–28.

Staines, G.M. and J. Craig. 1999. "Using Creativity: Creating a Hands-On Learning Environment in Times of Tight Budgets." *The Reference Librarian*, 65, 79–88.

Sullivan, K. and W. G. Taylor. Summer 1999. "Building a Partnership from the Ground Up." *Colorado Libraries* 25 (2): 12–14.

Swanson, T. A. 2001. "From Creating Web Pages to Creating Web Sites: The Use of Information Architecture for Library Web Site Redesign." *Internet Reference Services Quarterly*, 6 (1): 1–12.

Thomas, S. E. 2000. "The Necessary Library Revolution in Community College Development and Remedial Programs." *Community and Junior College Libraries*, 9 (2): 47–58.

Todaro, J. B. 2000. "Change for the Right Reason: What Is a Best Practice?" *Community and Junior College Libraries*, 11 (2): 27–36.

Tolle, A. L. 2001. "Reference and the Community College: Renaissance Librarians at Pikes Peak Community College." *Colorado Libraries*, 27 (Summer): 28–30.

Tolson, S. 2001. "Wireless Laptops and Local Area Networks." *THE Journal*, 28 (11, June): 62–67.

Tope, B. C. 1998. "South Florida Community College, Avon Park Florida: Campus on the Lake." *Ohio Media Spectrum*, 50 (1, Spring): 18–19.

"Unique College, Unique Public Library." 1999. *Unabashed Librarian*, 111: 14–15.

Vaughn, D. and B. Callicott. 2003. "Broccoli Librarianship and Google-Bred Patrons, or What's Wrong with Usability Testing?" *College and Undergraduate Libraries*, 10 (2): 1–18.

Visser, M. 2003. "Identifying and Caring for Rare Books in the Community or Junior College with No Special Collections Department." *Community and Junior College Libraries*, 11 (3): 29–34.

Walsh, R. 2002. "Information Literacy at Ulster County Community College: Going the Distance." *The Reference Librarian*, 77: 89–105.

Weintraub, T. and J. Cater. 1999. "Technology Partnerships on Community College Campuses: Something Old, Something New, and Something Borrowed from the Library/Learning Resource Center." *Community and Junior College Libraries* 9 (1): 5–20.

Wiggins, R. W. 2002. "Yesterday's Headlines." *School Library Journal* (Spring): 26–27.

Williams, C. and M. M. Corpus. (2002). "Serving the Homebound Learner: The Queensborough Experience." *Urban Library Journal*, 12 (1): 49–59.

Winston, S. J. 1999. "The Role of Recruitment in Achieving Goals Related to Diversity." *College and Research Libraries*, 59 (3): 240–47.

Woods, J. A. 2001. "Joint-Use libraries: The Broward College Central Campus Experience." *Resource Sharing and Information Networks*, 15 (1–2): 41–53.

Yang, E.L., C. Hashert, and L. Evans. 2001. "Auraria Library and Media Center: A Best Kept Secret? Not!" *Colorado Libraries*, 27 (4): 32–34.

Yorke-Smith, M. 2001. "Back to School." *Library Mosaics*, 12 (2, March/April): 19.

NOTE

1. Regional campuses are defined as campuses at locations other than the main campus of a university where at least 50 percent of an educational program is offered (Schneider 2001).

APPENDICES

Here in "short subjects" is good information, something like the movies use when the feature film isn't very long, or the transmitter malfunctions in the middle of the big game. Good authors and two guys you no doubt know contribute their helpful thoughts.

1 ASSESSMENT OF LIBRARY RESOURCES AND SERVICES AS PART OF THE COLLEGE PROGRAM REVIEW PROCESS

Andrine J. Haas

Academic librarians are in a constant quest for methods to involve faculty in the selection and use of library resources and services. Librarians send new book lists, provide instruction sessions, attend meetings, and actively request input from faculty in many other forms and methods. One method that has had success at Dawson Community College (DCC) is looking at library resources and services as a part of the assessment process for our Associate of Applied Science (AAS) and one-year certificate programs.

All of the DCC vocational/technical programs go through a periodic review process. The review process includes the following:

1. An annual review/revision of program goals and objectives;
2. Meetings with the program Advisory Committee twice per year;
3. An annual Quantitative Review, which includes data on enrollment, job growth potential, and placement over the past five years; and
4. A Qualitative Review every four years.

The Qualitative Review is designed to assess the role and scope, financial aspects, and support areas for each program. The support areas include an evaluation of faculty credentials, student success indicators, curriculum, library resources, facility and equipment, and support staff for each program. The section on Library Resources states:

> The Program Director will meet with the Library Director to assess the adequacy of existing library resources and services available for the program and to make recommendations for improvement.

The Program Director then writes a statement about the adequacy of and needs for library materials and services as a part of the Qualitative Review.

To facilitate the meetings with Program Directors, a one-page outline/worksheet was created to guide the assessment of library resources and services for each program. That outline follows this text. The Library Director arranged meeting times with each Program Director to go through the outline.

The meetings were met with a variety of attitudes from faculty—from "Let's just hurry and get this over" to very honest, detailed discussions. Some discussions lasted less than 30 minutes, and others lasted more than an hour. However, because the Program Director was required to write a statement about the library resources and services, most were serious and appeared to like the structure of the prepared outline.

Results of the outlined meetings were positive on both sides, partly because of the one-on-one nature of the meetings. The Program Directors were open to hearing about existing resources (especially online), even though they had received information about these resources in the past. Many seemed to appreciate the opportunity to discuss their programs and courses and gave recommendations regarding journal subscriptions, books, and videos for the library.

From the library point of view, librarians learned more about the curriculum and instructional methodologies for each program. Two items on the outline were especially helpful in gaining faculty assistance in making future collection improvements. The questions "Are there new areas you are adding to the curriculum/course?" and "Are there new 'hot topics' in your field?" elicited responses from all Program Directors. These responses gave specific subject areas to investigate for new library materials and—in several cases—gave suggestions the library might not have identified. For example, consider the following:

- The Program Director in Law Enforcement stated the need for materials on police ethics, racial profiling, and security issues;
- The Program Director in Office Technology requested changes to our journal subscriptions and suggested the purchase of more materials on office ergonomics;
- The Program Director in Business Management suggested the need for a few basic books on managerial accounting and was interested to see the library already owned several available in an e-book collection.

In addition to giving specific recommendations and subject areas for collection development, the discussions also led to other faculty-library collaborations. The Program Director for the Farm-Ranch Management program (which is mostly taught on site at individual farms and ranches) brought students to the library for instruction in using agriculture-related online resources and how to access them from off-campus. The Office Technology instructor asked a librarian to talk to a class about copyright issues in creating Web pages. Computer and business instructors asked technical questions about the set-up of library computers and if it could be changed to allow access needed by some of their students.

Overall, the library section of the Qualitative program review had very positive results. The one-on one nature of the discussions helped to provide this positive feedback and the review outline served to keep the conversations on task and to look at a variety of issues regarding library resources and services.

This Program Review process is currently in place for the vocational/technical degrees only. A similar process for review of the college's general education core requirements and transfer courses is being studied. If that process is approved, it will include a similar section for review of library resources and services in those areas.

Outline of Areas to Be Reviewed by the Library Director and a Program Director/Course Instructor in the Review Process of Applied Science Programs and Individual Courses

1. Research/Information needs
   a. What major subject areas are covered in your program/course? (Course/programdescription/syllabus)
   b. What research will you be asking your students to do? What information needs will they have? (for example—research papers, book reports/reviews, journal article abstracts, newspaper article summaries, statistics collection, information gathering for speeches/presentations, background reading/skills development)

2. Existing library collection/services
   a. Does the library have the books, periodicals, online resources, videos/AV materials, and other resources you and your students need for your program/class?
   b. Does the library provide the services you and your students need for your program/class?

3. Suggestions for improvement

   Materials/resources
   a. What new materials/access should be added to provide resources/information needed?
   b. Are there new areas you are adding to the curriculum/course?
   c. Are there new "hot topics" in your field?
   d. Have your students mentioned any problems with finding information on a certain subject?
   e. Are there resources such as videos that YOU need to help you teach your course(s)?

   Services
   a. Do you need informational literacy/library skills training provided for your students or yourself? If so, in what subject areas, time, place, format?

b. Do you have distance education/remote students who need library access that are not currently receiving it (through the Web page/proxy server/phone/fax/e-mail systems)?

c. Are there handouts, printed informational guides, etc. which we could provide for you and/or your students? (for example, on using a specific online database, on basic bibliographic citation, on remote access to the library resources)

d. Are there other services you need from the library?

Other

Are there any other suggestions you can make for the library to help you or your students with your program/course?

2 LAPTOP USE POLICY: MONTANA STATE UNIVERSITY—GREAT FALLS CAMPUS LIBRARY

Sheila Bonnand

The Montana State University (MSU)—Great Falls Campus Library serves primarily the MSU—Great Falls College of Technology, a two-year institution in Great Falls, Montana. The campus consists of one building and also houses branches of MSU—Northern and MSU—Bozeman, both of which provide upper division opportunities for local students. Because of an expanding student population, problems with space have become acute. Though the library was renovated and expanded in 2003, both the addition of the campus computer lab and increasing gate counts have kept space issues at the forefront.

A wireless network was recently added to the MSU—Great Falls Campus Library and a set of laptops was acquired. This wireless solution was the only way to solve the problem of increasing computer access without physically expanding the facility. Keeping pace with current technology was another factor in the decision to add the network. Students now have the option of computer access anywhere in the library, including group study rooms. Planning for this addition involved hardware and network issues as well as designing policies to govern laptop use. To start, the laptop units are for in-library use only. However, concerns over the expense and damageability of the units led to the development of rather stringent use policies as this venture began in the summer of 2004.

Although the MSU—Great Falls wireless network is progressive, the library is certainly not in the vanguard of this movement. Because of this, MSU—Great Falls was able to tap into the expertise at a sister library (MSU—Billings), and development of the laptop policies did not have to start from scratch. MSU—Billings Library was already providing wireless service and graciously shared its policies. By adapting these policies to the local situation and incorporating ideas gathered through an internet search of other libraries, the Great Falls document was created.

Devising policies is always an attempt to plan for eventualities that might arise in dealing with patrons. It can also be an opportunity to educate patrons about library and campus expectations. To these ends, MSU—Great Falls's policies were organized in to two parts. The first part addresses basic checkout/responsibility issues such as needing a current student ID and the checkout period. The second section was designed to educate users about computer access responsibilities, which range from the basics (food/drink issues) to the more complex (privacy and security issues) to the obscure (university computer use policies). The major concern addressed by the policies was making sure users understand their responsibilities in using the laptops and the consequences if problems arise. It was also important to create a document concise enough that patrons might actually read it.

A check-out document was created along with the policies. It duplicates basic policy information, putting it into agreement format. Because the form must be signed by users, the expectation is that it will be read by users even if the full policy isn't. The form also works as a backup to checking out through the circulation system. An additional protection for patrons was included by having a library staff member sign off when a laptop is returned.

After gaining some experience in the laptop trade, these policies will be reviewed and revised as needed. It is hoped that such revisions can eliminate duplication in both paperwork and checkout procedures. However, the long-term plan for the college is to expand access campus-wide; because of this, it may be necessary to retain the stringency of the original document.

Library Laptop Check-Out Agreement

I agree to accept *full financial responsibility* for failure to return the laptop and any accompanying equipment, and any damage incurred to the equipment while it is checked out to me. The approximate cost of the laptop is $2,000, but a replacement cost may be assessed.

I understand that this equipment is a *2-hour library loan* and *must not leave* the library. Laptops will be checked out for 2 hours or until the Library closes. Laptops should be returned 15 minutes before the library closes. A fine of $2.00 per hour will be charged if the laptop is returned late. One renewal may be allowed, depending on availability.

I *will not tamper* with existing hardware or software (this includes installing, deleting, modifying and/or downloading). I agree to protect this equipment from theft and/or damage. I will not leave the laptop unattended nor will I have food or drink in the immediate vicinity of the computer.

I must follow *MUS Board of Regents and MSU—GF policies* regarding computer and network use (see http://www.msugf.edu/helpdesk/security/default.asp for information).

I will immediately report any *problems* with the laptop to the library staff.

I will *return* the laptop and/or peripherals to a library staff member.

I understand that my laptop *privileges will be revoked* if I violate any part of this agreement. In addition, any blocks on a patron record (overdue fines, etc.) will also prohibit laptop borrowing.

Signed:_____

Name (please print):_____

Student ID number: _____ Date: _____

Circle one: Student   Faculty   Staff

Circle one: COT   Northern   Bozeman

• •

Library Staff Use Only

Checked out: Laptop number: _____ Power cord _____ Floppy drive _____

Time: _____ Renewal time: _____

Returned to (library staff member): _____

Comments:_____

_____

_____

Library Wireless Laptop Check-Out Policies

Laptop computers are available for check out at the MSU—Great Falls Library. These are equipped with wireless network cards which will allow for Internet access throughout the Library. Each laptop will be clearly marked with an MSU—Great Falls ownership symbol and will have a machine number, barcode and security tag.

Check out:

Users must agree to the terms of checkout by signing a Library Laptop Checkout Agreement. This includes assuming financial responsibility for the equipment.

Privileges will be revoked for any patron violating the use agreement. In addition, any blocks on a patron record (overdue fines, etc.) will also prohibit laptop borrowing.

A valid MSU ID card must be shown to check out a laptop.

Community library users (courtesy borrowers) will not be eligible to check out laptop computers, but will be directed to use Library desktop computers.

Laptops will be checked out for 2 hours or until the Library closes, if that is less than 2 hours; one renewal may be allowed, depending on availability. Laptops should be returned 15 minutes before the Library closes. $2.00 per hour overdue fines will be accessed.

Power cords and external floppy drives will be checked out with laptops by request. Laptops will have a battery life of up to 31/2 hours. Electrical outlets are available throughout the Library.

Laptop use:

Laptops are for use only in the Library and may not leave the Library.

Borrowers must agree to not leave a laptop unattended and to refrain from having food and/or drink around the unit.

Users must comply with MUS Board of Regents and MSUGF policies for computer and network use (for complete information see http://www.msugf.edu/help-desk/security/default.asp).

Borrowers are expected to refrain from installing, deleting, modifying, or otherwise altering any hardware, software or data on the laptops, including display and desktop configurations. Saving to an external pen drive is recommended, but files can be saved to a disk, emailed, or saved to assigned server storage space on the campus network.

Printing is available to laptop users. The default printer is the 4300 printer located in the computer lab.

Users should be aware that campus computers are not private or guaranteed secure and use of personal information should be kept to a minimum.

Users should immediately report any problems with a laptop to a Library staff member.

Each laptop must be returned to a Library staff member. Library staff will check each laptop in and complete the checkout agreement.

February 2004 / MSU—Great Falls Campus Library

3   THE COLLEGE HILL LIBRARY— WESTMINSTER, COLORADO

Warren Taylor

Front Range Community College—Westminster, Colorado, serves more than 23,000 students on three campuses and one center. The City of Westminster has a population of more than 106,000 persons.

The College Hill Library in Westminster, Colorado, began as a discussion between Front Range Community College and the City of Westminster in the early 1990s. We moved into the College Hill Library in April 1998. The discussions led to an Intergovernmental Agreement. In August 1995 the Colorado State Board for Community Colleges and Occupational Education and the Westminster City Council approved the Intergovernmental Agreement to jointly build and operate the library. Some of the basic points agreed to in the Intergovernmental Agreement include the following: the building would be located on the college campus; all public space would be open to use by all; the State of Colorado would own the building with the City's share would be in effect for 50 years; the College would pay 60 percent of the cost and the City would pay 40 percent; the City and College would share equally the cost of 200 additional parking spaces; the City and College would each purchase and own furnishings, equipment and supplies; the College would provide maintenance, utilities, and so on and bill the City; each party would purchase and manage their own library collections. In addition, the library would be operated with one computer network, to be agreed upon by the two library directors and the management of the two library operations would be determined by the two library directors, but with as little duplication of services and functions as possible.

College Hill Library

College Hill Library

Bennett, Wagner and Grody were hired as architects after a lengthy search process. The architects designed a two-story building with two entrances. The building is approximately 80,000 square feet. The College Hill Library is connected to the main college building by an enclosed walkway. The architects also designed a long, gently curved wall on the northwest side of the building with large windows to provide a view of the Front Range of the Rocky Mountains. The lower level includes a public meeting room, circulation services, the Children's Library, a New Books area. The upper level includes Circulation/Reserves, the Reference Desk and collection, the media services, a Library Instruction room, and additional public meeting rooms. The lower level also houses Technical Services and the Rocky Flats Reading Room, paid for and staffed by the U.S. Department of Energy.

Six years after we moved into the new facility, the College Hill Library continues to operate smoothly. The Front Range Community College staff and the City of Westminster staff work well together and provide a wide range of services to the public, faculty, and students. The College Hill Library serves approximately 600,000 patrons a year and has a yearly circulation of over one million.

4 SOME RECENT BUILDINGS

David R. Dowell and Gerard B. McCabe

A recent inquiry to the CJC Listserv asked for a list of new community college library/learning resource center buildings. Several responses were received, which are listed here. In looking for new buildings, certainly look at new public and other academic libraries. Take note of furniture and equipment and ask about comfort, wearability, and any advice that can be offered.

California

Columbia College, Sonora. www.gocolumbia.org/library
Cuesta College, San Luis Obispo.
Cuesta College, San Luis Obispo North County.
MiraCosta College, Oceanside.
Pasadena City College, Pasadena.
Riverside Community College, Riverside campus. www.rcc.edu

Colorado

Front Range Community College, c.80,000gsf, a joint-use facility with City of Westminster

Florida

> Brevard Community College Library, Cocoa—This facility is shared by the University of Central Florida, Brevard Community College, and the Florida Solar Energy Center.
>
> Brevard Community College Library, Palm Bay—This facility is shared with the University of Central Florida.
>
> Seminole/St. Petersburg College Library, Seminole.

Massachusetts

> Quinsigamond Community College, Worcester. Http://www.qcc.mas.edu/academicservices/new_qcc_campus_center_piece.htm

New York

> Westchester Community College, Valhalla. www.sunywcc.edu/library

5   OFFICE SUPPLIES: MARKETING YOUR LIBRARY

David R. Dowell and Gerard B. McCabe

The CJC Listserv provides a wealth of information on many useful topics. One such topic involved giving office supplies to students finishing term papers and similar assignments. In response to a query on this topic, several librarians replied with very useful suggestions, and this appendix summarizes these suggestions and adds some of our own.

SPACE PLANNING

If you're planning a renovation or even more fortunately a new building, program space for a supply table, about 40 square feet. Responding librarians agree in general that handing out these simple supply items from the Circulation service is not practical because it interrupts the circulation function. If you're not so fortunate with your building, try to find space to put a supply table such as those seen in Office Depot, Staples, or Kinko's.

FUNDING THE EXPENSE

For some libraries the operating budget is large enough to support the cost of incidental supplies. Not all libraries are so fortunate, and there is a limit on just what is affordable. For some items, referral to the campus bookstore is the only alternative. (Some examples are listed at the end of this text. The list also includes a means of handling certain items, including scissors, punches and paper cutters.)

To avoid collecting money for small supply items, consider asking for return of surplus supplies. A small sign can suggest this.

Office Supplies

These supplies and equipment are provided free-of-charge for your use.
The cost is charged to a limited budget. If you have some of these supplies that
you no longer require, please bring them to the library and place them here.
Supplies not available here can be found in the Campus bookstore.

There's no harm in impressing on students the need for replenishment and conservation. Common paper clips disappear by the hundreds, but they must be accumulating somewhere. At semester's end, thoughtful students can unclip their papers, return the clips to the supply table, and, it is hoped, recycle the paper.

EQUIPMENT

Paper cutter/trimmer: Avoid guillotine style; buy rotary or enclosed blade style.
Punches: two/three hole, secure by bolting to tabletop. One-hole hand punch, buy model with hanging ring and secure with chain to table.
Scissors: secure with chain to tabletop.
Stapler, electric: secure by bolting to tabletop.
Tape dispenser: difficult to secure but is heavy.

SUPPLIES

Binder clips
Paper clips
Plastic clips
Rubber bands

All of these are in containers.

6 ARCHITECTURAL FEATURES

Gerard B. McCabe

Many architectural and design features go into a building. Some are more prominent than others; some require explanation for understanding. There are features
that years ago were not considered desirable, but with technical changes or improvements have come into better reputations and so are worthy of consideration. This appendix presents a list of such features with brief remarks indicating
why they are important for consideration or in some cases why care should be
taken to avoid or modify them. There is some repetition in this list with my
chapter; this emphasizes the importance of certain items.

Air intakes: These are placed best well above ground level. Air pollutants
are less likely to be brought into the air handling system.

Atria, atrium: Up until recently many consultants recommended against an
atrium as wasteful of space. A carefully designed atrium, however, admits
natural light, a desirable feature, and so should be considered.

Beverage service: This requires a water supply, power, and trash disposal. Location is optional. Often including a snack service requires concern for
insects and rodents, so a lobby location is often preferred. If possible, this
service is highly recommended.

Canopy, exterior: Overhead protection from inclement weather is desirable
for entering and leaving the building. Using photovoltaic glass can help
with energy savings and can be an attractive feature.

Carpet: Electrostatic carpet is preferable for computer workstation areas. Carpet tile for high traffic areas reduces wear. Specifications should be very
specific regarding durability, stain resistance and colors fading.

Composting toilets: In some areas these are excellent. If your library is in such an area, raise the question of their use.

Copy machine placement: Options vary from a central copy room to alcove locations in collection areas. When line drawings are prepared, for whatever option is chosen, be certain there is a power supply and space for recycling receptacles; if in collection areas, prefer alcoves so the machines are not in traffic lanes.

Elevator: When elevators are required, placement occasionally becomes an issue. Ordinarily, public elevators are located near the main entry and not far from a main staircase. Sometimes a location on line drawings may be deeper into a building requiring the public to transit some distance through open floor space. This should cause an objection. Persons with mobility impairments will find this very uncomfortable and others will find it inconvenient.

When there is only one elevator, its size should accommodate loaded book trucks and even some furniture. For more detailed information about elevators and escalators see the Selected Bibliography.

Entry: The most convenient and safest entries have power activated sliding glass doors. These have the greater advantage over even push/pull doors with a power assistance feature.

Escalator: These are seen sometimes only in very large buildings. See the Selected Bibliography for more information.

Fire extinguisher placement: Don't leave this to chance. Fire extinguishers should be in receptacles clearly marked with overhead red lamps. Even if the library has or is to have a sprinkler system a fire marshal could insist on extinguishers. Later installation could result in ugly placement of brackets on walls and columns. This can result in brackets being pulled loose, leaving a damaged spot on a wall or column.

Flush valves: With low-flow commodes, these are essential. The recommendation is to insist on having flush valves installed.

Foundation: This must support a minimum of 150 pounds per square foot. See "Liveload" for more detail.

Glass: There is no reason to be "glass shy." Glass technology has produced some outstanding glass with superb technological features for many uses. Don't think of glass as a hard surface reverberating sound waves. There is acoustical glass that can be used in situations in which noise can be a disturbing factor.

Windows are an obvious need, and today's window glass can block ultraviolet waves, be impact resistant, or be bullet resistant and shatterproof. Windows admit light and there is no need to restrict size below what is best or to limit use on exterior walls facing city streets.

Safety glass can be used on entry doors on interior doors and walls, and with decoration as attractive dividers.

HVAC: The system must maintain comfortable levels in all areas and operate with minimal noise.

Lighting levels: For reading and work surfaces 50-foot candles is recommended. For other areas intensities are lower. See the Selected Bibliography for further information.

Liveload: The recommendation is for 150 pounds per square foot. Liveload calculation considers the weight of library material, storage equipment, and the average weight of people in the library during open hours. This factor is critical for all floor levels. If planning for a shared building with the library space on an upper floor, this requirement holds. If compact shelving is used then 300 pounds per square foot is the requirement.

Loading dock: If the site requires a loading dock then it should be four feet high and long enough to permit two trucks to load or unload. A ramp at one end permits the use of small hand trucks when a delivery van is used. If the receiving area is at ground level a concrete pad will suffice.

Mezzanine: Some older buildings will have mezzanines. I don't recommend them because of small size and the need to observe liveload requirements if any collections are placed on them.

Parking: Exhaust emissions can be a problem affecting air quality in the building if too many vehicles drive close. This is one good reason why air intakes should be at high levels. It may be inconvenient, but parking should be at a safe distance.

Pedimat: Every effort should be made to encourage people to wipe their feet as they enter the library. Using a mat like this is very helpful toward keeping the floors clean.

Power supply: Sometime libraries are found to be underpowered. Even with the low power usage equipment and energy efficient lighting, this can happen. The library runs on power, and everyone involved should understand this. Outlets and circuits should be sufficient to power even unforeseen equipment that might be added to services. For more information, please see the Selected Bibliography.

Precast concrete: You might not get the opportunity to propose use of precast concrete, but if you can, its components can be very attractive for the exterior and its use will speed construction.

Shelving: Manufacturers offer several options for shelving books, periodicals, and media. For books and some media lower shelves should tilt up for ease of reading titles and call numbers. Height of units and number of shelves for books will affect capacity, but there is a definite trend toward medium height, five feet, book shelving.

Skylights: Once ignored, with new technology, these are a good way to admit natural light. If it's possible for design of the building, definitely favor a skylight.

Sliding glass doors: See "Glass."

Trash/recycle receptacles: Here is where the attractiveness of an interior sign scheme is ruined by an oversight, and unattractive receptacles detract from the appearance. You should be certain that these are color coordinated with the interior design.

Wastebaskets: See "Trash/recycle receptacles."

Water fountains: The preferred practice is to pair fountains at two heights for convenience of all users.

SELECTED BIBLIOGRAPHY

Ingersoll, Patricia and John Culshaw. 2004. *Managing Information Technology: A Handbook for Systems Librarians.* Westport, CT: Libraries Unlimited, The Libraries Unlimited Library Management Collection

Lueder, Dianne and Sally Webb. 1992. *Administrator's Guide to Library Building Maintenance.* Chicago: American Library Association. See pages 52–54 for information on Elevators and Escalators.

McCabe, Gerard B. 2000. *Planning for a New Generation of Public Library Buildings.* Westport, CT: Greenwood Press. Greenwood Library Management Collection For Elevators and Escalators see pages 101–103.

McCabe, Gerard and James R. Kennedy, eds. 2003. *Planning the Modern Public Library Building.* Westport, CT: Libraries Unlimited. The Libraries Unlimited Library Management Collection see pages 206–08 for Lighting and Windows, see pages 209–10 for Power.

7 STRATEGIC PLAN BIBLIOGRAPHY

Francis G. Kuykendall

ACRL. 2000a. Standards for college libraries: the final version: approved January 2000. *C&RL News* 61 (3): 175–82.

———. 2000b. Information literacy competency standards for higher education: the final version, approved January 2000. *C&RL News* 61 (3): 207–15.

———. 2001. Objectives for information literacy instruction. *C&RL News* 62 (4): 416–28.

———. 2002a. Guidelines for instruction programs in academic libraries: approved by the ACRL Board. June 2003. *C&RL News* 64 (9): 616–19.

———. 2002b. Guidelines for instruction programs in academic libraries: final draft. *C&RL News* 63 (10): 732–35.

———. 2002c. Information literacy competency standards for higher education. Chicago: American Library Association.

———. 2003a. "Characteristics of programs of information literacy that illustrate best practice: a draft. *C&RL News* 64 (1): 32–35.

———. 2003b. "Guidelines for curriculum materials centers: approved by ACRL and ALA. January 2003. *C&RL News* 64 (7): 469–474.

———. 2003c. Guidelines for distance learning library services: a draft revision. *C&RL News* 64 (4): 265–271.

Alire, Camila, ed. 2000. *Library disaster planning and recovery handbook.* New York: Neal-Schuman.

American Library Association, Office for Intellectual Freedom, comp. 2002. *Intellectual freedom manual.* Chicago: ALA.

Appleton, Margaret, and Debbie Orr. 2000. Meeting the needs of distance education students. In *Information literacy around the world: advances in program,* ed.

Christine Bruce and Philip C. Candy, 11–24. Wagga Wagga, NSW: Centre for Information and Research Studies.

Arp, Lori, and Gerald Jay Schafer. 1992. Connecting bibliographic instruction and collection development: a management plan. *RQ* 31 (3): 398. Expanded Academic ASAP. Infotrac http://web6.infotrac.galegroup.com. Accessed 7 Nov. 2003.

Ashcroft, Linda. 2002. Issues in developing, managing and marketing electronic journals collections. *Collection Building* 21 (4): 147–53.

Baltzer, Jan A. 2000. Consider the four-legged stool as your plan for information technology. *Computers in Libraries* 20 (4): 4. Academic Search Elite. EBSCO-host. http://web19.epnet.com. Accessed 8 Sept. 2003.

Bauer, Kathleen. 2001. Resources for library assessment. *C&RL News* 62 (1): 12–14+.

Bertot, John, and Charles R. McClure. 2003. Outcomes assessment in the networked environment: research questions, issues, considerations, and moving forward. *Library Trends* 51 (4): 590. Research Library. ProQuest. http://proquest.umi.com. Accessed 28 Jan 2004.

Bielefield, Arlene, and Lawrence Cheeseman. 1994. *Maintaining the privacy of library records: a handbook and guide*. New York: Neal-Schuman.

Billings, Harold. 2003. Wild-card academic library in 2013. *College & Research Libraries* 64 (2): 105–9.

Bryson, John M. 1995. *Strategic planning for public and nonprofit organizations*, rev. ed. San Francisco: Jossey-Bass.

Bryson, John M., and Farnum K. Alston. 1996. Creating and implementing your strategic plan: a workbook for public and non-profit organizations. San Francisco: Jossey-Bass.

Casserly, Mary Frances. 2002. Developing a concept of collection for the digital age. *Portal*: Libraries and the Academy 2 (4): 577. Research Library. ProQuest. http://proquest.umi.com. Accessed 28 Jan 2004.

Catts, Ralph. 2000. Some issues in assessing information literacy. In *Information literacy around the world: advances in programs*, ed. Christine Bruce and Philip C. Candy, 271–83. Wagga Wagga, NSW: Centre for Information Studies and Research.

Cervone, Frank. 2001. Transforming library services to support distance learning. *C&RL News* 62 (2): 147–49.

Clougherty, Leo et al. 1998. The University of Iowa Libraries' undergraduate user needs assessment. *College & Research Libraries* 59 (6): 572–84.

Connaughton, Sue Ann. 2000. Developing virtual collection from the online smorgasbord. *Computers in Libraries* 20(6): 42. Expanded Academic ASAP. Infotrac. http://web4.galegroup.com. Accessed 7 Nov. 2003.

Courtois, Martin P. 2002. Crisis, disaster, and emergency management: Web sites for researchers. *C&RL News* 63 (10): 723–26.

Cowgill, Allison, Joan Beam, and Lindsey Wess. 2001. Implementing an information commons in the university library. *Journal of Academic Librarianship* 27 (6): 432–39.

Cronau, Deborah Ann. 2001. Lifelong learning and the library connection: a perceptual model for tertiary library customer education. Australian *Library Journal* 50 (4): 335. Expanded Academic ASAP. Infotrac. http://web4.infotrac.galegroup.com. Accessed 27 Aug. 2002.

Dodsworth, Ellen. 1989. Marketing academic libraries: a necessary plan. *Journal of Academic Librarianship* 24 (4): 320. Academic Search Elite. EBSCOhost. http://search.epnet.com. Accessed 27 April 2004.

Dougherty, Richard M. 2002. Planning for new library futures. *Library Journal* 1 (27): 9. Academic Search Elite. EBSCOhost. http://search.epnet.com. Accessed 8 Sept 2003.

Doyle, Charles. 2003. Libraries and the USA Patriot Act. CRS Report for Congress. Received through the CRS Web. The Library of Congress. Feb. 26, 2003.

Ducas, Ada, and Nicole Michaud-Oystryk. 2003. Toward new enterprise: capitalizing on the faculty / librarian partnership. *College & Research Libraries* 64 (1): 55–74.

Dugan, Robert E. 2002. Information technology plans. *Journal of Academic Librarianship* 28 (3): 152. Academic Search Elite. EBSCOhost. http://search.epnet.com. Accessed 16 April 2004.

Ebbinghouse, Carol. 1999. Library standards: evidence of library effectiveness and accreditation. Searcher 7 (8): 20–27.

Ellis-Newman, Jennifer. 2003. Activity-based costing in user services of an academic library. *Library Trends* 51 (3): 333–49.

FAQ Strategic planning. Nonprofit GENIE. 2001. CompassPoint Nonprofit Services http://search.genie.org. Accessed 30 Apr. 2004.

Feinman, Valerie Jackson. 1999. Five steps toward planning today for tomorrow's needs. *Computers in Libraries* 19 (1): 18. MasterFILE Premier. EBSCOhost. http://search.epnet.com. Accessed 27 April 2004.

Fernekes, Robert W., and William N. Nelson. 2002. How practical are the ACRL "Standards for College Libraries"? *C&RL News* 63 (10): 711–13.

Fradkin, Bernard. 2003. The community college library perspective in an age of opportunity. *C&RL News* 64 (11): 721–23.

Fraser, Bruce T., Charles R. McClure, and Emily H. Leahy. 2002. Toward a framework for assessing and institutional outcomes. *Portal: Libraries and the Academy* 2 (4): 505–28.

Gratch-Lindauer, Bonnie. 2002. Comparing the regional accreditation standards: outcomes assessment and other trends. *Journal of Academic Librarianship* 28 (1/2): 14. Academic Search Elite. EBSCOhost. http://search.epnet.com. Accessed 30 Jan. 2004.

Helfer, Doris Small. 1999. Has the virtual university library truly arrived? *Searcher* 7 (8): 62–65.

Hisle, W. Lee. 2002. Top issues facing academic librarians: a report of the Focus on the Future Task Force. *C&RL News* 63 (10): 714–15+.

Jacobson, Alvin L., and JoAnne L. Sparks. 2001. Creating value: building the strategy-focused library. Information 5 (9): 14–20. LookSmart's FindArticle. http://www.findarticles.com. Accessed 3 May 2004.

Jones, Chris. 2001. Development strategies for library collections in a digital environment. *Australian Public Libraries and Information Services* 14 (3): 101. Expanded Academic ASAP. Infotrac, http://web4.infotrac.galegroup.com. Accessed 7 Nov. 2003.

Kaufman, Roger et al. 2003. *Strategic planning for success: aligning people, performance, and payoffs.* San Francisco: Jossey-Bass.

Kluegel, Kathleen. 1997. Redesigning our future. *RQ* 36 (3): 330. Expanded Academic ASAP. Infotrac. http://web4.infotrac.galegroup.com. Accessed 7 Nov. 2003.

Kreitz, Patricia. 2004. Librarians as knowledge builders: strategic partnering for service and advocacy. *C&RL News* 65 (1): 8–10+.

Kyrillidou. Martha and Kaylyn Hipps. 2001. Symposium on measuring library service quality. ARL Bimonthly report 215 www.arl.org/newsltr/215. Accessed 30 Apr. 2004.

Lankes, R. David, Melissa Gross, and Charles R. McClure. 2003. Cost, statistics, measures, and standards for digital reference services: a preliminary view. *Library Trends* 51 (3): 401–13.

Lawrence, Stephen R., Lynn Silpigni Connaway, and Keith H. Brigham. 2001. Life cycle costs of library collections: creation of effective performance and cost metrics for library resources. *College & Research Libraries* 62 (6): 541–53.

Library safety & security: a comprehensive manual for library administrators and police and security officers. 1992. Goshen, KY: Campus Crime Prevention Programs.

Lindauer, Bonnie Gratch. 1998. Defining and measuring the library's impact on campus-wide outcomes. *College & Research Libraries* 59 (6): 546–63.

Lippincott, Joan K. 2002. Developing collaborative relationships: librarians, students, and faculty creating learning communities. *C&RL News* 63 (3): 190–92.

Lynch. Clifford. 2004. The future of libraries: six perspectives on how libraries, librarians, and library patrons will adapt to changing times. *Threshold* (Winter): 13–17.

McClamroch. J., Jacqueline Byrd, and Steven L. Sowell. 2001. Strategic planning: politics, leadership, and learning. *Journal of Academic Librarianship* 27 (5): 372. Academic Search Elite. EBSCOhost. http://search.epnet.com. Accessed 8 Sept 2003.

Melton, Emily, ed. 1989. Library confidentiality policies: computers for patrons. *American Libraries* (February): 126–27.

Morgan, Eric Lease. 1999. Stringboards for strategic planning. *Computers in Libraries* 19 (1): 32. Expanded Academic ASAP.Infotrac. http://web5.infotrac.galegroup.com. Accessed Oct. 2003.

Mundell, Jacqueline, Corly Celene-Martel, and Tom Braziunas. 2003. An organizational model for instruction support at a community college. *Information Technology and Libraries* 22 (2): 61–67.

Nelson, Sandra. 2001. *New planning for results: a streamlined approach.* Chicago: American Library Association.

Nelson, William Neal, and Robert W. Fernekes. 2002. *Standards and assessment for academic libraries: a workbook.* Chicago: American Library Association.

Newcomb, Doug. 2002. What every librarian needs to know about the USA Patriot Act (Public Policy). *Information Outlook* 6 (10): 38. Expanded Academic ASAP. Infotrac. http://web5.infotrac.galegroup.com. Accessed 2 Oct. 2003.

Penniman, W. David. 1999. Strategic planning to avoid bottlenecks in the Age of the Internet. *Computers in Libraries* 19 (1): 50. Expanded Academic ASAP. Infotrac. http://web3.infotrac.galegroup.com. Accessed 28 April 2004.

Perrault, Anna H. et al. 2002. Florida Community College statewide collection assessment project: outcomes and impact. *College & Research Libraries* 63 (3): 240–49.

Phipps, Shelley. 2001. Beyond measuring service quality: learning from the voices of the customers, the staff, the processes, and the organization. *Library Trends* 49 (4): 635. EBSCOhost . http://search.epnet.com. Accessed 8 Sept. 2003.

Poll, Roswitha. 2001. Performance, processes and costs: managing service quality with the Balanced Scorecard. *Library Trends* 49 (4): 709. EBSCOhost. http://search.epnet.com. Accessed 30 Jan. 2004.

Rader, Hannelore B. 2001. A new academic library model: partnerships for learning and teaching. *C&RL News* 62 (4): 393–96.

Ratteray, Oswald M. T. 2002. Information literacy in self-study and accreditation. *Journal of Academic Librarianship* 28 (6): 368. EBSCOhost http://search.epnet.com. Accessed Jan. 29, 2004.

Roberts, Stephen A. 2003. Financial management of libraries: past trends and future prospects. *Library Trends* 51 (3): 462. Research Library. ProQuest. http://proquest.umi.com. Accessed 28 Jan. 2004.

Rockman, Ilene F. 2003. Integrating information literacy into the learning outcomes of academic discipline: a critical 21st-century issue. *C&RL News* 64 (9): 612–15.

Ryan, Susan. 2003. Library Web site administration: a strategic model for the smaller academic library. *Journal of Academic Librarianship* 29 (4): 207. Academic Search Elite. EBSCOhost. http://search.epnet.com. Accessed 16 Apr. 2004.

Shuman, Bruce A. 1999. *Library security and safety handbook: prevention, policies, and procedures*. Chicago: American Library Association.

Smith, Erin T. 2003. Assessing collection usefulness: an investigation of library ownership of the resources graduate students use. *College & Research Libraries* 64 (5): 344–55.

Smith, Mark. 1999. *Internet policy handbook for libraries*. New York: Neal-Schuman.

Teper, Thomas H., and Stephanie S. Atkins. 2003. Building preservation: the University of Illinois at Urbana-Champaign's stacks assessment. *College & Research Libraries*. 64 (3): 211–27.

Terry, Ana Arias. 2000. How today's technology affects libraries' collection choices. *Computers in Libraries* 20 (6): 51. Expanded Academic ASAP. Infotrac. http://web5.infotrac.galegroup.com. Accessed 30 Apr. 2004.

Thompson, Hugh. 2002. The library's role in distance education: survey results from ACRL's 2000 Academic Library Trends and Statistics. *C&RL News* 63 (5): 338–40.

Wallace, Linda K. 2003. *Libraries, mission, and marketing: writing mission statements that work*. Chicago: American Library Association.

Wang, Jian. 2001. Promoting library services to campus administrative offices: a new approach and a new tool. *C&RL News* 62 (2): 193–97.

Westbrook, Lynn. 2001. *Identifying and analyzing user needs: a complete handbook and ready-to-use assessment workbook with disk*. New York: Neal-Schuman.

———. 1993. User needs: a synthesis and analysis of current theories for the practitioner. *RQ*. 32 (4): 541–549.

Winston, Mark D. and Lisa Dunkley. 2002. Leadership competencies for academic librarians: the importance of development of fund-raising. *College & Research Libraries* 63 (2): 171–82.

8 AACC POSITION STATEMENT ON LIBRARY AND LEARNING RESOURCE CENTER PROGRAMS

Community colleges are comprehensive institutions that provide a full array of educational programs. Library programs, as part of that full array, are indispensable to the teaching/learning mission of the community college. In today's world, libraries are not just a place, because many library resources and services are online and accessible from anywhere. Community colleges continue to need libraries as a physical space, as long as students need assistance to conquer the digital or information divide and there is a need to house and provide access to materials not available electronically. Whether the term used is Library, Learning Resource Center, or Instructional Resource Center, it describes a set of programs and services that provide an organized universe of knowledge to users. Library programs have long served a vital role in the mission of the community college. In fact, the concept of the learning resource center—one of creatively merging access to traditional library services with media and instructional support—had its genesis in the community college. From the beginning, library programs have promoted dynamic and efficient access to knowledge for all learners. Indeed, the management of these varied learning resources using limited budgets, consortial arrangements, and internal and external partnerships has added complexity, technical sophistication, and greater economic responsibility to librarians who staff these centers.

The term librarian describes a professional member of the academic community with, at a minimum, an appropriate master's degree in the disciplines of library science and information management. Librarianship is uniquely structured and systematized by its professional members to serve the constantly changing knowledge management needs of students, faculty, and the local community. The

319

library profession has long shown exceptional and immediate responsiveness to managing access to widely diverse knowledge resources. Today more than ever, librarians are educators and teachers of information literacy for faculty and students, as well as the local and worldwide community. A growing percentage of information resources are digital (online indexes, full-text databases, websites, e-books and e-journals). Yet this new format will not replace the large number of useful knowledge resources that will continue to be in print (e.g. books, newspapers, periodicals and other documents), or to be available in magnetic and optical media (e.g. tapes, CDs, DVDs). In collaboration and partnership with other faculty, librarians teach members of the community the information literacy skills necessary to access and to evaluate critically the myriad of available resources.

Learning resources programs that provide information literacy skills are essential to the development of the independent lifelong learner. Tenets of information literacy include the ability to:

- Determine the nature and extent of information needed
- Access and use needed information effectively and efficiently
- Evaluate information and its sources critically, and incorporate selected information into one's knowledge base and value system
- Use information effectively to accomplish a specific purpose
- Understand many of the economic, legal, and social issues surrounding the use of information.

Libraries and librarians help to establish the foundation on which all lifelong learners can build. An information-literate person has the ability to be a knowledgeable, active participant in the workforce, the community and the democratic society in which we live.

For these reasons, the Board reaffirms the vital role of library and learning resource center programs and librarians to formal education, information literacy and to lifelong learning as a core value.

Approved by the AACC Board of Directors November 8, 2002

http://www.aacc.nche.edu/Template.cfm?Section = Position_Statements&template = /ContentManagement/ContentDisplay.cfm&ContentID = 9634&InterestCategoryID = 224&Name = Position%20Statement&ComingFrom = InterestDisplay July 16, 2005

9 MIRACOSTA COLLEGE LIBRARY AND INFORMATION HUB—OCEANSIDE CAMPUS

Joseph Moreau

In January 2003, MiraCosta College opened its new Library and Information Hub on the Oceanside campus. This attractive and exciting new facility was designed to optimize the college's approach to providing learning support services to its students beyond that of simply a traditional library. Students are drawn to the Hub in record numbers, and often every chair in the building is occupied. This "one-stop shop" brings together the college's superb Library with a state-of-the-art large-scale computer lab, a computerized Math Learning Center, and the Tutoring Center. The building also houses all of the college's technical support staff and facilities. With two predominantly different environments in the building, virtually all student needs can be satisfied. The first floor contains extensive computing facilities and a variety of spaces that allow students to collaborate on projects and assignments. With almost a marketplace atmosphere, the first floor is a vibrant and energetic place that encourages student interaction. The second floor has more of a traditional library feel that offers students a quiet space for study, contemplation, and meditation. While reading or relaxing in a sunny spot under the unique spoked hub skylight or listening to the Las Vegas-style "rain forest" show during inclement weather, many find the second floor to be a peaceful retreat. Indoor planters filled with lush plantings and palm trees complete the illusion. Scattered throughout the building are group study rooms that can be utilized by students and faculty for secluded or private study sessions. In addition the fountain and plaza surrounding the main entrance have reenergized the cen-

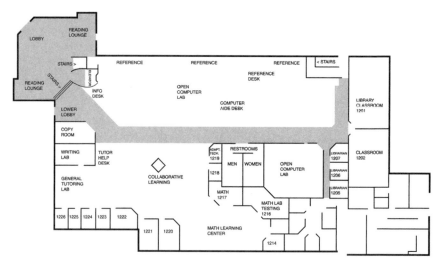

MiraCosta College Library and Information Hub, Building 1200, First Floor

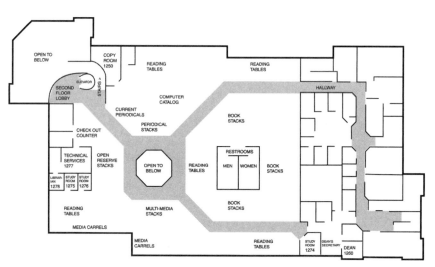

MiraCosta College Library and Information Hub, Building 1200, Second Floor

MiraCosta College Library Study Area

ter of the campus providing students with a wonderful new place to meet socially or simply relax and enjoy the sound of running water. On a campus attended exclusively by commuters, the plaza offers a comfortable home base to spend time outside of class. The Hub and plaza together have greatly enhanced the sense of community among the students.

10 PLANNING CHART

David R. Dowell

A Planning Chart for Budgeting

UNIT NAME:

DATE:

UNIT MANAGER:

UNIT MANAGER'S SIGNATURE:

List the programs/services covered by this unit plan:

List the names of those who participated in developing the unit plan:

PART I
Proposed Goals & Priorities 2005–06

Our unit goals should be measurable and must support the Board approved San Luis Obispo County Community College District Goals and Priorities for 2005–06 (listed below). In addition, they must directly support the overall goals of the cluster as they relate to the College Plan. Mark those goals that are the unit's top priorities with an asterisk to identify their importance and identify the college and/or cluster goal to which each goal relates. **Goals and Priorities must relate to institutional effectiveness outcomes and student learning outcomes.**

1. Increase employees' cultural competency to enhance students' likelihood of success and the sense of college community.
2. Begin implementation of the initial strategies to improve institutional effectiveness outcomes.
3. Complete the development of student learning outcomes for instructional programs and General Education requirements, student service functions, and administrative service functions and develop a plan for regular evaluation and implementation of change to improve student learning outcomes.
4. Begin analyzing the effectiveness of assessment of student learning outcomes in instructional programs.
5. Research and develop an implementation plan of student success models (best practices) that have had positive results (best practices) for student success.
6. Train District employees in responding effectively to emergency situations such as fire, earthquake, flooding, power outage, bomb threat, or similar emergency situations.
7. Revise, implement, and evaluate the enrollment management and marketing plan to achieve the District's funded growth and increase enrollment of under-served populations, incorporating student equity goals.
8. Revise the 2001 Educational and Facilities Master Plan to reflect strategic decisions responsive to changes in enrollment, county demographics, economic conditions, and workforce needs.
9. Position the District for a bond measure.

The District's Institutional Effectiveness Outcomes are listed below:

1. Students progress successfully to acquisition of degrees and certificates
   a. There is an annual increase in the proportion of students who successfully complete their goals of attaining a degree.
   b. There is an annual increase in the proportion of students who successfully complete their goal of attaining a certificate of proficiency or certificate of completion.
   c. Degrees for continuous-fulltime students are earned in a timely manner.
   d. There is an annual increase in the proportion of students who successfully complete transfer and vocational courses.
2. Students successfully acquire transfer-ready status and transfer.
   a. There is an annual increase in the proportion of transfer-ready students who declare transfer as their goal.
   b. Students transfer to a four-year college or university (public or private).
3. Students are employed in a job related to their vocational degree or certificate after program completion/graduation.
4. For ESL students who declare transfer or degree/certificate completion as their goal, there will be an annual increase in the proportion of students

who successfully complete ESL courses and successfully move from these courses into transfer and vocational courses. For basic skills students (English and math) who declare transfer or degree/certificate completion as their goal, there will be an annual increase in the proportion of students who successfully complete basic skills English or math courses and successfully move from these courses into college level courses in those disciplines.

   a. There is an annual increase in the proportion of ESL and basic skills students who successfully complete ESL and basic skills courses.

   b. There is an annual increase in the proportion of ESL students who persist from one semester to the next in the ESL course series.

   c. There is an annual increase in the proportion of ESL students who successfully matriculate from ESL courses into college level courses. There is an annual increase in the proportion of basic skills English and math students who successfully matriculate from basic skills English or math courses into college level English or math courses.

   d. There is an annual increase in the proportion of ESL and basic skills students who successfully complete college level courses in their next semester of enrollment.

5. There is an annual increase in the proportion of students in licensure or professional certification programs who successfully earn their license or certification.

6. Students completing degrees demonstrate achievement of general education outcomes, e.g., critical thinking, civic responsibility.

7. The District demonstrates responsiveness to changing demographics and cultural environment, as well as needs of business and industry.

   a. College programs and services reflect the current needs of the community as demonstrated through a College Needs Assessment.

   b. Student enrollment reflects the demographics of the service area.

   c. High school graduates in the service area select Cuesta College as their community college of choice.

   d. Local employers express a high level of satisfaction with Cuesta College offerings/programs.

Note: This note applied to Part II thru Part VI.

Immediate needs are for the next fiscal year 2005-06

Intermediate needs are for the following two fiscal years 2006-08

Long-term needs are for 4-5 fiscal years out 2008-10

PART II
FULL TIME FACULTY — PRIORITY ORDER

Within the justification for full time faculty, include data on full time to part time faculty hours calculated from the current semester; master planning information; and all other pertinent information related to the request.

Full Time Faculty	Position Title	Site	Salary and Benefits	New or Replacement	Justification
Immediate Needs 2005-2006	1. 2. 3.				
Intermediate Needs 2006-2008	1. 2. 3.				
Long Term Needs 2008-2010	1. 2. 3.				

Include in the justification a brief description of the role and responsibilities of the proposed management position and all other pertinent information related to the request.

Academic & Classified Managers	Position Title	Site	Salary and Benefits	New or Replacement	Justification
Immediate Needs	1. 2.				

2005-2006	3.
Intermediate Needs 2006-2008	1. 2. 3.
Long Term Needs 2008-2010	1. 2. 3.

Include in the justification a brief description of the role and responsibilities of the proposed classified position and all other pertinent information related to the request.

Classified & Confidential Staff	Position Title	Site	Salary and Benefits	New, Replacement or Restoration	Justification
Immediate Needs 2005-2006	1. 2. 3.				
Intermediate Needs 2006-2008	1. 2. 3.				
Long Term Needs 2008-2010	1. 2. 3.				

Overall Immediate (2005-2006) Unit Personnel Priorities:
1.

PART III
OPERATIONS

2.
3.
4.
5.

Student Help	Description	Site	Current Allocation and Requested Increase	Justification
Immediate Needs 2005-2006	1. 2. 3.			
Intermediate Needs 2006-2008	1. 2. 3.			
Long Term Needs 2008-2010	1. 2. 3.			

Hourly Workers	Description	Site	Current Allocation and Requested Increase	Justification
Immediate Needs 2005-2006	1. 2. 3.			

Intermediate Needs 2006-2008	1. 2. 3.			
Long Term Needs 2008-2010	1. 2. 3.			

Separate hardware and software licenses

Instructional Supplies	Description	Site	Cost	Justification
Immediate Needs 2005-2006	1. 2. 3.			
Intermediate Needs 2006-2008	1. 2. 3.			
Long Term Needs 2008-2010	1. 2. 3.			

Separate hardware and software licenses

Non-Instructional Supplies	Description	Site	Cost	Justification
Immediate Needs 2005-2006	1. 2. 3.			
Intermediate Needs 2006-2008	1. 2. 3.			
Long Term Needs 2008-2010	1. 2. 3.			

Overall Immediate (2005-2006) Unit Operation Budget Priorities:

1.
2.
3.
4.
5.

PART IV
EQUIPMENT

Instructional Equipment	Description	Site	Cost including Installation and Facility Modification (if Necessary)	Justification
Immediate Needs 2005-2006	1. 2. 3.			
Intermediate Needs 2006-2008	1. 2. 3.			
Long Term Needs 2008-2010	1. 2. 3.			

Non-Instructional Equipment	Description	Site	Cost including Installation and Facility Modification (if necessary)	Justification
Immediate Needs	1.			

2005-2006	2. 3.		
Intermediate Needs 2006-2008	1. 2. 3.		
Long Term Needs 2008-2010	1. 2. 3.		

Overall Immediate (2005-2006) Unit Equipment Priorities:

1.
2.
3.
4.
5.

PART V
FACILITIES

Deferred Maintenance	Description	Site	Entire Cost of Project	Justification
Immediate Needs 2005-2006	1. 2. 3.			
Intermediate Needs 2006-2008	1. 2. 3.			
Long Term Needs 2008-2010	1. 2. 3.			

INDEX

ABOUT THE EDITORS
AND CONTRIBUTORS

DAVID R. DOWELL, Director of Library/Learning Resources at Cuesta College, previously held library management posts at Pasadena City College, Illinois Institute of Technology, Duke University and Iowa State University. Active on management, personnel, and education issues in the American Library Association, he holds graduate degrees from the University of Illinois and the University of North Carolina.

GERARD B. MCCABE retired from Clarion University of Pennsylvania. His most recent work is co-editor of *Planning the Modern Public Library Building* (Libraries Unlimited, 2003). He is a past chairperson of the Executive Committee, Buildings and Equipment Section, LAMA.

SHEILA BONNAND is the Senior Librarian at the MSU—Great Falls Campus Library in Great Falls, Montana. Before moving into academic librarianship, she was teacher and school librarian and a community education director. She has an MA in Library and Information Science from the University of Arizona.

SHELLEY WOOD BURGETT has an MLS from Indiana University and has worked in special, professional school, academic, school, and public libraries in four different states. Currently she serves as Director of Library Services for Somerset Community College, a two-campus, three-center community and technical college serving 13 counties in south central Kentucky.

MARY M. CARR, Dean of Instructional Services and Telecommunications at Spokane Community College, holds a Masters in Librarianship (University of Washington) and a Masters of Science in Human Resources (Gonzaga University). She has been president of the Washington and Idaho library associations and chair of the National Council for Learning Resources and the Community and Junior College Libraries Section of the American Library Association. She was recently elected to the American Association of Community Colleges' Board of Directors.

LYN "MIMI" COLLINS is Director of Library and Learning Resources at Taft College, California. She and her coauthor have proposed a joint-use library with Kern County Library—Taft Branch.

CELITA DEARMOND is a Reference and Distance Learning librarian in the Library and Media Services department at San Antonio College. She is also active in library instruction and information literacy issues, and was selected to present at the LOEX 2003 Reflective Teaching: A Bridge to Learning conference.

WILLIAM DUNCAN is Vice President of Administrative Services at Taft College, California. He and his coauthor have proposed that Taft College and the Kern County Library plan a joint-use library as a Taft Branch.

W. JEANNE GARDNER is the Director of Library Services and Coordinator, Library Technician Program at Pueblo Community College, Pueblo, Colorado. Jeanne served as the Learning Resources Center Director at Lamar Community College in Lamar, Colorado, and the Media Center Coordinator, School of Nursing, University of Missouri, Columbia, Missouri. She received her MLS from the University of Missouri—Columbia.

CHRISTINE C. GODIN is Director of Learning Resources at Northwest Vista College, a new institution, in San Antonio, Texas. She has more than 30 years experience in community college libraries, having also served as Public Services Librarian at Kansas City Kansas Community College and Johnson County Community College in Overland Park, Kansas. In her present position she has watched the student body grow from a few hundred to more than 8,000 in just five years. Northwest Vista College is a comprehensive community college with academic, occupational, and developmental programs.

ANDRINE J. HAAS is Library Director at Dawson Community College, Glendive, Montana, where she also teaches a course in Children's Literature. She is an active member of both the Montana Library Association and the Mountain Plains Library Association and has held offices and committee appointments in both associations. Currently, she is serving on two statewide library task forces and a consortium.

SHARON D. JENKINS is currently Director of Library Services at New Mexico Junior College, Hobbs, NM. She earned her doctorate in Information Science from the University of North Texas and an MLS from the University of Missouri-Columbia. Prior experience includes working as a medical librarian/consortium coordinator for the Western Arizona AHEC.

RASHELLE KARP is Associate Vice President for Academic Affairs at Clarion University of Pennsylvania. Dr. Karp has published extensively in the field of librarianship and higher education. She has worked as a public, academic, and special librarian, and served as the Interim Dean of Libraries at Clarion University of Pennsylvania.

ROBERT KELLY, a Colorado transplant, lives with his wife and children in Hutchinson, Kansas, where he is Coordinator of Library Services at Hutchinson Community College/AVS. His enjoyment of sports and libraries reflect in his 1990 MLS from University of Kentucky and his 2002 Sport Administration MEd from Wichita State University. His interests include poker, basketball, NASCAR, and reading biographies and fantasy fiction.

FRANCIS G. KUYKENDALL has 30 years experience in public, school, and academic libraries. She is Library Director of South Arkansas Community College in El Dorado, Arkansas. She has held offices and board positions in state and national library and technology organizations and has been a conference speaker. She holds a MSEd from University of Central Arkansas and MLS from Texas Woman's University.

JOSEPH MOREAU is Dean of Academic Information Services at MiraCosta College, Oceanside, California. He has worked with technology and media for more than 20 years. Currently, he serves as president of the California Community Colleges Chief Information Systems Officers Association and on the board of directors of the PeopleSoft Higher Education Users Group.

ERIC E. PALO, MLS, is Library Director at Renton Technical College, Renton, Washington. He has also held supervisory positions in academic libraries in Kansas and North Carolina.

KATHY L. PETERSEN, a private practice human resources consultant, was formerly Associate Director of Human Resources at Bellevue Community College, Bellevue, Washington. She has an MBA and an MA in counseling.

BRANDI PORTER is Director of Library Services at Bucks County Community College in Newtown, Pennsylvania. Currently, she is a doctoral candidate in Information Science at Nova Southeastern University, Fort Lauderdale, Florida.

LINDA REEVES, MLIS, MA, provides library instruction and reference assistance to students both online and on campus at Northwest Vista College. A former college English teacher, Linda acquired her MLIS and her interest in online learning as a distance education student at the University of Texas-Austin.

MICHAEL D. RUSK is Dean of Learning Resources Center, Tulsa Community College, Tulsa, Oklahoma. He has worked for Tulsa Community College since 1981. Previously he was in charge of Engineering Technical Library for American Airlines. Before that he spent a number of years with Tulsa City-County Library System. Mr. Rusk was a member of the editorial board for *Community & Junior College Libraries* from 1988 to 1992 and contributed a number of articles for publication to this journal and others. His education includes a BA from the University of Tulsa (1971) and an MLS from the University of Oklahoma (1976). He has served as chair of the Oklahoma Council of Academic Library Directors (1991–1995) and coauthored state level initiatives for linking academic libraries in Oklahoma.

DONNA J. SMITH is Director of the Kankakee Community College's Learning Resource Center. She has a BS in Applied Computer Science from Illinois State University and a MALIS from the University of Missouri—Columbia. She combines these fields by promoting student and faculty awareness of information sources, regarding of the information format.

JOHN STANLEY, international conference speaker and retail and library consultant, has been consulting to retailers, growing businesses and their profits, as well as inspiring and motivating retail teams to achieve excellence in their daily lives for more than 25 years. He has authored several books, which have become best-sellers.

WARREN G. TAYLOR holds an MA in library science and a doctorate in higher education administration from the University of Denver. From the University of Colorado at Denver, he holds an MA in Anthropology. His prior experience included serving as a tenured library faculty member at the University of Colorado and Director of Facilities Use Planning at Auraria Higher Education Center. Recently, he retired as Director of the College Hill Library of Front Range Community College in Westminster, Colorado.

PATRICIA VIERTHALER has been Technical Services Librarian at Trident Technical College since February 2003. Previously she served as Director of Library Services at Hutchinson Community College and Cataloger at Morris College. She holds a MLS degree and an MS in Educational Media.

£27-95